Expanding Access to Financial Services in Latin America

Miguel Basch
Camilo Morales
Editors

Published by the Inter-American Development Bank
Distributed by The Johns Hopkins University Press

Washington, D.C.
1995

The views and opinions expressed in this publication are those of the authors and do not necessarily reflect the official position of the Inter-American Development Bank.

Expanding Access to Financial Services in Latin America

Inter-American Development Bank
1300 New York Avenue, N.W.
Washington, D.C. 20577

Distributed by
The Johns Hopkins University Press
2715 North Charles Street
Baltimore, MD 21218-4319

Library of Congress Catalog Card Number: 96-75386
ISBN: 1-886938-02-4

AUTHORS

Basch H., Miguel
Economist, School of Economic and Administrative Sciences, University of Chile.

Fernández, Raúl
Economist, Center for Studies of the State and Society (CEDES), Argentina.

Morales, Camilo
Economist, School of Economic and Administrative Sciences, University of Chile.

Noya, Nelson
Economist, Center for Economic Research (CINVE), Uruguay.

Rodríguez, Martha
Economist, University of the Pacific, Peru.

Rozenwurcel, Guillermo
Economist, Director of Research at the Center for Studies of the State and Society (CEDES), Argentina.

Sosa López, Lizardo
Economist, Association of Research and Social Studies (ASIES), Guatemala.

Velarde, Julio
Economist, University of the Pacific, Peru.

FOREWORD

The studies in this book were carried out by five different research institutions as part of the Centers for Applied Research in Economics Project, which was organized by the Inter-American Development Bank and is now completing its third successful year. In particular, it fell to the Economics Department at the University of Chile to coordinate this research project, as well as to produce its own corresponding country study. Representing Argentina, Guatemala, Peru and Uruguay, the national case studies were performed, respectively, by the Center for Studies of the State and Society (CEDES), the Association of Research and Social Studies (ASIES), the University of the Pacific, and the Center for Economic Research (CINVE). Three meetings and constant coordination permitted completion of the studies, which we hope will constitute an important contribution to the development of financial systems and the sustained growth of the small and medium-sized enterprises sector.

The central hypothesis of the book is that development of financial systems brings about more timely access to the services that this industry offers. A greater level of intermediation of loanable funds leads sectors traditionally left out of the formal financial system to become part of that system, transforming them into more attractive credit customers. In particular, small and medium-sized enterprises, which are often ineligible for credit for a variety of reasons, represent a sector whose needs will increasingly be met by new banking services. The unmet financing needs of these small businesses has led to development of activities designed effort to fill this vacuum outside the traditional system of intermediation.

In each of the five case studies, it has been observed that small and medium-sized enterprises have continued to develop despite their difficulties. The studies examine both successful as well as unsuccessful financing efforts. In sharing these results, the authors hope to contribute to development of this sector, which is so vitally important in countries throughout the region.

Nohra Rey de Marulanda, Manager
Integration and Regional Programs Department

CONTENTS

CHAPTER ONE

EXPANDING ACCESS TO FINANCIAL SERVICES AND SUPPORT FOR SMALL ENTERPRISE

Camilo Morales*

A wider range of financial services in Latin America could induce the region's small businesses to make greater use of banking and to become more attractive borrowers. This study describes how the development of financial systems in Argentina, Chile, Ecuador, Guatemala, and Peru could expand access to banking intermediation for small enterprises.

Such enterprises are a natural market for the new services that Latin America's banking industry is developing as it grows. The unmet financing needs of the small business sector, which was traditionally excluded from access to banking services, have prompted new activities to address that market. Such activities are receiving considerable government and multilateral support and have so far achieved various degrees of success.

In this chapter we first discuss the macroeconomic environment that encourages growth of small businesses and analyze the requisite conditions for their success. Second, we briefly describe the economies of the five countries, in light of global events that affected their overall performance and influenced the private financial intermediation markets in their monetary and banking sectors.

In the third section we summarize the primary causes of the economic crises and their effects on the region's financial system. In Chile and Uruguay, for example, outwardly oriented programs and financial liberalization had results different from those in Argentina and Peru, where recent hyperinflation was far more extreme. The economic adjustment programs applied in each country had different impacts on the operational framework and the institutional arrangement

* The author is grateful for the suggestions and contributions made by participants and outside evaluators during the third round of consultations of the Network of Centers for Applied Economic Research of the Inter-American Development Bank (IDB).

of each financial system. Much remains to be done to improve the operational framework, especially in Guatemala, a country now undergoing a profound structural adjustment.

One current change in international financial networks involves lowering of transaction costs, making it easier to bring together potential lenders and borrowers. That process, known as "financial disintermediation," has characterized more advanced banking systems like the Chilean, but in Guatemala and Uruguay it apparently arose due to lack of depth in the intermediary apparatus.

The fourth section describes the small enterprise sector, its credit potential, and its relationship to the financial system. The characteristics that reduce its attractiveness to the banking system are relatively similar from one country to the next—lack of guarantees, limited diversification and sales volume, and technological backwardness.

The fifth section presents some solutions outside the financial system that are offered by the market and by government initiative. Finally, this chapter's sixth section contains the main policy recommendations for small business, in three distinct levels. First are general recommendations concerning the healthy operation of the economic system. Next are recommendations directed at the financial sector and its relationship with small business. Third and last, we recommend measures aimed at making small businesses creditworthy.

While these recommendations are derived from each of the country studies, the conclusions at the end of chapter one are the sole responsibility of this author.

Macroeconomic Circumstances

The macroeconomic situation shapes the operating framework for the various financial systems studied. External shocks, internal administrative problems, and how each national economy handled them, had different consequences for banking operations in the various countries. Their adjustment programs differ in magnitude and intensity, but all address the same concerns: stabilizing prices, lessening the dependence of the fiscal apparatus, and assuring the proper management of external capital flows. Those objectives help establish a more stable framework for the financial system. Such stable conditions also allow financial intensification and a more developed intermediation to take place naturally, thus encouraging a growing level of savings and investment.[1]

[1] McKinnon (1973), Shaw (1973), and Díaz-Alejandro (1985) provide the analysis underlying that proposition.

Origins of Adjustment Policies

Uruguay and Chile: The Legacy of the 1970s

Both Uruguay and Chile adopted measures in the mid-1970s to make their economies more open to international trade. These measures had a strong impact early in the next decade, when worldwide economic activity declined during the international recession.[2]

A deregulation policy was applied in Uruguay between 1974 and 1977, allowing greater international mobility of capital resources. Contracts were often made in foreign currencies due to a more liberal composition of investment and debt portfolios. Finally matters reached a point where even basic restrictions like minimum required reserves were temporarily lifted. Deregulation clearly did not increase public confidence, since domestic economic policy did not establish the necessary stability, and thus the country's overall savings did not increase.

Nevertheless, the economy became more dollarized, which exacerbated the crisis. During the 1981–82 period, external shocks caused by the international recession placed the financial system in a difficult situation, made worse by inconsistent economic measures. The dollarization of debts and abandonment of the existing exchange guidelines caused many borrowers in the financial system to go bankrupt. The private banking system was backed by the government, which had to deal with a loss equivalent to 8 percent of GDP. Around 1987 the government finally took over the three largest private sector banks, thereby introducing "administered banking," or *banca gestionada*. Support for national banking not only involved the state as sponsor and part owner, but also required measures to prop up debtors. These measures continue to affect the behavior of the financial system to this day, as demonstrated by government-ordered reschedulings of debts. The Central Bank also initiated a program for buying portfolios of unrecovered loans, thereby improving the holdings of the entities involved. Foreign banks had direct support from their home offices, so that part of the financial system remained in private hands. Both groups, the administered banking system and foreign banks, today serve as the foundation of Uruguay's financial system.

Chile's structural reforms, beginning in 1973, were designed to reduce the financial repression and excessive government intervention then prevalent. Their effect was similar to that of the deregulation policies in Uruguay. The reforms began in 1974 with freeing interest rates and eliminating the credit controls built into the workings of the financial system. This latter move was only relatively successful, because the needed fiscal adjustment was slow in occurring. How-

---

[2] Based on Basch (1994), Held (1989), Noya (1994), Noya and Dominioni (1994), and Ramírez (1989).

ever, measures aimed at taxing the real portion of savings account interest and the gradual lowering of required reserves helped reduce intermediation costs substantially by 1984. Much like Uruguay, the economy of Chile was overly dependent on the external sector when the 1981 crisis struck. From 1979 to 1982 the Chilean currency was pegged to the dollar, thus generating a significant commercial debt, which was financed with foreign borrowing. The presence of an implicit state guarantee for deposits, and the moral risk involved in granting credit without preventive oversight, which led to the transfer of a significant level of resources to the economic groups, no doubt intensified the effects of the sudden reduction of outside financing caused by the international recession at that time.

Although these structural changes eventually led to the way Chile's economy now operates, their immediate results seemed rather mediocre at that time. For example, despite the significant increase in the money supply noted between 1973 and 1982 and the increase in credit, the real interest rate remained high and the level of savings declined from 16.3 percent of GDP in the 1970s to 12.4 percent in 1975–81. Something similar took place with public and private investment. Intervention by government economic officials during the 1982–83 period prevented the financial system from going bankrupt by adopting measures aimed at rescuing those profitable economic activities that had significant debts at high interest rates, and by other measures aimed at directly rescuing the net worth of banks. The legacies of these programs have continued to prompt political criticism, based on apparent distortions produced by the survival of entities that otherwise would have disappeared. But those criticisms have been mitigated by the creation of an efficient and competitive private financing apparatus that is governed by legislation and modern oversight agencies.

Inflationary Experiences in Peru and Argentina

Peru and Argentina face different circumstances, because the domestic component of their economies is far more important. In both countries, extreme hyperinflation and poor economic management—due basically to flawed and inconsistent government policy—led to the recent adjustment programs, whose effects cannot yet be regarded as definitive.[3]

Interesting liberalization efforts in Peru from 1980 to 1985 were interrupted by the political experiment of the García government. A costly result of that administration was the hyperinflationary process that plagued the Peruvian economy between August 1988 and July 1990. An additional cost arose from the thrust of that government's economic policy, which in effect sought to return to a system of direct, hands-on management by the government. For example, the

[3] Based on Rozenwurcel and Fernández (1994), and Velarde and Rodríguez (1994).

financial system returned to a system of controlled interest rates, and measures were passed to divide up credit by establishing sector quotas for loan portfolios.

In addition, a series of measures related to the external sector reduced the flow of international financing that Peru needed, as the payment of both dividends on foreign investments and outside debts were prohibited. The loss of confidence likewise affected local investors, since the government decreed that deposits in foreign currency had to be converted into national currency. Due to the segmentation mentioned above, noneconomic criteria were used for channeling credit. Support was renewed for the already declining development bank, which then became a significant channel for Central Bank resources. The high point of interventionist policy was reached in July 1987 when a law was created to nationalize the banks. Although the law was never applied, it revealed unmistakably what the executive power intended to do. The flaws and inconsistencies of economic policy culminated in hyperinflation, which translated into a rapid reduction in the real liquidity of national currency, mainly through declining levels of demand deposits. Likewise, the turnover of accounts increased significantly, thus increasing financial intermediation costs.

In 1990 the incoming government began an adjustment policy aimed both at combating inflation and clearly changing the philosophy of government management. It was decided to keep the level of legal reserves high and to allow the true interest rate to be charged, thereby causing a widespread decline of wealth. The central elements of the program introduced far-reaching changes both internally and externally. Among the internal changes, a program to adjust the fiscal gap was established, and obstacles to hiring and firing employees were substantially reduced.

In the monetary realm, Peru's Central Bank, exercising its legal autonomy, had been granting credits to the government. These credits were abolished, and the Central Bank began to apply an active monetary policy, supported by liberalization of the balance of payments capital account. This last step, together with eliminating the obligation to hand over foreign exchange obtained through export operations, unifying the exchange rate with a managed float, and reducing para-tariff restrictions, has reestablished the flow of outside funds into the country. The new measures adopted by the government had quite positive results: they created a propitious climate for applying the provisions of the 1991 Banking Law, which reinforces the task of supervising the banking sector and allows the establishment of full-service banking.

Much like Peru's experience, the recent economic history of Argentina's institutional framework derives largely from the hyperinflation of the late 1980s, which culminated in a two-step adjustment process. During the 1989–90 period, the application of the Bonex plan involved replacing domestic obligations in national currency with external bonds, government instruments issued in dollars with a ten-year maturity. This first stage of the adjustment plan caused a decline in the money supply and demonetization, making it possible to reduce inflation to more reasonable levels. Nevertheless, certain requirements absolutely necessary to achieve the plan's objectives were not fulfilled. The fiscal situation, for example, required a sustainable adjustment of the deficit. When that requirement was not met, the demonetization process was reversed and the results gained from the original plan went off course. That situation was only worsened by the fact that the country's relations with its foreign creditors had not been normalized.

Thus, March 1992 marked the adoption of the second stage of the adjustment program, the "Convertibility Plan," which was based on the support of the monetary base with international reserves. The basic focus of the program was the external situation, since the support for the monetary base became dependent on both the trade situation and the influx of foreign capital. The resources generated by the privatization of state companies were another key piece of the design. To assure normal payments to outside creditors, those resources have been channeled toward satisfying the requirements of the Brady Plan, the route by which Argentina has begun to normalize relations with its foreign creditors.

The Convertibility Plan obliges banks to return deposits in the same currency, and does not allow the Central Bank to make use of those resources. To maintain an adequate range of currencies, dollar instruments have been designed to capture more dollars domestically. This last point, in view of the banks' greater access now to foreign financing, will make it possible to secure adequate support for the dollarization that the plan seeks to achieve.

Even though the financial system has clearly improved, the measures adopted have not produced a decisive increase of savings. Thus far the Convertibility Plan has meant more change in the structure of portfolios rather than in their growth, just as in Uruguay. Nevertheless, officials hope that the greater productivity of investment will make it possible to resolve the growing current-account deficit Argentina is experiencing due to continuing overvaluation of the national currency. Thus far, the model follows the line of the monetary focus on the balance of payments, particularly the first phase of expansion. The second phase of contraction will probably bring about a contraction in capital inflows, a deflation of domestic prices, and an increase in the real interest rate. Nevertheless, the negative effects of the second phase could occur sooner if devaluation is expected, and that could translate into the possibility of a speculative move against the national currency. Officials thus far have guarded against that eventuality by issuing instruments in dollars.

The financial system, in which government bodies play a preponderant role, is facing a clear push toward privatization. Argentina's Central Bank does not offer any type of guarantee on deposits, and restricts itself to being a lender of last resort. The increase in deposits connected to stabilization programs has made it possible to lower the interest rate and the financial margin applied to loans. However, due to the special circumstances in banking there is an oversupply of plants and personnel, thus opening the possibility of significantly improving efficiency and thereby lowering intermediation costs.

With regard to the capital market, Argentina's modernization thrust is similar to Peru's—to restructure the pension system toward capitalization, making it possible to provide further needed savings. Privatizing state enterprises would also make it possible to improve the level of stock exchange capitalization. Full-service banking would provide the vitality needed for intermediation activities, and thus the price system would truly reflect the net worth of assets.

Changes Pending in Guatemala

Guatemala's economic situation differs substantially from the others. In those cases, although conditions and time periods differ, adjustment programs are building stable operating arrangements based on growing independence from state intervention, greater fiscal equilibrium, a monetary policy tied to price stability, and external connections in trade and finance. While results are incomplete, the direction is clear. Judging by events in Guatemala, however, that does not seem to be what its economic policymakers are seeking.[4]

From 1970 onward, the model employed in Guatemala has provided incentives for import substitution activities. The political and social crises affecting the country at the end of that decade brought about a decline in productive capacity and a consequent rise in poverty levels. Such were features of the behavior of the economic system until the mid-1980s. As in the previous cases, the crises of the world economy in 1980–81 further aggravated the situation in the country. Only in 1986 did Guatemala begin to show slight positive growth, due to the adjustment programs suggested by multilateral organizations. Inconsistent implementation of the proposed programs, which focus primarily on monetary and fiscal aspects, have brought further financing restrictions and have delayed the resolution of a series of important pending issues. Thus, certain measures like modernizing the financial system have been contingent upon meeting new goals, and only in 1993 have the first legal and regulatory measures aimed at resolving the problem been adopted.

Unfortunately, the Monetary Board that governs the Central Bank is constrained by operating under a law dating back to 1946. The same is true of the Banking Law, which was intended to regulate a financial system under a paternalistic type of state. Thus it should be noted that the interest rate and the foreign exchange measures adopted have been managed through transitory resolutions, while other activities have been organized informally from the standpoint of the Banking Law, because it does not allow banking to develop in a globalized framework.

---

[4] Compare Sosa (1994).

The decisions adopted clearly suggest the intention to put things in order, rather than to modernize. Guatemala's fiscal instability and balance of payments disequilibrium, which led to rising prices and a deteriorating currency in 1990, had improved substantially by 1991. Monetary officials have implemented a contractionist monetary policy, increasing reserves and raising the interest rate on open market operations. Hence the 1990s began with a substantial reduction in inflation and an increase in international reserves, which have also meant greater stability in exchange rates.

Results in the Financial System

This section takes up the main consequences of the crises described above and the measures taken to resolve them, which entail changes in regulation and in the workings of the financial system. Specifically in the Guatemalan case, the financial system clearly depends on measures connected to the restructuring process, which affects the overall operating framework of the economy.[5]

Direct Consequences of the Crisis

Uruguay and Chile: Experiences with Similar Origins

The situation in Uruguay described above had undeniable effects on the functioning of the financial system and its debtors. The heavy dollarization of the economy before the abandonment of exchange-rate parity became the main issue in the crisis, since the net worth of debtors affected the quality of banks' loan portfolios. That led to programs whereby the Central Bank would buy portfolios from financial institutions and to compulsory reschedulings by law. Even now these programs are affecting the financial position of the banks, particularly insofar as the last of these processes began in 1992, thus entailing significant uncertainty for potential investors in the banking sector.

Programs to support the financial system led to the absorption by the government of almost the entire national banking system, and thus the virtual disappearance of this segment of the market, which was replaced by a new system known as the "administered banking" sector. Private banks are now predominantly foreign, because when the crisis occurred those banks could rely on their head offices for support. By 1987 the financial system had declined in size, as the volume of credits handled by the sector fell by about 20 percent. Private banks

---

[5] The analyses presented in Frenkel (1994), Ramírez (1989), Held (1989), and Díaz-Alejandro (1985) complement the ideas presented in this section.

cut back on their number of branch offices and concentrated on a few major customers. Deposits nonetheless tended to remain at their level due to bailout programs. Thus the contraction of traditional activity has forced banks to make greater efforts to diversify their products by incorporating new activities that may not have to with banking, such as offshore operations and other activities that are connected to their traditional sphere but that until now have remained undeveloped, including credit card services and foreign trade support.

Much like what happened in Uruguay, the Chilean experience of the early 1980s has markedly influenced how the financial system now operates. When the widespread use of dollar borrowing at fixed parity suddenly had to be abandoned, Chile's main borrowers faced a crisis, which left the financial system with a significantly reduced net worth. The situation was aggravated by the large amounts of credit that the banks had issued to the economic groups that owned the financial institutions themselves. Resolving this situation meant adopting measures to support the financial condition of the borrowers, along with other measures to restore the banks' net worth. The former included reschedulings financed with resources provided by the state through the Central Bank, while under the latter, programs were established for selling portfolios and capitalizing financial entities.

The main difference in the policies adopted to resolve these crises is that in Chile the measures were aimed at keeping the financial system private. Thus Chile did not incur the efficiency costs that normally ensue when the state manages private resources, and has no need to carry out reprivatization. Nevertheless, the costs involved in the process are still affecting the financial system's performance: these costs are manifested in a heavy quasi-fiscal debt administered by the Central Bank, and by the maintenance of a subordinate debt due to the sale of portfolios. Both factors constrain the independence of monetary policy, and currently give rise to significant political disagreement over the future of the financial system.

Peru and Argentina: Responses to Hyperinflation

Both countries experienced shocks like those of other economies in the early 1980s. The most important factors that created pressure for implementing adjustment programs, however, were price instability and hyperinflation.

In Argentina the cost of financial intermediation increased significantly when the Bonex plan went into effect. From an estimated 1.9 percent in 1980, it rose to 6 percent in 1990. The Convertibility Plan subsequently restored liquidity by allowing an increase in the money supply, mainly in dollars, thus permitting the situation to normalize. Intermediation costs thus reached 1.4 percent, according to information available in June 1993.

Even by the new measuring methods, the liquidity level required is still lacking, and the savings rate too low to finance development needs. Although by certain measuring standards the level of penetration of the banking system seems adequate, the Argentine financial system has a weak infrastructure that impairs its efficiency. The Convertibility Plan has allowed the interest rate to rise, which enabled deposits to recover, spurred bank service activity, and increased the financial system's profitability. Moreover, this process has helped improve efficiency indicators.

Over the past decade, both because of the guarantees received and the significant amount of government bonds that banks are holding, financial institutions have tied up a high level of their own capital. The determination to reduce the fiscal deficit, part of the adjustment plan applied by government officials, is translating into a lesser dependence on investments in financial assets in state or municipal debts. A large part of the portfolios of Argentine government banks are concentrated in such debts, and these agencies help explain the degree of paralysis and delinquency toward the Central Bank.

Peru implemented its adjustment plan at the same time as Argentina. As noted in the previous section, Peru's plan sought to control the hyperinflation affecting the country from 1987 to 1990. The effects on the financial system were clear in the following sense: first, when the period of controlled interest rates and credit allocation policies ended, domestic savings began to increase, both because of the greater returns generated by deposit instruments and because of the greater public credibility resulting from the establishment of a more coherent economic framework. Moreover, the suspension of Central Bank financing to development banking meant the virtual disappearance of that sector, so the geographical and sector-specific concentration of credit pursued by the previous administration declined. Thus banking began to lean toward a notably private approach to operation involving less participation by the state. The declining influence of government banking has been crucial to the improvement of efficiency levels within the Peruvian financial system. Although geographical concentration shows that the capital city plays a leading role, the elimination of controls has allowed for an allocation of credit toward the productive sectors with what is essentially a market criterion.

The banking recovery was nonetheless abruptly interrupted in 1992, when domestic production fell 3.9 percent and the delinquency rate on loans reached 13 percent. Nevertheless, Peru's financial system made a significant recovery in 1993: its institutions were fully solvent, and GDP had been restored. The downward trend in prices has allowed levels of checking accounts and demand accounts to surpass historic levels. Another sign of the modernization and greater efficiency of Peruvian banking is the spread of automatic teller machines (ATMs).

Guatemala: Beginning a New Experience

Guatemala's current situation is not the result of a particular crisis. Nevertheless, in 1986 the multilateral banks conditioned their support for Guatemala upon the government's use of programs to reduce the fiscal deficit and the pursuit of price stability by the Central Bank.

No clear change in the behavior of price levels was achieved until 1990. Since then, open-market operations carried out by monetary officials have significantly reduced liquidity and the money supply, not only making interest rates positive but raising them. Thus, the intermediary role of banks diminished as the new monetary policy led to a change in the composition of bank assets. The amount of credit created by the banks was reduced, and replaced by instruments issued by the Central Bank. Many of the positive results achieved in Guatemalan banking are due to recently applied monetary policy measures. Of late, the financial system's profitability has risen considerably, in contrast to its negative operating margin over the previous five years.

High reserves and high interest rates have increased the cost of bank intermediation, and the latter have been an important source of bank profits. The sector has begun to show a change in its composition of credit, with a greater concentration on major clients. The change in the orientation of business is more evident in the fact that the level of delinquency has declined considerably, while management costs of the financial system have increased.

Rising interest rates have caused some decline in the use of banking services. Because banks are concentrating their operations on large-volume customers in metropolitan areas, who require sophisticated guarantees, other intermediaries have begun to fulfill roles traditionally played by banks.

Principal Institutional Changes Due to Adjustment Programs

Even though common elements link the arrival of the crisis and the way it was handled, the legal, regulatory, and operational consequences in these five countries do not fit a single pattern. Accordingly, each experience merits separate examination.

Consequences in Argentina

The situation in Argentina involves issues of internal management. Because the adjustment plan has been applied only recently, the Banking Law itself has not changed significantly. Nevertheless, the existence of government-owned commercial, mortgage, investment, and development banks has resulted in too many branches and too many employees. Privatization will not only reduce such dependence, but also improve standards for financial services. Public sector banks account for 44 percent of the branch offices and 50 percent of the total personnel in the financial system. That is perhaps why their credit represents only 17.3 percent of the total, indicating a low level of financial deepening. Likewise, credits are still chiefly granted on a short-term basis, especially when government banking is excluded. A primarily private system would make it possible to improve both the level and the duration of loans, by drawing on domestic and international funds deposited for longer terms.

Consequences in Chile

Chile's experience made it possible to consolidate a financial oversight system based on the classification of bank loans by borrowers, to establish "early warning" indicators. Similar procedures aided the adoption of a series of regulations to safeguard banking management from its ownership consortia by monitoring the loans to parent or related companies. The 1986 changes in the General Banking Law allowed for the application of more sophisticated economic concepts such as limits per borrower and economic debt. The change in the Organic Banking Law provided the Superintendency of Banks with the ability to effectively exercise oversight over the new legal provisions.

An important element in the 1986 legal changes was the addition of new activities to those carried out by the traditional banking system. These innovations, known as bank affiliates and support companies, have made it possible for the Chilean banking system to engage in activities proper to its competitor industry, investment banking. Through check servicing companies, the banks have also introduced modern developments such as ATM networks, credit card operations, and data transmission networks.[6]

Consequences in Guatemala

In contrast to the other experiences examined here, the legal and regulatory changes in Guatemala are still pending. The financial system operates within a legal framework consisting of a Banking Law and an Organic Central Bank Law that date from the 1940s, when the state was heavily involved in the country's economic activity. Both laws are out of tune with the contemporary situation of a modern financial market with global needs. The requirements for minimal capital, guarantees, and individual credit limits are additional costs for the already burdensome process of providing traditional financial services. These costs have led to the appearance of nonbank entities organized to satisfy real credit needs that cannot be met within the existing regulatory framework.

The Superintendency of Banks carries out auditing primarily to protect fiscal interests, but it has no staff qualified to carry out preventive oversight. By

---

[6] See Morales (1989).

means of the agreement signed with multilateral banks to restructure the financial system, a more deregulated and modern financial market should be established. Strengthening the Superintendency of Banks, diversifying banking products, and liberalizing financial operations within a framework of greater monetary stability are among the objectives of Guatemala's modernization process.

Consequences in Peru

Peru's financial system today reflects a series of profound changes that culminated in the 1990s with broad reforms, followed by a new regulatory framework. A generation earlier, during the 1960s, heavy state intervention extended from controlling interest rates to setting salaries for bank employees. In 1981 a crisis due to interest rate adjustments affected debtors severely and had such an adverse impact on some banks that the government had to take them over. The basic laws for state banks were eventually reformed and gradually to reflect the true cost of credit under inflationary conditions like those before 1985. Other liberalizing measures, such as reducing legal reserves in both national and foreign currency, were adopted.

Peru returned to market practices after the 1985–90 crisis, eliminating the development bank and permitting discrimination among types of banks. New regulations establish minimal requirements for diversification, thereby avoiding concentration of credit. Full-service banking now allows financial institutions to engage in factoring, financial leasing, mutual fund management, selling securities, and other functions typical of investment banks. Even though Peru's Superintendency of Banks had experience in development matters and preventive supervision, the change of government made it possible to reduce its size. To improve risk control procedures, a deposit insurance system was created. The concept of "maximum debt" was changed to "net worth adjustment," as defined by the Basel Committee, thus internationalizing risk measurement in the industry.

Consequences in Uruguay

Uruguay's severe crisis led to a government takeover of a significant portion of national banking. Unlike Chile and Peru, however, the outcome did not lead toward a private operating framework. Nevertheless, the Superintendency of Banks is trying to measure the portfolio risk of loans more adequately, adopting methods of preventive oversight and establishing risk control. There is a new plan to analyze accounts and ensure greater compliance with information standards for tax law purposes. Currently the system involves obligatory customer classification and the use of credit ratings—essential information for the central risk office. Small customers are not included, making the costs more suitable for the intermediation apparatus. The information obtained is basic for evaluating net worth, and makes it possible to shift from a system based on delinquency to one based on evaluating estimated losses.

As for the overall framework for evaluating financial entities, Uruguay's regulatory system seeks to shift overall debt toward a limit based on adequate capital, as indicated in the Basel Committee rules. This creates a system like that of Peru, oriented toward internationalized banking. Finally, officials intend to eliminate government influence by privatizing the banks currently under state ownership, so as to restore Uruguayan banking to private hands.

Disintermediation and Nonbank Developments

An important conclusion from all these experiences is that creating competitors for the traditional financial system reflects both the capital market's natural development and the banking system's failure to provide precise instruments. In the capital market's natural development, "financial disintermediation"[7] is based on lower transaction costs flowing from improved communications systems and technologies allowing suppliers and customers to locate one another. The Chilean capital market is a case in point, and the experience may soon be repeated in Argentina and Peru. However, the lack of organizations linked to the financial system prompts the rise of parallel institutional arrangements, as in Guatemala and to some extent in Uruguay.

Chile: The Clearest Example of Banking Disintermediation

The change in the 1986 General Banking Law contemplates the possibility that the financial system might develop activities within its own proper sphere. Such a change then reflected clear signs of a more developed capital market connected both to significant privatization of state-owned enterprises and to success in the pension fund system, based on the capitalization of individual retirement accounts. Both ideas entailed an expansion of stock market activities and greater sophistication in capital markets. Thus both the short- and long-term bond markets expanded, causing the volume of intermediation handled by the banking system to decline significantly by 1991. The involvement of this industry in managing mutual funds, investments, securities, trading shares, financial leasing companies, and consulting companies has stimulated the growth of capital markets and has unquestionably spurred its modernization.

---

[7] The term refers to alternatives that replace functions usually performed by the traditional financial system.

Argentina and Peru: Noteworthy Events

Although the stock exchanges in both these capital markets have grown more sophisticated over years of operation, two major changes are still to come. Only very recently (1993 for Peru and 1994 for Argentina) were retirement systems based on interest-earning accounts established in these countries. Similarly, there are still many state-owned companies not yet privatized. After that happens, the level of capital in the stock exchanges will rise. In this context a significant development in Peru is the recent change allowing full service banking. Mutual stock funds, risk analysis companies, and securities clearing and settlement institutions have been created. The deregulation process envisioned in the operating framework of the Argentine financial system also makes it foreseeable that banking revenue sources are going to diversify in an interesting way, thus allowing for significant development of stock market opportunities.

Guatemala and Uruguay: Opposite Situations

The capital market in Guatemala is admittedly not very developed. The existing securities exchanges basically trade bonds issued by the government or the Central Bank. Bank and government have become more important since the adoption of an adjustment policy based on open-market operations. A second source feeding the process has been the increased issuing of bonds by Guatemala's major companies. High interest rates and rigid banking legislation have led to a "quasi-disintermediation," in the sense that companies connected to banking ownership groups have arisen. Such companies appear as finance companies, financial leasing companies, and factoring companies (which are more agile and flexible) and are financed basically through bank loans. In addition, credit card companies, export-oriented companies, and offshore banking centers are serving other needs that traditional banks cannot meet.

The security exchange situation in Uruguay is comparable, since those markets have been used mainly for handing fixed income bonds. The lack of development is due primarily to the macroeconomic instability that characterizes Uruguay's economic system. Moreover, the small size of the companies and their heavily family-oriented management discourage potential issuers and investors. There is no sign of interest in attracting institutional investors other than those in traditional banking, a situation not likely to change soon.

Definition of Small and Medium-Sized Enterprises and Their Relationship to the Financial Sector

This section summarizes the situation of the small enterprise sector in each country considered, and seeks to outline the features of this sector in its relationships with the traditional financial system. Existing studies tend not to use a common definition for classifying companies in this sector, although the terms they use are quite similar.[8]

Features of Small and Medium-Sized Business

The countries under study undoubtedly have features in common, although they also have certain clear differences due to the specific nature of each economy. The informal quality of this sector of the economy made it necessary to devise measuring procedures quite specific to each case, making comparison between countries difficult.

According to available information, Argentina's small and medium-sized business sector includes 30,000 enterprises, accounting for about 45 percent of employment and representing about 33 percent of industrial production volume. Most of these enterprises began after World War II and have not modernized much since. As this sector is technologically backward and operates in an informal manner, the financial system has long neglected its needs. Consequently, efforts to support it have come primarily from the state.

In Chile also, small and medium-sized enterprises have played a significant role in job creation and represent 36.5 percent of the total. Calculations suggest that its effect on production is less important, since it does not account for even 24 percent of gross sales. Small and medium-sized Chilean enterprises are flexibly organized, often ignoring labor and tax laws. Since the traditional financial system does not serve them, they obtain financing through informal markets. Recently, foreign assembly and licensing procedures, which are fully operational in Chile, have spurred this sector. Nevertheless, these companies continue to be suppliers for large enterprises; when they do manage to export, they do so through specialized agents.

Estimates from 1987 showed that Guatemala had 356,000 micro, small, and medium-sized enterprises that created about 800,000 jobs. Contrary to the earlier cases, in Guatemala there has been a more focused development in financing the sector, actively involving nongovernmental organizations (NGOs) and financial system support. Guatemala is thus an exception to the general rule among the case studies. Even so, the country faces a significant shortfall of domestic savings, and its small and medium-sized enterprises have chronic unmet financial needs.

---

[8] In this book the terms *small business* and *small enterprise* are used to mean all smaller companies. To refer to a subcategory we have used the following criteria: A *microenterprise* has no more than ten employees, no more than US$10,000 in assets, and sales of less than US$45,000. A *small business* employs no more than twenty persons, its assets may reach US$50,000, and its sales may rise to US$200,000 a year. A *medium-sized business* employs no more than fifty workers and has assets of no more than US$300,000. (Source: Inter-American Development Bank).

Preliminary information gathered by Peru's Central Reserve Bank for 1989 listed around 775,000 businesses as small enterprises, providing approximately 1,330,000 jobs. Most of these companies were connected to commerce (66.7 percent), while only 9.5 percent were industrial. The recent fall in levels of economic activity has increased the relative importance of this sector, since it absorbed a significant fraction of existing unemployment. Such flexibility is rooted in the very informality with which the sector functions. In financial terms, neither the banking system nor existing NGOs have offered efficient support, and the virtual disappearance of development banking has only aggravated the situation. The structure of these enterprises is therefore along family lines and financing comes from suppliers, money lenders, pawnshops, and other informal sources.

Finally, Uruguay's 1988 Economic Census recorded 158,000 urban enterprises with fewer than ten employees; these small firms, which represented 94 percent of the number of urban enterprises in the country, created 32 percent of urban jobs. Those companies were concentrated primarily in commerce and services. Moreover, agricultural operations of less than 200 hectares (the standard used to identify small producers) represented 73.2 percent of the total, employed 56 percent of the labor force, and occupied 13.7 of the farming area. Unlike the other countries, small businesses in Uruguay's cities are not a form of disguised unemployment. Concentrated in Montevideo, they are owned by well-educated businesspeople using their own capital to finance investments, limiting their need to use the banking system. The situation is different in rural areas, which have 60 percent of the microenterprises.

Small Enterprise and the Financial System

These country studies reveal common features in the relationship between small enterprises and the traditional financial system. Lack of credit is not the only problem, however; the small business sector has other specific concerns related to the demand for financial services.

With respect to credit supply issues, at least three kinds of barriers unquestionably contribute to segmenting credit. First, persistent macroeconomic problems due to monetary or fiscal imbalances lead both to high interest rates and to significant government involvement in the capital market. High interest rates increase the cost of banking services, so that marginal borrowers who represent greater risk are excluded. Likewise, excessive government involvement in the credit market tends to restrict the flow of resources to the private sector.

Second, in response to macroeconomic problems, most countries have gradually adopted preventive monitoring practices. These procedures, which give priority to controlling risk, ultimately penalize shortcomings in the areas of net worth, guarantees, and information, and limit individual and overall risk exposure through margins. In addition, such practices plainly make monitoring small loans burdensome.

A third set of factors related to the credit supply are legal difficulties. Some countries are obliged to accept forced loan reschedulings, which further discourage the granting of loans. Similarly the enforcement conditions of loan agreements, the possibility of enforcing the guarantees, and slow judicial process all reduce the likelihood of recovery in case of delinquency. That predisposes banks to avoid customers who do not fully meet the established requirements.

Besides these external barriers, certain characteristics of small enterprises also reduce their prospects for credit. First, the small business person is often inexperienced in management, due to gaps in education or training. He or she may know little about how the financial system works and how to approach creditors. Finally, the enterprises themselves have low sales volumes, are less diversified, and use obsolete and inefficient technology. All these factors weaken their credit applications.

A brief description of the relationship between the small enterprise sector and the financial system in each country follows.

Argentina

The Argentine experience has much in common with the conclusions stated above. Although stabilization programs have increased the lending capacity of the financial system, the loans granted are for large-scale operations handled primarily through private banks. Smaller customers use government banking in urban areas and the municipal banks in rural regions. Nevertheless, these two providers of services focus their credit portfolios primarily on loans to the public sector and to municipalities. That explains their relatively small impact on small enterprises.

Though some private companies have created specialized services in small credits, obstacles remain to granting small enterprises more attention. For example, these companies are said to need substantial technological change, given the structural change they must face in order to participate in an increasingly privatized, market-based economy. Second, the banks themselves lack experience in evaluating small enterprise investment proposals. Standards for distributing loans more broadly, which would increase the value of small businesses as borrowers, are still not being applied, so the Argentine financial system remains highly concentrated. Finally, small enterprises are thought to be not sufficiently prepared to handle credit properly. Nevertheless, lines of refinancing are being channeled through government banking, and they help explain why participation in the financial system remains narrow, as explained further in chapter two.

Chile

Chile's traditional financial system has virtually ignored small business, as the segmentation of credit makes plain. The reasons for that are certainly linked to the banks' credit evaluation procedures, which are clearly biased toward the preventive monitoring standards of oversight officials. Such procedures place a premium on the amount of information available about businesses and on guarantees as a second source of loan repayment.

Monitoring costs are lower for large companies that use the capital market and produce their own information, in order to obtain the lowest financing costs. Collecting information is more expensive for small companies, and few financial agencies are willing to become involved in the initial evaluation process. Furthermore, since these are small credits, the unit costs for handling loans are high, and the lack of security collateral entails additional costs and specific provisions for the operation. Thus when private banks grant credit to this sector, the loan agreements have high interest rates, and in practice these operations have a higher average risk. However, disintermediation is now changing bankers' appreciation for small business. Moreover, the State Bank (Chile's only government bank) maintains lines of credit for small enterprises, so the banking system deals with this sector to some extent. Some financial companies are offering special lines that reflect their interest in developing new businesses.

Guatemala

As noted above, a monetary policy aimed at recovering macroeconomic stability is being applied in Guatemala. Interest rates now motivate banks to act more selectively, so they are even less likely to serve small enterprises. Guatemala's outdated Banking Law imposes administrative patterns on financial intermediation, which also explains the lack of financing for small enterprises. There are strict requirements for minimum guarantees, registration requirements, accounting records, and a minimum history of operation—requirements that reduce the chances of access for groups who cannot afford them. Nevertheless, some indirect efforts have enabled them to participate successfully in the financial system, even if on a small scale. One is the case of FUNTEC-Génesis Empresarial, an NGO that since 1990 has obtained financing with the support of ten banks and two finance companies that supply credit for working capital, machinery, and equipment.

Peru

Peru's recent adjustment policy, in effect since 1990, abruptly curtailed funds that the Central Reserve Bank granted for development banking. After this banking disappeared, the financing problems of small enterprises were aggravated.

Long-range funding is virtually unavailable, due to the country's recent history of instability, compounded by uncertainty over property rights. This basic problem has a serious impact on small enterprises. Their access to private bank credit, as in the other countries studied, is limited by high costs and insufficient information. For example, due to their informal manner of operation, small businesses often lack up-to-date financial statements.

Nor are there adequate registries of guarantees to facilitate the writing of loan agreements. Judicial enforcement processes are tedious and unreliable. The high cost of processing and monitoring small loans based on incomplete information translates into a high financing cost for those companies receiving credit, creating a counterproductive cycle of risk.

Uruguay

Because of the features already mentioned, small enterprises in Uruguay have circumstances different from those of the other countries examined, because their financing comes largely internal resources. Uruguay's microenterprises, however, have greater difficulty gaining access to financial resources, due to insufficient information.

The financial sector believes that micro-, small, and medium-sized enterprises encounter problems because they cannot meet the banking industry's criteria for risk evaluation. In many instances, figures are changed for tax purposes, thus producing information that does not properly reflect the true situation of the companies. There are also problems in complying with requirements for guarantees. Nevertheless, Uruguay is moving away from a system based on delinquent credit and is adopting a process of preventive oversight based on risk analysis. Obtaining small amounts of credit is becoming easier, and the stages of granting and renewing lines of credit are becoming more significant.

Finally, the state-owned Bank of the Republic, the main financial entity that issues small loans, is maintaining a high level of coverage in the countryside and other specific areas. Unfortunately, that institution has no professional procedures for allocating and monitoring those loans.

Proposed Solutions for Small Enterprises without Access to the Financial System

The tradition of segmented credit facing small companies is connected to the use of public resources through state programs or refinancing arrangements implemented through financial intermediaries. To this day the same principle has been at work in multilateral support provided by international lending agencies.

Financing mechanisms for small business have moved toward greater private sector involvement and are now grounded in market-oriented principles. One effective system for serving those needs is that of NGOs not tied directly to state agencies, although not entirely independent of them. Another successful set of experiences is that of producer associations and cooperatives that obtain loans with group collateral posted as security, granted primarily with funds from the financial system. Subsidy allocating mechanisms have shifted from granting them directly toward procedures that reduce the interest rates of loans refinanced through the banking system or other intermediaries. Occasionally such programs are complemented with procedures for helping persons in small businesses to qualify for credit, including training in how to obtain bank credits. The aim is to legitimize small businesspeople as creditworthy borrowers, enabling them to meet their future financing needs more independently.

Certain alternatives such as financial leasing or factoring are gradually resolving the problem faced by small enterprises in terms of collateral and their needs for working capital. Although these alternatives represent higher financial costs than those of obtaining bank loans, they are faster, and provide services for industries that market to small enterprises. In some cases they benefit from government or outside refinancing, thereby lowering costs to reasonable levels.

Finally, the fact of financial disintermediation has created a new situation for small enterprises, which has now begun to emerge as an alternative and attractive source of revenue for banking, which is facing more competition from other intermediaries. There are some interesting experiments in classifying small customers only by information for granting and monitoring the loan, and evaluating it primarily by whether due payments are made.

Such experiences are not entirely alike in all the countries surveyed, so each situation requires its own brief treatment.

Alternative Responses: Argentina

Two interesting lines of support stand out prominently in the Argentine experience: (1) measures aimed at the use of the financial system and (2) measures to encourage use of mechanisms elsewhere in the capital market.

Among those that apply to the financial system, changing financial regulations to reduce the individual credit margins applied to borrowers is an interesting effort, but cannot yet be judged successful. The complementary "Three-Year Development Program" uses the intermediation capability of the financial system to make public funds available to meet the investment and working capital needs of small businesses. This program employs a bidding process for funds based on the interest rates charged by each bank, and is the most effective of those applied to small enterprises.

In measures that involve mechanisms such as stock markets, the initiatives currently underway are also interesting, although not yet successful in practice. For example, the Central Bank allowed the issuing of negotiable debts in order to direct resources toward investments in fixed assets, working capital, refinancing liabilities, and even financing personal and mortgage loans. Small businesses have been allowed to issue debt instruments that do not need to be classified. The National Securities Commission also formulated a policy allowing small businesses access to the stock exchange and has created a section for new projects. As innovative and modern as such initiatives might be, they have not had a great impact.

Alternative Responses: Chile

Solutions to the financing problem of small businesses belong to two large groups: support for financing processes, and actual financing. Those alternatives arise from the state's concern to create an innovative kind of aid. Until recently, interventionist attempts had led to a high level of delinquency and a selectivity that constrained credit. Current policies are attempting to make accepted borrowers of small businesses: to encourage them to use public resources and take advantage of the banking system's loan evaluation and administrative capability.

Notable among support measures are those set up by CORFO (*Corporación de Fomento para la Producción,* the Corporation for Production Development), which seek to guide small businesspeople as well as financial intermediaries. An outstanding example is the SUAF (*Subsidio a la Asistencia Crediticia,* Credit Assistance Subsidy), which directs state resources toward the collection of more financial information from small enterprises by using specialized consultants, who also train businesspeople to take advantage of the alternatives offered by the traditional financial system.

There has been some success in attracting funds from the financial system and the financial leasing industry by using "discount coupons" that can be applied to loan-credit premiums, and support for the production credit card program adopted by at least one bank in the system. Based solely on criteria for granting loans and delinquency, the credit card program is intended to meet needs for working capital. But a lack of adequate monitoring agencies and the banks' practice of selection based on net worth has restricted the actual use of these funds by small businesses.

The experience of providing public sector resources is not different from that of other countries. Thus, for example, CORFO puts up for bid funds obtained from multilateral financing agencies, such as lines established by the IDB. Probably the most novel development in this area has been the incorporation into these programs of the growing and increasingly successful industry of financial leasing. Due to the bias of the credit issuing process, however, large companies have absorbed much of the funding. A second interesting example is that of State Bank support programs for small business, involving soft credits ranging from investment finance to working capital, including finance of imports and exports. The latter have shown notable growth, especially in the agricultural sector.

Private initiatives connected to financing small enterprises in Chile are primarily connected to the financial leasing industry. It has even been estimated that 40 percent of leasing contracts are in this area. Efforts at risk capital investment funds have been less successful, probably because they demand a very short operation period. Both intermediaries, financial leasing and investment funds, depend largely on resources tied to pension funds, which primarily use bonds issued by them.

Alternative Responses: Guatemala

In Guatemala, NGOs and various kinds of cooperatives have probably been most successful in obtaining funds with support from the government and even from private banking, as was noted previously.

Various NGOs operate in the Guatemalan market with funds obtained through the Bank of Guatemala, thereby assuring government backing and a certain coverage for exchange-rate risk. Though the amounts involved are not large, what has been done thus far is regarded as successful. Among the most outstanding experiences is that of FUNTEC-Génesis Empresarial, which furnishes not only financing but technical training and on-site consulting for small businesses. Its financing sources include the lines of credit mentioned and support from ten banks and two private finance companies.

Among the cooperatives is FENECOAC *(Federación Nacional de Cooperativas de Ahorro y Crédito,* National Federation of Savings and Loan Cooperatives) devoted primarily to farmers. However, it makes loans at high interest rates, thus limiting its scope. There are also community credit programs, such as the association CEDRO *(Cooperación para el Desarrollo Rural,* Cooperation for Rural Development), which operates with funds from their community members and from national and international aid organizations.

Also noteworthy in NGO and private banking experience is the establishment of solidarity groups with mutually shared collateral posted as security. In such a procedure the volumes of credit are maintained at amounts determined by the credit granted; payment is also collected where people work. That procedure has been successful thus far. Among the informal financial alternatives are coffee exporters and producers who make advances made to small enterprises and informal financial companies working with extremely high interest rates.

Finally in Guatemala, as in most of the countries studied, the results obtained from guarantee funds are meager, primarily due to lack of analysis when loans are made and to inadequate collection procedures.

Alternative Responses: Peru

In Peru, formulas for financing outside the banks are primarily connected to the work of NGOs and to maintaining guarantee funds. Probably the most novel aspects are procedures for credit operations with group guarantees and complementary technical assistance.

Acción Comunitaria, CARE, and IDESI have been the most successful. The first two are NGOs which grant loans, while the third administers guarantee funds and rates and supervises loans aimed at small enterprises. A series of activities connected to financing small business are centered within Acción Comunitaria and CARE. Acción Comunitaria receives funding from multilateral banks and provides guarantees to assist microenterprises or poorer companies, adding training services and technical assistance. CARE focuses primarily on training and loan supervision, but also grants loans whose average repayment periods are longer than those commonly offered to small enterprises.

These organizations have provided effective services for small enterprise, and delinquency has been low. Collateral guarantee funds have been maintained in an effort to make small businesses creditworthy borrowers. The disappearance of development banking after the 1990 adjustment policies made the operation of NGOs all the more important. Since then, significant restructurings have defined even more clearly the lending process maintained by this sector of the financing market.

Alternative Responses: Uruguay

Uruguay's financing system reflects the strong influence of the Bank of the Republic (BROU), which supports small credits through a broad distribution network. BROU focuses specifically on various sectors of activity and maintains a significant coverage in the countryside. As noted earlier, the quality of loan allocation is unsatisfactory because this institution is government-owned.

NGOs in Uruguay do not handle a significant amount of lending to small businesses, and their activity is devoted primarily to creating enterprises and to technical assistance. Their loans are more costly than those offered by traditional banking and credit unions. Due to the particular market structure of the small enterprise sector in Uruguay, credit unions are its main support, but this financing is seriously flawed, primarily in the countryside. However, CONAPROLE (*Cooperativa Nacional de Productores de Leche,* National Dairy Producers Cooperative) and other producer cooperatives take on debt and then pass the loans on to their members, thus reaping the advantages of group guarantees.

Other alternatives developed by the market for resolving the issue of financing small enterprises are expensive and inefficient. Credit provided by suppliers, for example, carries interest rates much higher than market rates. Postdating checks presents similar problems. The financial lending industry is little developed, since their services, unlike those of the banks, are subject to value-added tax (VAT). Finally, although in Uruguay the invoice is a tradable instrument, factoring is unreliable, given the ease of eliminating invoices by issuing credit notes.

Main Policy Recommendations

Although small enterprises may differ in the various countries examined, the kind of treatment they receive from the financial system is alike in many ways. Their alternatives for satisfying the financing shortage are similar, so these policy recommendations are applicable to most of the cases. This section presents the main conclusions, and strives to formulate general propositions on the different areas in which regulatory or other changes are needed to improve financing possibilities for small enterprises.

General Recommendations

Proper management of the macroeconomic apparatus remains a basic element for reducing the credit segmentation facing not only small enterprises, but all those with a net worth insufficient to allow them access to financial markets.

In this sense, it is generally believed that stimulating savings and striving to eliminate any kind of financial repression are important, and that doing so indirectly helps improve the situation of small business. Making central banks independent would allow greater freedom to apply monetary policies aimed at assuring price stability and gradually lowering interest rates. These are crucial measures for establishing more efficient financial systems, resulting in a greater volume of available funds. Stability allows stock markets to develop further, creating spaces that make investment in all kinds of companies more attractive.

The state's presence, whether in the credit market or as a creator of debt instruments, is a second source of distortion. The size of the public sector indicates its level of involvement, as in Argentina's government banks, preventing others who demand credit from satisfying their financing needs at a suitable cost. Therefore reducing the size and the deficits of the public sector are unquestionably an incentive for the financial system to diversify its loan portfolio. From another angle, the stabilization goal of Guatemala's monetary policy has been achieved by using high interest Central Bank instruments, which now represent a significant portion of the banking system's credit portfolio.

Several of these countries' experiences indicate the need to improve the legal means for efficient execution of contracts. The debt instruments and mandatory rescheduling encouraged by the Uruguayan government are a good example. Measures aimed at increasing trust in the institutional framework can effectively reduce the risk level of financial operations. Initiatives to improve the information about potential users of financial services, and about the intermediaries themselves, have a similar effect. In certain cases, the use of fiscal requirements may improve tax collection and provide more reliable and useful information for decisionmaking.

Recommendations Regarding the Financial System

Here, again, supporting arguments of a general nature should be clearly differentiated from those measures that would have a concrete impact on the small enterprise sector.

In all countries considered, small businesses find it difficult to obtain bank credit due to the barriers raised by regulations governing how they relate to the monetary system. That connection is partly a result of the Central Bank's role as lender of last resort due to the need to keep the economy's payment system functioning. In practical terms, banking regulations require prior approval from supervisory bodies in order to operate within a particular financial system. That measure clearly restricts competitive financing by financial intermediaries, and therefore affects the cost of providing services. With Uruguay's situation particularly in mind, that restriction can be reduced by improving access to the finance industry, and thus improving competitiveness and the transaction costs entailed in requirements. Argentina's experience points to encouraging greater efficiency in the operation of the financial system by reducing government ownership through privatization and reducing costs of providing services.

The cost of intermediation, however, depends on more than the number of institutions or the level of privatization of the financial system. A determining element of that cost is the quality of the loan selection and monitoring process. A loan portfolio with a high default ratio will no doubt make it necessary to finance non-revenue generating assets which must be covered with resources, thus affecting costs. In this sense, preventive oversight is justified in economic terms, since it makes it possible to reduce the problem of resource allocation caused by a poorly structured credit process. It also reduces the potential cost of state intervention when that is justified. Both approaches entail a lower intermediation cost and therefore a more efficient resource allocation process.

In circumstances like those in Chile, two restrictive aspects of regulation must be reduced. First, the exchange controls applied by monetary officials artificially raise the overall cost of domestic credits. Second, it is impossible to provide the full service banking activities established by the Banking Law, which limits the possibility of creating a broad spectrum of businesses and so reducing the industry's marginal costs. Thus eliminating exchange controls and diversifying bank asset portfolios would raise bank productivity, and the ensuing economies of scale would lead to significant cost savings.

Finally, Peru's success with deposit insurance systems may be mentioned, along with Uruguay's intention to do the same. These are being proposed as a way of raising the domestic savings level, and in at least one of these countries the effort has been successful.

Specific Recommendations for Financial Services to Small Enterprises

As indicated in the previous point, a system for preventive oversight must be established. Due to the financial crises of the 1980s, portfolio classification procedures exist in Chile and Uruguay at least, and risk evaluation processes based on the net worth of potential borrowers are being established. Although such procedures are quite useful for the overall operation of the financial system, they have unfortunately become a major obstacle hindering small businesses from obtaining credit, since the characteristic traits of this sector include lack of information, low levels of capital, and a perennial lack of guarantees.

The first specific recommendation is that a different evaluation procedure should be devised for smaller credits than is used for most loans. Uruguay's method, for example, is based solely on granting and monitoring the credit, acknowledging not only the costs for small businesses to generate information, but also their difficulty in obtaining sufficient guarantees. In Chile, small businesspeople have begun using credit cards, in which risk is evaluated from previous behavior or potential delinquency by loan recipients.

Another way of providing access to the financial system for small business is to expand the use of credit insurance programs that eliminate the excessive cost currently facing such companies. The use of mechanisms for allocating subsidies, such as those successfully used in Chile under the name of CUBOS, is another notable example.

In Argentina, where the most successful experiences have to do with channeling government resources toward lowering the interest rates charged to small enterprises, one new idea is to establish participatory guarantee funds in which the finance entity also shares the risk. In this approach, the small enterprises that use the benefit pay in proportion to their use, thus assuring that the system is self-financing. Such a relationship would maintain interest on both sides, that of small enterprises and that of the financial system, throughout the life of loan agreements.

On the other hand, in Guatemala, Peru, and Uruguay, the experience of using joint community guarantees has been successful and could be used widely and as a complement to the initiative posed in the Argentine example.

Finally, in those financial systems where government plays a significant role as owner of the institutions, the argument for privatization cannot always be translated into an immediate solution. Based on Uruguay's experience, it is proposed that in such cases measures be adopted to improve the management of such agencies, decentralizing decisionmaking, improving incentives for the employees, and professionalizing the different levels involved in approving credits. The proposed decentralization of decisionmaking likewise creates momentum for reducing the political influence exerted by members of the boards of directors who are closely allied with government agencies.

Recommendations Directly Related to Small Enterprises

To complement what was said under the previous point, there is a series of recommendations aimed at stimulating demand for credit by small enterprises, since there are often significant obstacles on this side. The first type of measure that can be applied directly to small enterprises has to do with the spread of programs to stimulate the use of bank credit, based on providing training for businesses and using consultants, like the SUAF program in Chile.

That stimulus can be complemented by strengthening management capacity either by setting up specialized centers or by designing activities to complement such training efforts. That would encourage greater appreciation of small businesspeople as creditworthy borrowers. To extend such centers and activities is among the most important recommendations of this study. Direct assistance is another important complement, particularly in aspects such as technological innovation in countries like Argentina, where this sector is significantly outdated.

Support for retail operations and for other specializations within small business are another important alternative, as is the encouragement of producers' associations like those operating in Guatemala and Uruguay. This support becomes even more important where the financial system is less able to deal with small companies, as has happened in rural areas of Chile and Argentina. Indeed, the spread of procedures that contemplate the use of joint guarantees complements the proposals to open the financial system up to the possibility of being involved as second-level banking. The successes of a Guatemalan NGO and a Uruguayan cooperative demonstrate that banking can play an important role when the issue of risk is handled appropriately.

Finally, changes in pension fund management systems and the spread of support by multilateral agencies make it possible again to consider risk capital as a financing alternative for small business. Argentina, Chile, and Peru are now at that stage, and some complementary efforts are underway to support small enterprises with the possibility that they might issue publicly traded or other types of bonds that could become part of the portfolios of various institutional investors.

Conclusions

An examination of the experiences of Argentina, Chile, Guatemala, Peru, and Uruguay leads to a series of conclusions that are set forth briefly in the paragraphs to follow.

Macroeconomic adjustment programs were already underway in most cases, whether prompted by external shocks, management problems, or simply inadequate monetary or exchange rate policies that plainly resulted in a crisis. Such adjustments had consequences for the financial situation of companies and for the agencies providing their financing. In the more complex cases, such as those of Chile and Uruguay, programs were set up to support both debtors and banks, with the consequent fiscal and monetary cost. These were part of a useful learning process during the experiences of liberalization and financial intensification. The outcome was a financial system that was decidedly private in Chile and primarily state-dominated in Uruguay. Depending on the intensity of the crisis, the experience led to conservative approaches of preventive oversight based on the gathering of predictive information and processes of portfolio classification that are now being adopted by most Latin American financial systems. Such practices have imposed relatively demanding standards for loan approval under the control of oversight officials. Thus, the result of financial intensification and the crisis within banking systems has been a particular kind of segmentation based on risk.

In the more recent adjustment experiences—in which interests rates were raised in order to lower the money supply and stabilize prices—segmentation took place more naturally, as illustrated in Argentina, Peru, and more recently, Guatemala. The procedures used by the banking system generally penalize lack of information and guarantees. Small businesses, which operate informally due to insufficient guarantees and a perennial lack of information, have therefore sought to obtain alternate financing sources, which include government, multilateral, and market efforts. However, reduced asymmetries of size and information have led to a process of disintermediation, forcing banks to seek new business alternatives, including personal credit and credit for small companies.

Thus the situations that impair the small business sector can be viewed as forming two groups: those of a general nature and those proper to their particular segment. The most important of the first group are those aspects of segmentation caused by persisting macroeconomic problems, such as restrictive monetary policies, inflation, high interest rates, or a high degree of government involvement. Similarly, legal issues such as mandatory reschedulings or contract enforcement involve general aspects that significantly harm smaller borrowers. Finally, the preventive supervision processes limit exposure to individual risks, demand levels of guarantees and information that small and medium businesses cannot fully meet, and raise the financial and administrative cost of credit.

The situations specific to this sector that harm small and medium-sized business have to do with the low education level of businesspeople in the sector. Such businesses are often undiversified, low-volume operations that are technologically obsolete and fail to meet fiscal and labor standards.

The approaches that have partially resolved the financing problems of small and medium-sized businesses are primarily state- or multilateral-supported programs. One aspect is becoming increasingly important as such support programs begin: the use of market-based allocation tools. Government funds are generally offered for bidding so that the resources may reach the user adequately through specialized intermediaries and the risk may be properly covered. Banks and other formal intermediaries are prominent in this effort, although NGOs have been most efficient in implementing aid programs for small enterprise. Such entities have operated at different levels of the credit management process, ranging from obtaining funds and evaluating risk to applying those funds. They differ from traditional intermediaries, in that they often teach the businessperson not only how to obtain the loan, but also what technology to use.

The problem of information and guarantees, which was originally confronted unsuccessfully by creating special funds from government sources, is also finding different approaches to a solution based on market considerations. A number of advisory service programs now encourage the small businessperson and the traditional banking system to develop joint activities for creating information. In the area of guarantees, there are noteworthy efforts at using loan insurance, some using group collateral as security. The latter has even been used through cooperative experiences in which businesspeople connected to a particular area of production act as co-signers.

Such alternatives seek to improve the creditworthiness of the small businessperson. Other activities such as financial leasing and factoring, although they are still expensive and uncertain, have resolved the questions of guarantees and the financing of working capital. Credit directly from suppliers, advances granted by exporters, and credit cards for buying supplies all indicate how the market is directly organizing solutions without need for government support.

Finally, the policy recommendations that flow from this study place the emphasis on the role of the market in solving the chronic financing shortage of small enterprise. Hence it is extremely important that economic systems not be repressed, that monetary officials be independent, and that government influence in the capital market be limited so as to allow new actors to enter the financial system. On this last point, it is crucial to lower the access barriers, to increase competition and lower intermediation costs. The use of preventive oversight for small customers represents an excessive cost that must be examined. Here the idea of granting and monitoring credit should prevail over the traditional idea based on rating credit in terms of the risk of nonreturn. To support the involvement of neglected sectors, efforts such as the establishment of funds that use participatory collateral as security (and share risks between businesspeople and financial entities) are a crucial form of support. Similarly, it is advisable to encourage the spread of loan insurance systems, which solve the problem of the excessive cost that small companies are forced to incur.

Strengthening management capability by the formation of groups to provide advice and direct assistance should stimulate demand for bank credit by small businesses, thus breaking the vicious circle of financing. Creating agencies or cooperative entities to post group collateral guarantees or provide other services could have a similar effect. Multilateral credit based on capitalization through risk-capital procedures, about which there is not yet much evidence, might stimulate the formation of new companies or support existing ones.

Bibliography

Basch, Miguel. 1994. La Desconcentración del acceso a los servicios financieros: el caso chileno. Washington, D.C. Inter-American Development Bank. Working Papers Series No. 170.

Díaz-Alejandro, C. 1985. "Good-Bye Financial Repression, Hello Financial Crash." *Journal of Development Economics* 19 (1).

Frenkel, Roberto. 1994. El fortalecimiento del sector financiero en el proceso de ajuste: un análisis de Argentina, Brasil, Colombia y Uruguay. In *El Fortalecimiento del Sector Financiero en el Proceso de Ajuste: Liberalización y Regulación,* Roberto Frenkel, editor. CEDES-BID: Buenos Aires.

Held, Günter. 1989. Regulación y supervisión de la banca en la experiencia de liberalización financiera en Chile (1974–1988). ECLAC, Santiago, Chile.

McKinnon, R. 1973. *Money and Capital in Economic Development.* Washington, D.C.: The Brookings Institution.

Morales, C. 1989. Filiales bancarias: la experiencia chilena. Información Financiera, SBIF, Chile.

Noya, Nelson. 1994. La desconcentración del acceso a los servicios financieros: el caso de Uruguay. Washington, D.C.: Inter-American Development Bank. Working Papers Series No. 173.

Noya, N., and D. Dominioni. 1994. El fortalecimiento del sector financiero en el proceso de ajuste: liberalización y regulación. El caso uruguayo. In *El Fortalecimiento del Sector Financiero en el Proceso de Ajuste: Liberalización y Regulación,* Roberto Frenkel, editor. CEDES-BID, Argentina.

Ramírez, Guillermo. 1989. Política bancaria y legislación financiera: la experiencia chilena de los años 80. *Información Financiera,* SBIF, Chile.

Rozenwurcel, G., and R. Fernández. 1994. La desconcentración del acceso a los servicios financieros: el caso argentino. Washington, D.C.: Inter-American Development Bank. Working Papers Series No. 169.

_______. 1994. El fortalecimiento del sector financiero en el proceso de ajuste: el caso argentino. In *El Fortalecimiento del Sector Financiero en el Proceso de Ajuste: Liberalización y Regulación,* Roberto Frenkel, editor. CEDES-BID, Argentina.

Shaw, E. 1973. *Financial Deepening in Economic Development.* Oxford University Press.

Sosa, L., et al. 1994. La desconcentración del acceso a los servicios financieros en Guatemala. Washington, D.C.: Inter-American Development Bank. Working Papers Series No. 171.

Velarde, J., and M. Rodríguez. 1994. La desconcentración del acceso a los servicios financieros: el caso peruano. Washington, D.C.: Inter-American Development Bank. Working Papers Series No. 172.

CHAPTER TWO

ARGENTINA: OVERCOMING PERCEPTIONS OF CREDIT RISK

Guillermo Rozenwurcel
Raúl Fernández*

Financial market segmentation and unfavorable treatment of small enterprise have long been recognized as serious problems in the Argentine economy. Not surprisingly, the adverse effects of these problems have become more acute in the present macroeconomic environment, which demands that these businesses retool their operations.

This chapter examines the difficulties that Argentina's small businesses face in obtaining credit and other financial services. The study concludes with specific policy recommendations for overcoming these difficulties.

In the first of four sections, we discuss the general financial environment of Argentina's economy in the 1990s, focusing on the period after the 1991 Convertibility Plan. We also address in detail the challenges confronting smaller businesses in light of changing economic circumstances.

Next we analyze the structure and operation of Argentina's current financial system—its monetary and physical size, and the distinctive features and operations of its financial institutions. Then we examine the degree of bank concentration and review the performance indicators of the financial system: efficiency, liquidity, and solvency.

The third section discusses the functioning of capital markets in today's economy. Close attention is paid to the financing restrictions imposed upon small businesses and to the government's financial assistance programs. In the final

* The authors wish to express their appreciation for the comments received from participants at a seminar of the Network of Applied Economic Research Centers, sponsored by the Inter-American Development Bank in Buenos Aires during April, 1994, and especially to Camilo Morales, Glenn Westley, and Jose Luis Machinea.

section we present the study's main conclusions and list a series of policy recommendations.

Small Enterprise in the Macrofinancial Context of the 1990s

During the 1980s, the Argentine economy suffered from an underlying financial disequilibrium: As private-sector funds for loans were being reduced, the public sector's need for domestic financing grew disproportionately. This imbalance grew progressively worse throughout that decade before culminating in the hyperinflation of 1989–90 and in the Bonex Plan introduced in 1990,[1] which reduced money supplies in the economy to a bare minimum (Table 2.1).

By the start of the 1990s, however, the country's financial system was stronger and the public sector no longer demanded excessive domestic financing. This set the stage for achieving three objectives: sustainable fiscal adjustment; reversal of the demonetization process; and normalization of Argentina's relations with its foreign creditors. Since the second round of hyperinflation ended, the current government has adopted specific measures in all these areas.

With implementation of the Convertibility Plan in March 1991, the government began a comprehensive tax reform aimed at public accounts. Once major improvement in the area of tax administration was under way, eliminating the fiscal deficit became possible. The Bonex Plan had virtually wiped out the quasi-fiscal deficit by eliminating the remunerated reserve obligation. Additionally, a bold privatization policy launched in 1990, based on the principle of debt conversion, helped clear up the deficit and reduce the public sector's external debt. Despite some success, however, provincial disequilibrium persisted. Uncertainty about the functioning of the new social security system caused serious concern over the sustainability of fiscal equilibrium, especially once the resources generated by privatization are exhausted.

Rather than attempt to reverse the extreme dollarization of 1980s, the government adopted a strategy to expand the dollarized segment within the domestic financial system, in order to remonetize the economy. In 1989, Law 23.578 provided greater security for foreign exchange deposits by requiring financial institutions to return deposits in the same currency as received, and prevented the Central Bank from gaining access to those resources. Other institutional changes also helped strengthen this strategy. For example, at the outset of 1991, Argen-

[1] The Bonex Plan consisted of a mandatory restructuring of domestic public debt through the forced exchange of most deposits in the financial system (chiefly short-term financing to the public sector, due to Central Bank restrictions and requirements) and of short-term public securities in domestic currency for "external bonds" (Bonos Externos, which were ten-year, dollar-denominated public securities).

Table 2.1. Money Supplies and Inflation Tax, 1985–93
(In percentages of GDP)

Period		M1	Inflation tax[1]	M3	Total monetary resources (M3 + deposits in dollars)
1985		2.8	3.0	9.6	10.6
1986		3.7	1.6	11.2	12.0
1987		3.2	2.6	11.2	12.2
1988		2.2	2.7	10.3	11.5
1989		2.2	4.1	9.3	10.8
	I	2.4	0.5	10.6	12.0
	II	1.7	1.3	8.3	9.8
	III	2.0	1.7	9.2	10.4
	IV	2.7	0.6	8.9	10.8
1990		2.1	3.1	3.8	5.0
	I	2.0	1.7	3.0	4.3
	II	2.1	0.5	3.6	4.6
	III	2.3	0.6	4.3	5.5
	IV	2.1	0.2	4.3	5.5
1991		2.8	1.3	5.0	7.6
	I	2.2	1.1	4.4	6.3
	II	2.7	0.1	4.7	7.0
	III	3.1	0.1	5.3	8.1
	IV	3.4	0.0	5.7	8.8
1992		4.3	0.4	7.4	11.4
	I	3.9	0.2	6.4	9.8
	II	4.1	0.1	7.0	10.9
	III	4.7	0.1	8.1	12.5
	IV	4.5	0.0	7.9	12.4
1993[a]		5.0	0.2	9.2	14.8
	I	4.7	0.1	8.6	13.4
	II	4.9	0.1	9.1	14.6
	III	5.5	0.0	10.0	16.3

[1] Computed on the basis of the Combined Price Index.
[a] January–September 1993, provisional data.
Source: Prepared using data from the Central Bank of the Argentine Republic (BCRA) and of the National Institute of Statistics and Census (INDEC).

tine currency became freely convertible, backed 100 percent by foreign exchange from the available monetary base. After a new charter for the Central Bank took effect in 1992, financial institutions were granted complete freedom to make loans in pesos as well as dollars. The securities market was deregulated, most notably with the authorization of financial institutions and companies to issue negotiable bonds in foreign currency. Greater access by Argentine banks to international capital markets also bolstered the strategy to remonetize the economy.

The remonetization strategy contributed greatly to the growth of deposits and credits in dollars, particularly with the stabilization achieved through the

Convertibility Plan. Clearly, however, it cannot alone reverse the phenomenon of segmentation among credit markets, which limits the availability of resources for small enterprise. Nor can it reverse the chronic insufficiency of medium- and long-term financing. These crucial problems must be successfully resolved if investment and growth are to be stimulated and sustained in Argentina.

The Brady Plan, through the renegotiation of foreign agreements with private creditors, enabled the country to normalize its external financial relations. Radical shifts in the flow of international capital in the early 1990s, which greatly favored Latin American countries, helped relieve their financial problems. Although the "debt crisis" of the past decade is less intense, it is too early to assume that Argentina has definitively overcome its long-standing problem of external restrictions. But using privatization to reduce external public debt, as is feasible under the Brady Plan, will significantly affect the structure and rigidity of the factor services account in the near future.

After the second round of hyperinflation ended, the financial system began to show signs of recovery. The critical process of remonetization (see section two) began to unfold slowly, due to the relief created by eliminating short-term public debt and a slight improvement in the fiscal situation during 1990, and then more rapidly in March 1991, with implementation of the Convertibility Plan. Nonetheless, a key problem facing Argentina's economy today is that domestic savings have virtually stagnated. Consequently, the main source of remonetization has been the inflow of external capital.

These capital inflows cannot go on forever, of course. Privatization, an important autonomous factor in attracting capital to Argentina, is nearing its end. The other factor for capital inflows—the progressive adjustment of private-sector financial portfolios to the Convertibility Plan—will not continue indefinitely either.

If the fiscal situation remains under control, continuation of the Convertibility Plan will depend largely on resolving the problems of exchange arrears and the growing external disequilibrium in current accounts. The government is confident that the current international financial boom will last for a long time. According to official opinion, that would allow time to resolve the problem by a general rise in the economy's productivity, through investments financed first with external savings and later with domestic savings. Past experience, as well as solid theoretical arguments, suggest that this solution is highly improbable.[2] In particular, the flow of external financing could be abruptly interrupted due to changes on the international scene.[3]

---

[2] See McKinnon (1991).

[3] See Calvo and others (1992).

Furthermore, the capital markets in Argentina are still in the embryonic stage. The financial system remains fragile, as indicated by short fixed terms for loans and low levels of current-account deposits. Against this backdrop, if the private sector suspects the external situation is worsening and doubts that adjustment mechanisms will kick in fast enough, it may react by reducing holdings in pesos and "Argendollars" (dollars on deposit in Argentina) and increasing dollar holdings "under the mattress" or outside the country. Such a move would cause a strong contraction in domestic credit, higher interest rates, recession, and major financial imbalances. It is possible to imagine several scenarios that could bring about another collapse of the financial system.[4]

Small Enterprise and Challenges of the New Economic Reality

With the postwar emphasis on import substitution, small and medium-sized enterprises gain increasing importance in the economic structure, particularly in the area of manufacturing. Of the 110,000 industrial enterprises registered in the last National Economic Census taken in 1985, roughly 30,000 are small or medium-sized businesses. These enterprises accounted for 40 to 45 percent of total employment in the sector (between 550,000 and 700,000 workers) and generated one fourth to one third of manufacturing production.[5] Their presence in agriculture and service sectors has traditionally been very important.

Since the postwar period, however, two distinct stages in the development of small enterprises have become apparent. The emphasis placed on the import substitution model during the 1950s and 1960s enabled these enterprises to expand, especially in the industrial sector. Through a highly irregular process, these companies learned new techniques and slowly and indirectly gained access to international technology similar to that of large corporations.[6]

However, a closed economy and a limited domestic market imposed obvious limitations on small enterprises in terms of equipment, organization, scale, training, and information. These limitations also negatively affected their productivity indices and product quality, which prevented them from attaining international standards.

Macroeconomic instability and a decline in production, starting in the mid-1970s and deepening with the debt crisis of the 1980s, continued to worsen. The

---

[4] See, for example, Zahler (1988).

[5] Although the number of microenterprises is significant, their share of industrial employment in the 1985 census did not exceed 10 percent of the total. In terms of production, it reached only 4 percent. See Gatto and Yoguel (1993) for a more thorough analysis of small and medium-sized industrial enterprises.

[6] See Katz (1993) for a description of post-war Argentine industrial development.

new economic reality forced small enterprises to forget about growth and development and to concern themselves primarily with survival.

Since the early 1990s, however, renewed availability of external financing and improvements in the domestic economy indicate that a new phase is beginning. Laws to liberalize the economy and a series of structural changes that limit government interference and promote private enterprise have led to a more competitive and internationally integrated economy. As stated previously, these processes must still overcome major obstacles, but already they have drastically changed the operating conditions of the Argentine economy.

The recovery now underway, which does not equally affect all sectors or economic actors, is clearly different from the ascending phase of an economic cycle. As the initial impulse of stabilization subsides, a far more serious concern for many enterprises will be not how to boost their production, but rather how to plan their growth in keeping with the new incentives.

Only within the framework of a thorough organizational and technological retooling can continued economic growth be assured. This retooling must be carried out in close collaboration with the entire productive apparatus and is essential to maintaining the economy's new momentum.

Retooling is a slow and fragile process. For small enterprises, it is a particularly compelling challenge, but its importance is not purely microeconomic. The trajectory of small enterprises has had a strong impact on job creation and wealth distribution, two of the most problematic aspects of economic reform.

A central objective of this study is to propose specific policies to help small and medium-sized enterprises expand their access to credit and other financial services. The concise diagnosis presented below has two fundamental consequences arising out of retooling requirements.

Financial market segmentation and unfavorable treatment of small and medium-sized enterprises vis-à-vis large enterprises are, as mentioned earlier, perennial problems widely recognized in the Argentine economy.[7] These two problems are more or less common to any capitalist economy, resulting from the lack of adequate information inherent to financial markets. Nonetheless, the poor development and lack of diversification of these markets in Argentina have caused these problems to assume far more serious proportions than in the industrialized economies. Even in the most successful development experiences, domestic financial markets have barely been able to keep up with the advances achieved in other areas of the economy.[8] This fact alone justifies consideration of specific financial measures to aid small and medium-sized enterprises. This issue has immediate importance, since the retooling of these enterprises has been assigned high priority for economic progress.

---

[7] See Rozenwurcel and Fernández (1993).

[8] McKinnon (1991) and Stiglitz (1993) both emphasize this fact.

Retooling will of course require a wide range of private incentives and public policies. Promoting access by small and medium-sized enterprises to adequate financing for this purpose (acceptable amounts, conditions, and costs) is a fundamental requirement of the process, but it is not the only one. Thus, in order for their effects to be fully felt, the measures adopted for this purpose must not produce isolated results, but rather must form part of an comprehensive retooling policy.

In our opinion, the policy direction that has been pursued up to now has failed to give adequate consideration to these requirements. While it is true that in the financial sector a set of specific measures designed for small and medium-sized enterprises is now in place, the resources for these measures are clearly inadequate, as we argue later on, and their conditions have generally not adapted to the needs of the retooling process. Furthermore, although consideration of this issue will lead us beyond the limits of this study, the absence of a comprehensive strategy for retooling these enterprises (which would consider not only the financial aspects of the problem, but also the technological, organizational, training, and informational aspects) has contributed to the limited impact these measures have had up to now.

Current Structure and Operation of the Financial System

Monetary and Physical Size

The periods of hyperinflation experienced in 1989–90 and the launching of the Bonex Plan on New Year's Day 1990 caused disarray among the financial conditions of the Argentine economy by reducing the level of the money supply to a bare minimum. From that point, and even more noticeably since the start of the Convertibility Plan, a significant process of remonetization began to unfold.[9] This process included both the peso and dollar segments of the financial system and caused all monetary resources, including deposits in foreign currency, which had fallen to 4.3 percent of GDP in the first quarter of 1990, to reach 16.3 percent of GDP in the third quarter of 1993 (Table 2.1). Furthermore, the spectacular growth of dollar deposits, which in October 1993 represented nearly 48 percent of total deposits, has created a virtual bi-monetary financial system (Table 2.2).

It is interesting to note, however, that although the remonetization caused by the Convertibility Plan was rapid and significant, the reference point was exceptionally low. However, liquidity ratios in the economy are still far below those observed, not just in industrialized countries, but in other economies at similar

---

[9] A more detailed analysis of the issues discussed in this section can be found in Rozenwurcel and Fernández (1993).

Table 2.2. Total Deposits, 1988–October 1993
(In millions of current dollars)

Period		In domestic currency	% of total	In foreign currency	% of total	Total
1988		9,334	88.3	1,231	11.7	10,565
1989		5,505	84.0	1,051	16.0	6,556
1990		3,998	70.1	1,705	29.9	5,703
1991	January	6,219	66.4	3,150	33.6	9,369
	February	4,630	58.6	3,274	41.4	7,904
	March	5,156	60.4	3,387	39.6	8,543
	April	5,535	59.7	3,741	40.3	9,276
	May	5,796	57.5	4,278	42.5	10,074
	June	6,036	56.8	4,594	43.2	10,630
	July	5,973	55.2	4,838	44.9	10,811
	August	6,452	55.3	5,209	44.8	11,661
	September	6,789	54.3	5,720	45.7	12,509
	October	7,185	54.1	6,108	45.9	13,293
	November	7,615	54.5	6,363	45.5	13,978
	December	8,096	55.2	6,560	44.8	14,656
1992	January	8,471	54.9	6,970	45.1	15,441
	February	8,692	53.9	7,446	46.1	16,138
	March	9,027	53.3	7,898	46.7	16,925
	April	9,535	53.8	8,201	46.2	17,736
	May	10,566	55.0	8,652	45.0	19,218
	June	11,532	56.0	9,078	44.0	20,610
	July	11,859	55.7	9,437	44.3	21,296
	August	12,726	56.0	9,989	44.0	22,715
	September	13,031	55.7	10,344	44.3	23,375
	October	13,190	55.3	10,673	44.7	23,863
	November	13,342	55.0	10,921	45.0	24,263
	December	13,841	55.9	10,936	44.1	24,777
1993	January	15,451	57.3	11,524	42.7	26,975
	February	15,913	57.0	11,982	43.0	27,895
	March	16,687	56.7	12,768	43.3	29,445
	April[1]	16,762	55.4	13,475	44.6	30,237
	May[1]	17,402	55.2	14,138	44.8	31,540
	June[1]	17,423	54.1	14,778	45.9	32,201
	July[1]	16,935	52.2	15,532	47.8	32,467
	August[1]	18,860	53.6	16,296	46.4	35,156
	September[1]	19,032	52.7	17,074	47.3	36,106
	October[1]	19,252	52.0	17,774	48.0	37,026

[1] Provisional data.
Source: Prepared using data from the Central Bank of the Argentine Republic.

levels of development. They are, in fact, even below those recorded in Argentina before the financial crisis of the early 1980s.

Another indicator of the lack of progress in financial deepening is the supply of financing to the entire system, which is on the order of 17.3 percent of GDP. Worse still, more than half of that sum is granted in foreign currency (Table 2.3).

Despite the limited volume of resources that it intermediates, the Argentine financial system maintains a relatively high number of institutions and branches.

Table 2.3. Loans from the Consolidated Financial System, December 1989–September 1993
(In percentages of GDP)

	Pesos	Dollars	Total
December 1989	3.4	9.4	12.8
December 1990	3.9	3.7	7.6
March 1991	1.8	5.4	7.2
June 1991	4.6	4.9	9.4
September 1991	4.9	5.7	10.6
December 1991	5.1	5.8	10.9
March 1992	5.3	6.0	11.3
June 1992	5.8	7.4	13.1
September 1992	6.6	8.2	14.9
December 1992	6.7	8.8	15.5
March 1993	7.2	9.3	16.6
June 1993	7.1	9.2	16.3
September 1993	7.5	9.6	17.1

Source: Central Bank of the Argentine Republic.

At the end of 1992, for example, it was composed of 210 financial institutions that had 4,006 branches in addition to their main offices. Out of this total, 167 were banks that operated with 3,986 branches. Additionally, there were 43 were non-bank financial institutions that operated with 20 branches (Table 2.4).

This implies a ratio of just less than 8,000 inhabitants per bank or a bank utilization rate equal to that of industrialized countries. The situations are hardly comparable, however, since the level of money supply, as mentioned, is far below that of any industrialized country. In fact, despite the significant growth in deposits caused by the Convertibility Plan, total growth per branch by the end of 1992 amount to barely US$7 million.

The number of personnel employed in the system tends to confirm the diagnosis that it is overstaffed. In fact, even though major adjustments began to be made in 1990, total employment by the end of 1992 still amounted to almost 119,000 persons (Table 2.5). Thus, by the end of 1992, the volume of deposits received per employee could be estimated at only US$270,000, a number incompatible with the reduced levels of receipts per branch.

Characteristics and Operations of Financial Institutions

The institutionalized financial system is comprised of the monetary authority (the Central Bank) and the following categories of financial institutions: commercial banks, mortgage banks, investment banks, development banks, and even non-bank financial institutions.

Table 2.4. Trends in the Number of Institutions and Affiliates of the Financial System, 1989–92

Type of institution	1989		1990		1991		June 1992		December 1992	
	No. of institutions	No. of affiliates	No. of institutions	No. of affiliates	No. of institutions	No. of affiliates	No. of institutions	No. of affiliates	No. of institutions	No. of affiliates
Public banks	36	2,003	36	1,911	35	1,841	35	1,825	36	1,765
Private banks	141	2,481	133	2,282	132	2,211	131	4,202	131	2,221
Total banks	177	4,484	169	4,194	167	4,052	166	4,027	167	3,986
Nonbank institutions	59	48	51	36	47	28	46	27	43	20
Total financial system	236	4,532	220	4,230	214	4,080	212	4,054	210	4,006

Source: Central Bank of the Argentine Republic.

Table 2.5. Personnel Employed in the Financial System, 1989–92

Financial institutions	1989	1990	1991	June 1992	December 1992
Public banks	82,666	75,710	67,706	61,940	58,984
Private banks	64,365	57,876	54,375	56,652	58,464
Non-bank financial institutions	2,344	1,678	1,493	1,583	1,539
Total	149,375	135,264	123,574	120,175	118,987

Source: Central Bank of the Argentine Republic.

The Central Bank (BCRA) is autonomous and its authority is legally independent of the Executive Branch of Government[10]. Its management of monetary policy, however, has been greatly limited by the Convertibility Law as well as by its own charter. Additionally, the deposit guarantee system has been eliminated and new legislation has been enacted, strictly limiting the duties of the Central Bank as the "lender of last resort." Accordingly, limits have been established on the amount and term of discounts and advances that the Central Bank can make to financial institutions.[11]

Commercial banks offer "full service banking" by conducting the traditional financial transactions of receiving deposits and investing funds as well as providing a full range of other services. According to the share structure of the capital, commercial banks are classified as either public banks, national private, or foreign. National private banks may be established either as corporations or as cooperatives.

Although current legislation also permits other institutional forms (investment banks, mortgage banks, and non-bank financial institutions), it in fact stimulates the expansion of commercial banks. In mid-1993, these banks operated about 99.5 percent of all offices and accounted for a similar proportion of total employment of the sector. The official banking sector maintained an overwhelming position within this sector, controlling 44 percent of the branches and accounting for 50 percent of the total salaried employees in the system (Tables 2.4 and 2.5). The distribution of basic financial transactions among the various categories of institutions is closely related to the physical structure of the system.

The short-term nature of its deposits reveals the insufficient development from which the financial system still suffers. For example, the average period for deposits in domestic currency is 15 days. Foreign currency deposits average 39 days. Loans are also primarily short-term in nature, although a major disparity

[10] Central Bank authorities, who hold their posts for six years, are appointed by the President, but they must receive Senate approval.

[11] These may only be requested to handle temporary cash flow problems, in limited amounts with guarantees in securities or real assets for a period no longer than 30 days. Renewal is not automatic.

exists between the average terms granted in domestic currency (331 days) and foreign currency (76 days). In private banking, the averages are 50 days for domestic currency and 60 days for foreign currency. Public banks, however, assume greater risk by operating with average terms greater than 700 days for credits in pesos and nearly 200 days for those denominated in foreign currency.[12] The latter, however, basically benefit the public sector, which takes up about half of the loan portfolio of the official banking sector.

Additionally, the pace of concentration in the system picked up throughout the 1980s. As Table 2.6 shows, by the end of 1979 the five largest banks in the system received 27.7 percent of total bank deposits. This share increased to 40.2 percent for the ten largest, and to 56.6 percent if the 20 largest banks are considered. In December 1990, this share had risen to 41.2 percent for the first group, to 54.1 percent for the second group, and to 67.8 percent for the group of the twenty largest banks. Government institutions are predominant among the larger banks. In March 1993, three public institutions (Banco de la Nación, Banco de la Provincia de Buenos Aires, and Banco de la Ciudad de Buenos Aires) were among the five largest banks in the system in terms of the number of deposits, while the remainder were national private banks.[13] Of the ten largest institutions, five were official (two national, two provincial, and one municipal), two were national private banks, and the remaining three were foreign.

Concentration of assets is also high in the private banking sector. The top five banks received 31 percent of total private bank deposits, the top 10 received 49.6 percent, and the top 20 received 66.8 percent. (Note that the total number of private banks exceeds 133.) Seven of the top 20 banks were founded with foreign capital.

Financial System Performance Indicators

Changes in Argentina's macroeconomic conditions, along with the adjustment and restructuring of financial institutions between 1989 and 1993, explain the significant improvements in the financial system during that period.

To evaluate this improvement in greater detail, we have grouped indicators in three categories: 1) cost structure and efficiency; 2) asset structure and liquidity; and 3) quality of financial portfolio and solvency.[14]

---

[12] Data based on the latest information available from August 1992.

[13] The two first banks (Banco de la Nación and Banco de la Provincia de Buenos Aires) held nearly 25 percent of total bank deposits in August 1992.

[14] Definitions of the indicators are set forth in the appendix to this chapter. Although these indicators are calculated for both the entire system and the different institutional groups, the latter are not analyzed in this article due to limited space.

Table 2.6. Distribution of Deposits by Bank Group, December 1979–March 1993
(Percentages of total in banking system)

	End of year			March 1992		March 1993	
Bank group	1979	1985	1990	Domestic currency	Foreign currency	Domestic currency	Foreign currency
The biggest 5	27.7	42.5	41.2	39.3	28.9	43.5	32.2
The biggest 10	40.2	54.6	54.1	53.0	47.5	55.5	49.4
The biggest 20	56.6	66.7	67.8	67.7	67.6	69.3	67.3
Others	43.5	33.4	32.2	32.1	32.4	30.7	32.8
Total banks	219.0	198.0	170.0	166.0	166.0	167.0	167.0

Source: Prepared using data from the *Estado de Entidades Financieras*, Central Bank of the Argentine Republic.

Cost Structure and Efficiency

Under this heading we consider indicators on yield and efficiency for financial institutions as well as average costs incurred in converting deposits to credits (Table 2.7).

The Bonex Plan of January 1990 greatly increased the average cost of intermediation. Soon after the launching of the Convertibility Plan, that cost began to fall, until it reached 1.4 percent in June 1993. Higher efficiency was the result of two concurrent events: great expansion of total deposits and a reduction of operating expenses. This lower overhead was the outcome of the adjustment and restructuring underway since 1990, which was particularly effective in the national public banking sector.

Argentina's most intense financial activity since 1991 was reflected in an increased yield from equity throughout the entire financial system. In June 1993, the ratio between total net earnings and total net worth had reached 0.82 percent per month. Productivity of service personnel also increased during that period, but the ratio between labor cost and total cost has increased among all institutional groups except provincial and municipal banks. This is due to both salary increases and the addition of qualified staff to perform new financial activities (securities market operations, insurance transactions, and other commercial services).

Real financial yield per deposit, used to measure the economic results of the institution for each peso deposited in the system, dropped sharply, from 5.8 percent in December 1990 to 0.9 percent in June 1993. The decrease in the financial margin was the result of a drop in interest rates and a strong expansion in the total number of deposits. This expansion accounted for an increase of 390 percent in deposits received by the banking sector between the end of 1989 and June 1992. This increased productivity was also reflected in the growth of deposits per employee, which between November 1989 and March 1993 rose from 159,000 to 271,000 pesos.

Table 2.7. Cost Structure and Efficiency Indicators, December 1990–June 1993
(In percentages)

Type of institution	Average cost of financial intermediation		Yield on capital		Real financial yield per deposits		Structure absorption with yield		Efficiency of service personnel[1]		Labor cost/ Total cost	
	Dec. '90	June '93	Dec. '90	June '93	Dec. '90	June '93	Dec. '90	June '93	Apr. '91	June '93	Apr. '91	June '93
1. Banking institutions												
- National public	3.28	0.93	–0.05	0.95	9.39	0.95	31.83	59.94	0.83	1.66	66.24	70.65
- Provincial and municipal	6.43	1.88	0.47	–1.46	5.82	0.41	91.22	158.68	0.49	1.41	69.36	61.28
- National private (Fed. Cap.)	3.66	1.47	0.58	1.73	3.42	0.91	72.76	79.66	2.11	3.45	47.16	51.81
- National private (Interior)	4.58	1.87	0.44	1.19	3.94	1.05	86.51	94.78	0.94	1.88	49.15	53.60
- Foreign	3.94	1.48	0.11	0.67	3.13	0.89	87.74	91.73	2.20	3.20	49.56	61.78
2. Non-bank institutions	5.00	1.56	2.19	–0.32	10.64	0.96	41.18	118.42	0.61	1.20	40.72	49.32
3. System total	4.09	1.42	0.19	0.82	5.76	0.87	58.18	86.53	1.11	2.19	56.84	59.08

[1]In thousands of pesos of June 1992.
Source: *Indicadores del sistema financiero*, Central Bank of the Argentine Republic.

Asset Structure and Liquidity

This category includes indicators on the sunk cost of assets and the degree of liquidity shown by financial institutions (Table 2.8).

At present, the financial system shows a high level of capital sunk cost. Although this indicator has shown some improvement, 59 percent of the financial system's net worth in June 1993 was still tied up in physical assets (sunk cost). This is attributable primarily to the following: (a) the strong incentive to open branches throughout the country, due to the 1977 financial reform ; (b) the accounting revaluation of fixed assets undertaken by financial institutions, because of inflation; and (c) the financial crisis in the early 1980s, which forced institutions to settle uncollectible loans with their customers' physical assets.

Furthermore, the financial system's degree of liquidity, as measured by the immediate liquidity index on deposits (i.e., availability plus public securities in foreign currency as a percentage of total deposits), dropped from 38 percent in April 1991 to 25 percent in June 1993.

With respect to public securities in domestic currency, their share in the financial net worth of the system decreased 62 percent during the first year that the current stabilization program was in force. This reduced sunk cost of liquid capital was due mainly to the fact that the government not only ceased issuing public securities to finance the budget, but also began paying off its debt.

Portfolio Quality and Solvency

The indicator of financial portfolio quality (the percentage of loans delinquent or risking insolvency, receivership, bankruptcy, or liquidation) revealed an unfavorable trend for the system as of October 1990. In other words, portfolios became more risky. As Table 2.9 shows, the negative development of this indicator is greatly influenced by the irregularity of the portfolio of public banks.[15]

Furthermore, government participation in the loan portfolio (the percentage of loans to the nonfinancial public sector out of total loans made by public institutions) fell 47.6 percent throughout the system between December 1990 and June 1993.

Central Bank loans generally represented a higher proportion of the total deposits in the Argentine financial system. In recent years, however, financing by the monetary authorities diminished substantially. Improved public finances and greater

---

[15] The negative trend of this indicator is seen chiefly in the national public banking sector. This sector has delinquencies that are in fact far more serious if the accrued interest on the delinquent loans is taken into account. Furthermore, the delinquency index began to rise following the liquidation of several institutions (Banco Nacional de Desarrollo) and the restructuring of others (Banco Hipotecario Nacional).

Table 2.8. Asset Structure and Liquidity Indicators, April 1991 and June 1993
(In percentages)

		Capital sunk cost		Immediate liquidity of deposits		Liquid capital sunk cost		Share of deposits in foreign currency	
Type of institution		April '91	June '93	April '91	June '93	April '91	June '93	April '91	June '93
1.	Banking institutions								
	- National public	75.36	66.25	43.44	23.33	63.50	11.45	30.04	34.07
	- Provincial and municipal	47.05	52.89	35.41	24.84	20.80	19.31	18.06	24.08
	- National private (Fed. Cap.)	61.61	56.48	39.29	26.69	79.04	27.90	59.10	57.22
	- National private (Interior)	62.02	49.65	31.00	22.17	18.90	15.36	50.94	48.05
	- Foreign	62.89	53.20	32.90	26.65	90.95	57.00	72.50	64.90
2.	Non-bank institutions	53.07	33.10	33.08	10.06	35.47	22.19	44.81	65.09
3.	System total	64.75	58.90	37.92	24.63	56.68	25.53	45.56	46.11

Source: Indicadores del sistema financiero, Central Bank of the Argentine Republic.

Table 2.9. Financial Portfolio Quality and Solvency Indicators, December 1990–June 1993
(In percentages)

Type of institution	Quality of financial portfolio		Share of the public sector in loan portfolio		BCRA financing to the financial system	
	Dec. '90	June '93	Dec. '90	June '93	Dec. '90	June '93
1. Banking institutions						
- National public	25.25	34.63	42.23	27.75	175.97	18.55
- Provincial and municipal	40.48	36.81	37.26	23.20	96.70	22.91
- National private (Fed. Cap.)	6.55	6.45	1.82	0.59	6.97	2.11
- National private (Interior)	7.94	11.87	0.69	0.95	3.49	0.40
- Foreign	4.31	5.39	0.24	0.14	6.68	1.28
2. Non-bank institutions	7.08	13.36	5.91	2.07	7.50	0.45
3. System Total	22.02	21.73	28.88	13.75	73.67	9.36

Source: Indicadores del sistema financiero, Central Bank of the Argentine Republic.

monetary control implicit in the Convertibility Plan had a considerable impact on the official banking sector. Table 2.9 shows that both the public sector's share in the loan portfolio and the degree of financing by the Central Bank decreased substantially between April 1991 and June 1993. Both amounts remain high, however.

In the private banking sector, both the degree of solvency and the quality of the financial portfolio were satisfactory as of June 1993. The financial portfolio's irregularity remained low and the portion of loans granted to the public sector was less than 1 percent. Moreover, discounts and advances made by the Central Bank did not exceed 2.2 percent of the total deposits received by private banks.

Access to Financial Markets for Small Enterprise

Recent Bank Credit Trends

Since the launching of the Convertibility Plan, bank credit has expanded significantly. Between April 1991 and June 1993, total loans routed through the system tripled, reaching an amount equal to more than US$42.2 billion by the end of that period. Fifty-six percent of that total had been granted in foreign currency, which constitutes further evidence of the system's high level of dollarization.

Stabilization and Expansion of Lending Capacity

The increase in lending capacity by institutions during this period can be explained by a combination of factors: increase of deposits in pesos (339

Table 2.10. Distribution of Loans by Line of Credit, May 1993

	Millions of pesos	Percentage
Advances	9,515	23.3
Instruments discounted and purchased from one company	9,796	24.0
Mortgages	6,082	14.9
Collateral	2,069	5.1
Personal	3,371	8.2
Documentary credits	636	0.6
Public bonds	1,622	4.0
Others	8,145	19.9
Total	40,863	100.0

Source: Prepared using data from the *Estados contables de entidades financieras*, June 1993, Superintendency of Financial Institutions and Foreign Exchange of the Central Bank of the Argentine Republic.

percent) and in foreign exchange (235 percent); decrease in the average reserve ratio for deposits; growth in negotiable bonds issued by banks, and the increase in the lines of credit from abroad. Although to a lesser extent, discounts and advances granted by the Central Bank—which rose from US$18 billion to US$25 billion due to refinancing of previously granted credit—also explains the increase in lending capacity.[16]

The increase in the volume of bank credit was accompanied by a substantial increase in the number of loan customers processed through the system, which rose from 1.8 million to 3.1 million between the end of 1990 and 1992 (Table 2.10).[17] This increase can be explained mainly by the soundness of the loan portfolios involving individuals. In fact, the amount of personal loans granted accounted for 8.2 percent of total loans. To this amount may be added most of the mortgage and chattel loans, which were granted to private individuals to buy and/or renovate housing or to purchase automobiles. The sum of the three headings listed amount to 28 percent of the total volume of credit granted (Table 2.10).

The remainder is set aside for private companies and public agencies with emphasis on current account advances (23.3 percent of the total) and instruments discounted and purchased from one company (24 percent of the total). Nearly one-quarter of the total portfolio of the institutions and more than one-third of

[16] Credit growth was partially offset by a sharp decrease, on the order of 36 percent, in the funds accrued on loans, as recorded on the balance sheets of the financial institutions. This decrease reflects a certain degree of improvement among the portfolios of public institutions resulting from the adoption of various restructuring measures.

[17] It should be noted that the information available has not been consolidated. Consequently, the debts of each debtor at different financial institutions are calculated as belonging to different loan customers in the system.

Table 2.11. Distribution of Loans by Group of Institutions, June 1993

	Millions of pesos	Percentage
Public banks of the nation	8,287	19.6
Public banks of provinces and municipalities	11,572	27.5
Private banks established as corporations	11,933	28.3
Foreign banks	7,545	17.7
Cooperative banks	2,905	6.9
Total banks	42,242	100.0

Note: 1 peso = US$1.
Source: Prepared using data from *Estados contables de entidades financieras*, June 1993, Superintendency of Financial Institutions and Foreign Exchange of the Central Bank of the Argentine Republic.

non-personal credit is channeled through current account advances. This form of financing can be utilized on an extremely short-term basis by financial institutions in accordance with the existing liquidity conditions.

Table 2.11 reveals that the combined share of the domestic public and provincial banking sector accounts for 47.1 percent of total credit. Local private banks established as corporations process 28.3 percent of total loans, foreign banks 17.7 percent, and cooperative banks 6.9 percent.

The average size of loans in the system is slightly over 13,000 pesos (Table 2.12), although this indicator shows marked differences among the various groups of institutions. At provincial and municipal public banks, the average loan size is 24,000 pesos. At national public banks, it is nearly 15,000 pesos. These figures are strongly influenced by the large sums involved in earlier loans by public banks to various agencies in the nonfinancial public sector. However, it is well known that the public banking sector processes a large quantity of small loans for enterprises and individuals. In the private banking sector, the average size of loan transactions is 15,400 pesos at foreign banks, 11,400 pesos at local banks established as corporations, and 5,000 pesos at cooperative banks.

Concentration of Loan Portfolio

The Central Bank publishes statistics on credit granted to "principal debtors" of the financial system, which provide us with information on loan portfolio concentration. "Principal debtors" are defined as those customers in the private or public sector that, as of June 1993, had an average debit balance (in domestic and foreign currency) greater than 352,000 pesos at any given financial institution or that were among the fifty principal debtors of any given institution.[18]

[18] The institutions furnish information on the debt of each customer, but do not consolidate the debt by group or economic sector.

Table 2.12. Average Size of Loans, June 1993
(In pesos)

Type of Institution	Amount
Public banks of the nation	14,958
Public banks of provinces and municipalities	24,351
Private banks established as corporations	11,384
Foreign banks	15,421
Cooperative banks	5,020
Total banks	13,394

Source: Prepared using data from *Estados contables de entidades financieras*, June 1993, Superintendency of Financial Institutions and Foreign Exchange, Central Bank of the Argentine Republic, as well as from the *Boletín Estadístico*, April 1993, Central Bank of the Argentine Republic.

These statistics reveal that, out of the more than three million customers in the system, around 9,800 "principal debtors" receive 48.5 percent of total bank credit. The available data does not allow us to consolidate the total credit granted by all the financial institutions to each enterprise or economic group. However, the sheer weight of these numbers leaves no doubt about the degree of customer concentration in the loan portfolios of the Argentine financial system.

In the public banking sector, the loans granted to "principal debtors" equal 50.4 percent of the total credit and 373 percent of calculable net worth of these institutions (Table 2.13). This concentration is largely influenced by credit support granted to the public sector of national, provincial, and municipal jurisdictions. The private banking sector also shows a high level of concentration, but still less than that of the public banking sector. For the entire banking sector, support to "principal debtors" accounts for 45.7 percent of total credit and 159.8 percent of the calculable net worth of the banks.

However, there are major disparities between different segments of the private banking sector. In foreign banks, support to the "principal debtors" accounts for 78.9 percent of total financing and is equal to 310 percent of the calculable net worth. In national private banks established as corporations, the figures are 48 and 199.9 percent; in cooperative banks, they are 28.3 and 87.5 percent, respectively.

The delinquency level for credit granted to "principal debtors" is not radically different from the total portfolio, except for public banks in provinces and municipalities, where the proportion of credit to "principal debtors" in irregular condition is substantially higher than for the rest of the portfolio (Table 2.14).

Cost of Bank Credit

Although domestic interest rates fell sharply at the outset of the Convertibility Plan, the noticeable differential between domestic and foreign interest rates has persisted, albeit with a descending trajectory. As Table 2.15 shows, this differential was a result of the significant reduction of devaluation expectations caused

Table 2.13. Distribution of Credit Extended to the Principal Debtors of the System, February 1993

	P.D. debt / Total system debt (1)	P.D. debt / Net worth (2)	10 P.D. debt / Net worth (3)	30 P.D. debt / Net worth (4)	H-H index (5)
Public banks	50.4	372.6	177.7	268.7	0.0166
Private banks (established corporations)	48.1	199.8	86.9	143.0	0.0098
Foreign banks	78.9	310.3	366.6	205.4	0.0185
Cooperative banks	28.3	87.5	37.4	67.6	0.0057
Total private banks	45.7	159.8	74.8	123.7	0.0083

Listed are the mean values of the distributions of the variables indicated.
(1) Debt of the principal debtors/total system debt.
(2) Debt of the principal debtors/calculable net worth.
(3) Debt of the 10 principal debtors/calculable net worth.
(4) Debt of the 30 principal debtors/calculable net worth.
(5) Herfindahl-Hirschman Index.
Source: Indicadores del sistema financiero, June 1993—Central Bank of the Argentine Republic.

Table 2.14. Principal Debtors: Distribution of Credit and Delinquency by Groups of Institutions, June 1993
(In percentages)

	Indebted banks	Irregular P.D. portfolio/ Debt of principal debtors	Irregular portfolio/ Total portfolio
Public banks of the nation	32.23	20.54	34.63
Public banks of provinces and municipalities	16.55	47.32	36.81
TOTAL PUBLIC BANKS	48.78	29.63	
Private national banks (corporations) of the Federal Capital	22.72	4.12	6.45
Private national banks (corporations) of the interior	3.37	8.39	11.87[a]
Foreign banks	20.27	4.62	5.39
Cooperative banks	3.66	10.33	11.87[a]
TOTAL PRIVATE BANKS	50.02	5.07	
Non-bank institutions	1.20	13.28	13.36
SYSTEM TOTAL	100.0	17.15	21.73

[a] Corresponds to the total number of banks of the interior established as corporations and as cooperatives.
Source: Indicadores del sistema financiero, August–October 1993—Central Bank of the Argentine Republic.

by the difference between the average deposit rate for peso deposits and the internal rate of return (IRR) of Bonex bonds (dollar-denominated public securities) and, to a lesser extent, by the decrease in country risk, which we have estimated as the difference between the IRR of Bonex bonds and the LIBOR (London interbank offered rate). In any case, by the end of 1993, the domestic deposit rate for pesos was still equal to more than double the LIBOR.

Table 2.15. Rate of Interest, of Country Risk, and of Expected Devaluation, March 1991–December 1993
(In percentages, in annual terms)

Period	(1)	IRR Bonex 89	Libor	Estimated rate of country risk	Rate of expected devaluation
1991					
March	193.33	20.89	6.50	13.51	142.64
June	28.23	17.01	6.56	9.81	9.59
September	18.86	10.80	5.69	4.83	7.27
December	19.83	10.17	4.38	5.55	8.77
1992					
March	15.57	10.81	4.56	5.98	4.30
June	14.60	9.94	4.06	5.65	4.24
September	15.57	10.51	3.25	7.03	4.58
December	25.31	12.68	3.63	8.74	11.21
1993					
March	13.02	10.34	3.38	6.74	2.43
June	9.91	7.38	3.50	3.75	2.36
September	8.84	6.59	3.38	3.11	2.11
December	8.67	6.33	3.50	2.73	2.20

(1) Rate of interest in pesos for fixed terms of 30 to 89 days.
Source: Boletín Estadístico (BCRA). Economic Report (Secretariat of Economic Programming).

With deposit rates greater than international rates and differentials (which, although decreasing, remained high due to continued high intermediation costs), lending rates stayed at high levels on the average, especially when measured in real terms (Table 2.16). Based on available information, the Banco de la Nación discount rate, considered a reasonably representative lending rate, stabilized at 1.6 percent per month (21 percent annually) in the second half of 1993.

In addition to the above disparities, the cost of credit in the Argentine financial systems also varies greatly according to the size of companies and their geographic location, among other factors.

To illustrate this point, we refer to the classification of financing that has been established for the financial system in accordance with the lending rates drawn up by the Central Bank.[19] In June 1993, the composition of all loans in terms of interest rates charged was as follows: 42 percent of the credit was granted at effective annual rates of up to 20 percent in pesos and 17 percent in dollars. Twenty-five percent was loaned at a cost that varied between 20 and 27 percent in pesos, and between 17 and 20 percent in dollars. The remainder, 33 percent of the total, was granted at rates above 27 percent per year in pesos and 20 percent

[19] The classification is used by the Central Bank to weigh the capital requirements of financial institutions vis-à-vis the risk level involved in the financing they grant.

Table 2.16. Monthly Effective Interest Rates and Financial Differential, March 1991–December 1993
(In percentages)

Period	Nominal rates		Real rates[1]		Financial differential
	Lending rate[2]	Deposit rate[3]	Lending rate	Deposit rate	
1991					
March	17.10	11.60	10.79	5.58	5.50
June	5.00	1.60	2.84	-0.49	3.40
September	3.00	1.10	1.88	0.00	1.90
December	3.00	1.10	3.21	1.30	1.90
1992					
March	2.50	0.90	0.70	-0.87	1.60
June	2.30	0.80	1.49	0.00	1.50
September	2.10	0.92	1.24	0.07	1.18
December	2.00	2.00	2.21	2.21	0.00
1993					
March	1.90	1.07	1.75	0.92	0.83
June	1.60	0.81	1.30	0.51	0.79
September	1.60	0.72	1.20	0.32	0.88
December	1.60	0.72	2.21	1.33	0.88

[1] Deflated by combined price indices (IPCOM).
[2] Corresponds to Banco de la Nación discount rate for instruments up to 30 days.
[3] On deposits in pesos at average fixed term.
Source: Prepared using data from *Análisis de las estadísticas monetarias y bancarias* (ADEBA—various issues).

in dollars. Within the most expensive segment, 14 percent of total loans had an annual cost of more than 43 percent in pesos and 24 percent in dollars. On the same date, a survey conducted by the Central Bank on interest rates for loans to first-tier enterprises indicated that the annual nominal value was 9.9 percent for 30-day loans in pesos and 7.66 percent for the same loans in dollars.

A comparison of both statistics makes it possible to get a clear picture of the broad differentials in financial costs between enterprises viewed as first-tier and the other borrowers in the system. This phenomenon, together with loan portfolios being concentrated on "principal debtors," suggests obvious segmentation in the availability and cost of bank financing. This problem is far more serious now that large economic groups have almost unrestricted access to external financing, as well as to the domestic capital market. This is certainly not the case for small enterprise, as we will see below.

Recent Capital Market Developments

Historically, the capital market in Argentina has not played a major role in financing. However, since the launching of the Convertibility Plan in 1991 and, coincidentally, the arrival of large inflows of external capital, the securities market has grown dramatically.

The following developments, among other things, reveal the new importance of the capital market: the total number of public securities increased from US$7 billion to over US$40 billion between late 1991 and 1993; stock market capitalization has grown substantially due to the rise in share prices of existing securities and in the number of public offerings for new shares; and the negotiable bonds market (medium- and long-term debt securities) is developing rapidly.

Law 23962, approved in 1991, amended the legislation governing the negotiable bonds by granting more tax advantages and improving the conditions for minimizing exchange risks when issuing these securities. Furthermore, the Central Bank authorized financial institutions to issue negotiable bonds, so that resources secured through this means can be used to finance investments in fixed assets, integrate working capital, refinance loans to enterprises located in Argentina, and grant personal and mortgage loans. Additionally, financial institutions were permitted to participate in the placement of negotiable bonds issued by companies as well as to guarantee them and take part in their underwriting.

With the changes introduced through legal regulations and favorable domestic and international economic conditions, the market for negotiable bonds underwent marked growth. While only US$644 million were placed in the 1989–91 period, that volume later increased to nearly US$1.6 billion and exceeded US$4 billion in 1993. The total amount of these financial assets had reached US$6.8 billion by November 1993.

A new social security system beginning mid-1994 will also have a major impact on the development of the local capital market. In the new social security framework, a public distribution system will coexist with a privately managed system of capitalization. Official projections indicate that, in accordance with the new regulations, the savings routed in the first few years through the *administradoras de fondos de jubilaciones y pensiones* (AFJP, Retirement and Pension Fund Administration) will exceed US$2 billion annually. Based on the legislation governing the AFJP investment system and the experience of the similar Chilean plan, it is forecast that the funds will chiefly be channeled first toward government securities and then toward securities in private corporations whose net worth and solvency so warrant.

Financial Assistance Policies for Small Enterprise

During the 1980s the number of financial restrictions imposed upon small and medium-sized enterprise had increased noticeably. However, the stability attained through the Convertibility Plan somewhat reduced these restrictions. This improvement was aided, among other factors, by the strong increase in the lending capacity of financial institutions, the lower demand for resources by the public sector, a certain interest by some institutions in increasing their placements in that segment to take advantage of larger financial margins obtainable within the context of greater certainty, and the opportunity to add new customers to business services now offered by banking. Some government measures related to deregulation and financial system reform have also brought improvements.

Concurrently, several private institutions adopted certain measures designed to help small enterprises secure credit assistance. These institutions have formed specialized departments and launched promotional and advertising campaigns. Other nongovernmental groups have established foundations and implemented programs to provide training for small-business owners.

Despite these changes, only a small fraction of the new resources available in the financial system and on the capital market was channeled to small and medium-sized enterprises. Among the many obstacles currently limiting financing to these enterprises, from the viewpoint of both supply and demand, the following should be highlighted:

- The perception by the institutions that there is a higher credit risk on transactions with small and medium-sized enterprises, due to the structural adjustment process that affects most of the economic branches to which these enterprises belong.
- The relative inexperience or lack of personnel at most banks who are trained to evaluate investment plans from these enterprises.
- The lack of training or adequate advice on the proper management of the credit needs of small and medium-sized enterprises. The training programs conducted by banks or foundations are still quite general and are not specifically directed at credit management.

Below, we comment on the key aspects of official policies to reduce the concentration of credit and expand the access of small enterprises to the financial system.

Regulations Affecting Credit Concentration

Central Bank regulations seek to prevent any excess risk concentration in loan portfolios that might affect the solvency of financial institutions. In addition, the general recommendations contained in BCRA Circulars OPRAC 1-356 and LISOL 1-68 set forth stricter, more specific regulations on the subject. Below is a summary of current regulations.

Limits on transactions with customers. The total number of non-guaranteed transactions with a company or individual not connected to the financial institution may not exceed 15 percent of the institution's calculable net worth. The total number of operations, including those with guarantees, may not exceed 25 percent of the institution's calculable net worth. The total holding of unlisted shares, excluding holdings in companies that provide services complementary to financial activities, may not be greater than 15 percent of the institution's calculable net worth.

For companies or individuals that are connected to an institution, the total number of non-guaranteed operations may not exceed 5 percent of the institution's calculable net worth. Nor may the total number of operations with or without guarantees exceed 10 percent of the same. Finally, the total number of operations with all the private companies or individuals connected to the institution may not exceed 20 percent of its calculable net worth.

Limits on risk concentration. The sum total of operations established with companies, persons, economic units or groups—whether connected to a financial institution or not—that individually are greater than 10 percent of the calculable net worth of the institution may not exceed three times the institution's calculable net worth. For customers that are connected, the aforementioned 10 percent minimum will not apply.

Limits related to net worth of the debtor. The total amount of operations in domestic and foreign currency that each financial institution grants may not exceed 100 percent of the calculable net worth of the customers, whether such operations be with individuals or corporations, economic groups or units, connected or unconnected to the financial institution. Loans up to 200,000 pesos granted to unconnected individuals and corporations are exempt from this regulation. This exemption is essential to avoid excessive restrictions on credit support to small enterprises and on personal loans. It also allows debts to be backed by means of guarantees other than the debtor's net worth.[20]

Banks have until July 1994 to adopt the new limits. Full enforcement of these regulations may lead to a decrease in the level of concentration of the institutions' loan portfolios, but it is not yet possible to quantify their effect.

Three-Year Program

Recognizing the difficulties facing small enterprises, the federal government in May 1993 announced a three-year program to promote and develop the small business sector, along with other measures to bolster domestic production. The program includes a financing package for a total of US$2.05 billion and has different subsidy mechanisms for the two different credit lines involved. The first is formed by resources from public and private commercial banks, to which an official subsidy of 4 points per year is added to the lending rate. The second credit line is comprised of funds from the Banco de la Nación, which has an

---

[20] For purposes of the limits indicated in the text, the economic units or groups in the nonfinancial private sector should be considered as a single customer.

official nominal bank subsidy of 2 percent per year on amounts granted within the established quota.[21]

The first credit line has two tranches: one for acquiring capital goods, along with the complementary "soft" technology and working capital associated with their purchase, and the other designed to provide the funds needed to develop the enterprise. To access this line of credit, banks submit competitive bids, and the quota of subsidized loans are distributed on the basis of the interest rate proposed by each bank. The second line of credit is for retooling the sector or for productive investment and export financing for small enterprises.

This program's preliminary results, when compared with the credit line of funds from the commercial banking sector, were as follows:

- By October 1993, 881 million pesos had been bid, although only 9,705 credits in the amount of 346 million pesos (139 million pesos for the purchase of capital goods and 207 million pesos for working capital) had been granted. Maximum interest rates accepted in the bidding were 16 percent per year during the first two competitive biddings, and 15 percent during the third.[22]
- The distribution of loans by activity reveals a high level of participation by the agricultural sector (45.5 percent for capital goods and 56.5 percent for working capital). This contrasts sharply with the reduced participation of the industrial sector (21.6 percent for capital goods and 15.7 percent for working capital).
- The geographical distribution of loans reveals a low level of participation of the Federal Capital (10.3 percent for capital goods and 6.2 percent for working capital) and high concentration in the provinces of Buenos Aires, Córdoba, and Santa Fe, which collectively received more than 60 percent of the credit.

The Role of the Public Banking Sector

Official banks retain significant weight in the Argentine financial sector. Since 1991, however, they have undergone a comprehensive restructuring process, at both the national and provincial levels. This restructuring process will substantially modify their form of operation and participation in the market.[23]

The national public banking sector. As a result of institutional restructuring, the Banco de la Nación Argentina (a first-tier bank) and the Banco de Inversión

---

[21] See Table 2.18 for details on credit conditions.

[22] This means that with the official subsidy, the rates paid by the loan recipients were 12 percent in the first two cases and 11 percent in the third.

[23] For a more detailed analysis of this process, see Rozenwurcel and Fernández (1993).

y Comercio Exterior (a second-tier bank) are now the only national public institutions dedicated to financing productive activity.[24]

In 1991, the national government began restructuring the Banco de la Nación, Argentina's largest financial institution. A principal objective of this initiative was to enable the Banco de la Nación to regain its support role for small enterprise, while at the same time the bank would work toward improving its solvency and yield with a view to consolidating its credit capacity in the medium and long term.

The Banco de la Nación recently established a maximum credit limit of US$1.5 million per enterprise. Thus the loan portfolio became less concentrated and priority attention was given to small and medium-sized enterprise.

Among the institution's credit lines for financing specifically aimed at small enterprise are the following:

- A line of US$100 million for investment projects and productive retooling, and another US$150 million to finance exports of capital and durable goods within the framework of the aforementioned three-year plan.
- A line of pre- and post-export financing for small and medium-sized enterprise in the amount of US$300 million.
- A program designed to refinance the debts of small and medium-sized enterprise in the agricultural sector. Launched in September 1992, this program issues rural mortgage bonds for the granting of credit to rural producers. The first underwriting of these securities was for US$500 million. The effective loan cost for the producer is approximately 10 percent per year, substantially lower than the market rate for similar operations. In addition to this advantage, the seven-year amortization period (which may be doubled) is far superior to those currently available on the market.
- The institution has also actively participated in the placement of subsidized lines for the purchase of capital goods and the provision of working capital, as contemplated under the three-year plan.

Banco de Inversión y Comercio Exterior (BICE) was created in January 1992 as a second-tier institution dedicated to securing external funds to finance investments and activities related to foreign trade. This institution, which recently began operations, will route its credits through commercial institutions acting as first-tier banks.

As recently announced, BICE recently concluded financing agreements with the World Bank for US$500 million, with Eximbank of Japan for US$300 million, and with the Inter-American Development Bank for US$300 million dol-

---

[24]The Banco Hipotecario Nacional continues to operate as a national public wholesale bank, specializing in the financing of housing.

lars to finance its operations. Through a bilateral agreement signed with Spain, BICE also has access to financing worth US$250 million to import capital goods and services of Spanish origin. Additionally, the Secretariat of Finance will make US$250 million available to finance activities related to foreign trade.

Beginning in 1994, BICE will grant financing to small enterprise, initially to export firms. Currently under study is a line of credit to purchase capital goods, technology, and working capital for small export enterprises.

The provincial public banking sector. The difficult financial and net worth situation experienced by most of these institutions prevents them from playing a major role in the financing of small business. The high levels of delinquency, over-concentration, and the sunk cost of loans, absorbed in good measure by provincial public administrations and the sheer size of obligations to the Central Bank, drastically reduce the financing available for smaller customers. Furthermore, the small business sector's administrative inefficiency and low yield substantially drive up the cost of what little financing is available.

To cope with this crisis, most provincial banks are now in the final process of allowing private capital to be included in their equity capital (in different forms and proportions). This should help these institutions become independent from the provincial governments, which have often used them irresponsibly to finance their own budget deficits. The two largest provincial banks, however, the Banco de Buenos Aires and the Banco de Córdoba, still maintain their status as public institutions.

In any case, almost the only purpose for provincial bank restructuring until now has been to depoliticize its management. Nonetheless, provincial banks have yet to develop a policy for their future role in financing small enterprise, despite (1) their extensive networks of branch offices in the most marginal of localities, (2) the clear advantages they have in terms of information about the areas in which they operate, and (3) the high proportion of their private sector customers that are small and medium-sized businesses.

The Role of the Capital Market

Last year, the *Comisión Nacional de Valores* (CNV, National Securities Commission) created a number of programs designed to facilitate access by small and medium-sized enterprise to the capital market. The most important of these programs are summarized below.

Negotiable bonds for small enterprise. In September 1993, some of restrictions on the offering of negotiable bonds[25] were eased to allow these bonds

---

[25] Negotiable bonds are a new option for medium- and long-term financing. See the section on recent capital market developments for additional information.

to be used exclusively by businesses that adjusted their operations to fit the Ministry of Economy's definition of a small or medium-sized enterprise. The amounts of these bonds were not to exceed 5 million pesos.

First of all, information requirements were reduced. Accordingly, greater responsibility for analysis was transferred to investors deemed qualified. Furthermore, small enterprises were no longer required to obtain two analyses by different risk-rating agencies, which eliminated a high fixed cost.

To date, however, only one offering has been made in accordance with these regulations. This was for US$600,000, with a mortgage guarantee for two years and an annual interest rate of 12 percent. Although this financial instrument has worked well for large corporations, the market for the negotiable bonds of small and medium-sized enterprises is not expected to develop significantly. Despite the facilities granted, these offerings entail high fixed costs (professional fees, commissions for guarantees and placement, etc.), which substantially drive up the total cost of these funds compared with the alternative of bank financing.

Special section for over-the-counter trading. In 1990, the *Bolsa de Comercio de Buenos Aires* (Buenos Aires Stock Exchange) set up a special section for companies not listed on the Exchange but interested in raising financing for new investment projects in goods and services. Companies requesting the listing of their shares would, if accepted, receive a commitment from the Bolsa to conduct one or more equity issues through a subscription open to the public. The funds secured would then be used to develop the investment project. However, in the three years since its creation, this section has received no requests for listings.

In summary, despite the best efforts of the National Securities Commission and private institutions like the Buenos Aires Stock Exchange to expand the access of small enterprise to the capital market, the various initiatives launched have achieved very little. Although some of these programs are relatively new, there is little hope that they will ever become popular instruments for financing small enterprise.

External Financing of Small and Medium-Sized Enterprise

Comprehensive Credit Program

At the end of 1993, a comprehensive credit program for micro- and small enterprise was launched with funds from the Inter-American Development Bank (IDB) and complementary resources from commercial banks participating in the program. Its principal objective is to expand access to credit and technical assistance by micro- and small entrepreneurs throughout the country. At the same time, it seeks to develop and strengthen governmental and non-governmental technical support organizations that provide training and technical and financial assistance to microentrepreneurs. The program also works to promote greater participation by banking institutions in granting credit to small enterprises.

The initial amount allocated for the program is only US$60 million, of which US$45 million will be contributed by the Inter-American Development Bank and the remainder by commercial banks. This amount constitutes an initial fund; provided the first disbursement goes smoothly, a second disbursement is anticipated. The IDB credit consists of a 20-year revolving fund. According to official statements, the Bank is willing to offer an additional US$90 million for the program.

The program's credits will be distributed as follows: the IDB grants the resources to the Central Bank (BCRA), which routes them through official financial institutions, private or cooperative, previously selected on the basis of indicators developed by the BCRA's Superintendency of Banks.

Loan recipients will be microenterprises (up to five employees) and small enterprises (up to 20 employees). In both cases, the annual invoicing and net worth of these enterprises—whether new or existing, rural or urban, or dedicated to agriculture, industry, mining, commerce, or services—may not exceed US$200,000. These credits may used for working capital or investment. The maximum amount per credit operation will be US$20,000 per loan recipient. In addition, each bank involved with the program will participate with its own funds, which will average around US$10,000 per credit operation.

The interest rate charged by the BCRA to participating banks will be set every six months and based on the rate determined by the IDB for that period. At the beginning of the program, the fixed rate was 8.5 percent per year. The average interest rate for users will be 13.5 percent per year (with a minimum of 12 percent and a maximum of 15 percent). The maximum term envisioned is 48 months. Guarantees will be given to the satisfaction of the participating banks, since they will assume the full credit risk. Preference in the distribution of funds will be given to those banks that channel these resources to the regions with the lowest level of relative development.

Other Financing Sources

Eximbank. The risk portfolio in Argentina of the Export-Import Bank of the United States amounts to US$1.7 billion. Of this sum, US$300 million is for credit lines made available to small and medium-sized enterprise through local banks. The terms for loans used to import capital goods from the United States range between 5 and 10 years, depending on the volume of the operation. The cost of the loan is equal to the U.S. Treasury rate.

International Finance Corporation (IFC). To date, the IFC has allocated US$130 million to small and medium-sized enterprises through five local banks that operate as its financial intermediaries. The IFC also plans to allocate US$15 million to finance and underwrite the negotiable bond issues of small and medium-sized enterprises, also to be handled through local banks.

Inter-American Investment Corporation. This organization has granted loans to a number of medium-sized and large enterprise projects, the total sum of which now exceeds US$20 million. The Corporation has also agreed to make a capital contribution to the Banco Mayorista del Plata, a banking institution recently established by 20 bank cooperatives. The purpose of this new bank will be to expand the access of these bank cooperatives and their associated companies to the capital market.

Other lines of credit. A few private banks have set up lines of credit for the importing of capital goods that have been guaranteed by international organizations, such as Coface of France and Hermes of Germany, as well as by foreign private commercial banks.

New Financial Instruments

Time bills. In October 1993, the Central Bank authorized banks and finance corporations to issue dollar- and peso-denominated time bills to be used for settlements at clearinghouses.

This instrument, which works like a bank loan, is designed to replace other forms of credit like post-dated checks, promissory notes, and credit cards which are widely used by small and medium-sized enterprises, the use of which entails greater risk as well as higher costs. The risk of noncompliance is also reduced since time bills are accepted by the drawee. Furthermore, collection is very flexible since it is accomplished through check clearinghouses when the bills are deposited in either checking or savings accounts. Lastly, the bills may be discounted at a financial institution under better conditions than promissory notes since they are guaranteed by financial institutions.

With the repeal of the stamp tax proposed by the Fiscal Pact signed between the federal government and the provinces in 1993, the outlook for development of this financial instrument has improved greatly.[26]

"Small and medium-sized enterprise window." In November 1993, the opening of a "window for small and medium-sized enterprise" was announced. It will begin operating, alternately, three weeks in the Federal Capital and one week at different locations throughout the country. This initiative will provide information and assistance for small entrepreneurs to access data on the status of international markets, financing possibilities, and new technologies.

These information offices will consult with small and medium-sized enterprises on various subjects. Consultation will cover hedging resources, the report-

---

[26] The Fiscal Pact is an agreement signed between the federal government and the provinces to repeal taxes on goods production and financial services (gross receipts, seals, etc.).

ing of alleged dumping, industrial specialization systems, and access to lines of financing available to the sector.

Additionally, the government of the Province of Buenos Aires signed an accord with the Secretariat of Industry to create an Information Center for Small and Medium-sized Enterprise (CIP), with 11 offices throughout the province. These centers will provide information on tax rules, procedures, services, publications, lines of credit, and trade opportunities abroad.

Investment funds in enterprise development. The goal of the Fund for Investment in Enterprise Development (FIDE) is to provide venture capital to those enterprises which, due to their size or characteristics, have trouble entering the capital market. This fund allows the investor to invest capital in companies that offer a high financial return, but entail higher investment risk.

The fund portfolio will consist of equities, debt instruments, or warrants, if organized as a closed corporation (with no public offering of shares). If organized as an open corporation, it may not be listed in the special section of the Buenos Aires Stock Exchange, where the shares of the listed companies with a greater net worth are traded.

It is hoped that the banks will organize these funds, thereby providing an implicit guarantee to the participants with respect to evaluation of the operations they conduct. Practical application of this initiative, however, will require overcoming a number of legal and tax obstacles. This situation casts doubt upon on any forecast concerning the usefulness and future of this instrument.

Factoring. International experience shows that factoring can become an important supplementary instrument for financing small and medium-sized enterprise. It can also serve as a tool enabling these enterprises to upgrade their administrative skills and improve their practical, administrative, and business knowledge.

The main obstacle currently blocking its development is the stamp tax levied in many provinces on the "conformed invoice." As a result of the Fiscal Pact being negotiated by the federal government with the provinces, this tax will probably be repealed nationwide. That will allow widespread use of the "conformed invoice," and its popularization and discounting by banking institutions will promote the use of factoring. A number of banks are planning to use this mechanism and the International Finance Corporation has decided to set up a factoring company in Argentina.

Evaluation of Existing Programs

Recent policies have only partly reduced the difficulties faced by small enterprise. Limited access to financing due to a concentration of bank credit, high costs and short terms for the resources available, and rigid requirements for collateral guarantees still persist.

Currently the most important initiative for credit assistance to the sector is the three-year program to promote and develop small enterprise. A preliminary evaluation of its operation allows us to identify the following features:

- The subsidy bidding plan seems appropriate both for maximizing leverage of funds budgeted for the program and for reducing loan costs to the end user.
- A survey conducted of the participating institutions indicates, however, that the resources were used chiefly to refinance existing debt, a use not contemplated in the goals proposed for the program.
- The sectoral distribution of credit lines shows little support for industry. This may be partly explained by the public banking sector's large-scale participation in the program, which gave priority to refinancing problem debts in the agricultural sector, and by the agricultural sector's ability to offer real guarantees.
- Given that the funds were used mainly to refinance existing debt, it is not surprising that they mirror the geographical distribution of the institutions' general portfolio.
- Perhaps the main defect of the program is that it has not yet found a satisfactory solution regarding bank guarantees. In the case of credit for the purchase of capital goods, the program's official guidelines initially provided for a single collateral security. In turn, banks were required to make reinsurance arrangements with an insurance company. The latter, in turn, agreed to accept a federal subsidy obtained through competitive bidding. In practice, however, it becomes impossible to contract the guarantee reinsurance, given the absence of a proper legal framework and, consequently, of insurance companies with experience in this type of operation. Accordingly, the Secretariat of Industry and Commerce, which heads the program, had to authorize banks to charge an advance premium for noncompliance risk of up to 3.7 percent of the amount of the credit. In the case of loans for working capital, financial institutions were authorized to demand guarantees to their satisfaction, electing, in nearly all cases, mortgage securities. In short, the high cost of the requirement to post guarantees continued, thereby subverting the announced goal of drastically reducing the total cost of bank financing.

Financial support from the public banking sector is quite limited. On the one hand, the activities of BICE are still only in the embryonic stage. On the other hand, the Banco de la Nación, now amidst restructuring, is seeking to play a leadership role in providing credit assistance to small and medium-sized enterprise. Although in recent years its performance has improved, it is still far from completing the financial reorganization of its portfolio. Moreover, it still has to make the investments required to revamp its facilities and technology. For the moment, the policy of the Banco de la Nación is concentrated on these two activities.

As for the financing available to the sector through the capital market, various initiatives have in fact produced very few results. While some are relatively new, there is little to suggest that these instruments will ever become important in future financing of the small business sector.

After considering all available sources, it becomes clear that credit in Argentina is not available for initiating activities in the small enterprise sector. Financing from external sources is only complementary, and support from the public banking sector is still quite limited. The proposal to create incentives for these enterprises to enter the capital market does not solve the problems these enterprises face when looking for financing.

In sum, we may conclude this section with two basic observations concerning the current financial programs. First, these programs are not fitted into a comprehensive policy aimed at providing assistance to small enterprises. Second, the funds channeled to small enterprises are clearly insufficient to support the development and productive retooling required by the sector at this time.

Conclusions and Policy Recommendations

Principal Difficulties in Financing Small Enterprise

Credit rationing affecting small business is a longstanding problem in Argentina. Though the Convertibility Plan created a strong money supply and the government recently enacted programs to aid small business, these have not appreciably changed the situation.

The principal problems for small business in obtaining access to financial services may be summarized as follows:

- These enterprises are perceived as a credit risk for banking institutions, particularly in those sectors most affected by the liberalization of the economy.
- Lending interest rates are high, especially on funds intended for small enterprises or when the resources are routed outside the Greater Buenos Aires Metropolitan Area.
- Banks have rigid requirements for real guarantees from these enterprises, which causes a large number of enterprises to be excluded from the loan market, or substantially increases total loan costs for those applicants not excluded.
- Both public and private banks lack specialized departments with personnel properly trained in granting credit to small enterprises.

- Financing for new investment projects, particularly for starting new enterprises, is scarce; government programs and private bank credit policies are focused on existing enterprises, whose credit risk is easier to evaluate.
- The inadequate training of small entrepreneurs and their administrative staff hinder their compliance with the increasingly complex information requirements of banking institutions.
- The official policy to increase fiscal receipts, which force banks to apply increased controls at the time credits are granted, has had the undesired side-effect of restricting access to credit by many small and medium-sized enterprises due to their inability to comply fully with their tax and social security obligations.
- Despite the recent formulation of new legislation that enables small and medium-sized enterprise to access the capital market, experience shows that this source of financing is of little importance to the sector.
- Access by small or medium-sized enterprise to external credit is still quite limited. It is restricted almost exclusively to financing imports of capital goods using bilateral credit from official agencies that promote foreign trade and, to a lesser extent, from private commercial banks. Nonetheless, economic authorities are working hard to arrange for external financing through the public banking sector. The credit program for small and medium-sized enterprise, with funds coming chiefly from the IDB, is the first concrete result of this effort.

In sum, it may be stated that the small and medium-sized enterprise sector encounters a vast number of restrictions relating to the volume, terms, and cost of available financing, not to mention the security guarantees and other conditions demanded by intermediaries. Despite the liberalization of the financial system taking place in Argentina today, these restrictions continue to negatively impact small and medium-sized enterprises.

Appropriate state intervention could minimize the effects of these restrictions. Abundant international evidence, in both industrialized and developing countries, illustrates the importance of state intervention, especially in Southeast Asia. Many programs in that region to aid small businesses, particularly financial enterprises, are still operating today, despite the rising trend elsewhere to place greater priority on market forces.[27]

Specific programs for direct assistance—as well as more general policies aimed at reducing loan costs, expanding access to financing, and enabling small enterprises to post guarantees—differ greatly from country to country. Nonetheless, a number of common features are discernible.

---

[27] See, among others, Stiglitz (1993), Harm (1992), Layne (1993), Baek (1993), and Chen (1993).

- Special credit lines for small enterprises with some degree of government subsidy, at interest rates and terms more favorable than those available on the market. These terms are granted in exchange for meeting pre-established requirements and complying with simple supervision rules.
- Export financing, technological innovation and retooling, new projects, and establishing new enterprises.
- Credit policies complemented by other policies focused on assistance, training, and dissemination of information.
- Retail public institutions specialized in providing financial assistance to small enterprise (strictly defined and screened in order to avoid ineligible "infiltrators"); collaboration and assistance through wholesale public institutions, to the private banking sector most connected to the sector.
- Use of guarantee funds with government participation or other similar mechanisms to complement those offered by the enterprises themselves.

Instruments to Reduce the Cost of Credit

Despite the presence of macroeconomic and other factors permitting the improved functioning of the financial system that caused a major decrease in the lending rates at the beginning of the Convertibility Plan, these rates still remain too high, especially for small enterprise.

In addition to a series of specific tax measures and certain deregulatory provisions,[28] the Central Bank adopted two direct regulatory measures at the outset of the Convertibility Plan to reduce costs. First, on the national and provincial public banking system, the BCRA imposed a maximum charge of 2 percent per month for discounting instruments and a maximum charge of 3 percent monthly for overdrafts and personal loans. Second, in the formula for computing minimum capital requirements, the BCRA introduced a risk indicator keyed to the lending rate level, which raises capital requirements when rates over a certain level are charged.

The first measure succeeded in lowering rates in the public banking sector, although not in the provincial banking sector. The second measure had only minor impact. Moreover, this measure had no practical consequences for banks with a high calculable net worth. Furthermore, some institutions were able to offset the reduced lending rates by instituting increases concealed as commissions.

---

[28] Noteworthy among the specific provisions for reducing cost at financial institutions are elimination of taxes on bank debits and on the transfer of securities and foreign exchange, substitution of the tax on financial services with the VAT, adoption of certain deregulatory measures as well as streamlining certain aspects concerning deposits, banking hours, and rules for installing automatic teller machines.

By 1993, a set of innovative measures designed to achieve the same objective was announced. Most important was the ban on fixed terms of less than 30 days, which was offset by the authorization to open savings accounts with unlimited withdrawals. Concurrently, measures were introduced to simplify the structure of reserve requirements by reducing their dispersion and attempting to neutralize their impact on the amount of money. The easing of restrictions on the granting of credit to small and medium-sized enterprise, with real guarantees and elimination of the stamp tax on loans and other contracts, were also included among these measures.

Elimination of mini-terms for loans will tend to lessen the differentials by reducing illiquidity risks and administrative costs. Costs will also be reduced by the elimination of the stamp tax as well as by a number of specific deregulatory measures included in the package. Competition among the new financing alternatives (swaps, credit guarantees, and 30-day commercial securities) should also reduce the intermediation margins of financial institutions. As seen in Table 2.17, bank differentials have been significantly reduced since the introduction of the Convertibility Plan. By 1993 they were tending to stabilize, but still remained at high levels (just below 1 percent per month).

Other specific initiatives may be adopted to help bring down the high cost of intermediation by the institutions. First of all, without affecting the rules that preserve the solvency and liquidity of this system, it is possible to reduce operational costs by deepening the process of deregulation of financial activities. Simplifying and computerizing information for the Central Bank, easing the rules related to the composition of minimum cash requirements, and streamlining the regulatory framework governing collateral security are a few examples of this.

Second, a review of specific tax policy affecting the sector could help reduce this component of operating expenses. The contribution to the *Instituto de Servicios Sociales Bancarios* (Banking Social Services Institute)—2 percent of lending rates and commissions paid into the bank staff's social foundation, added to the standard employers' contributions—and the gross receipts tax (a provincial tax whose rate varies in each jurisdiction) are obvious candidates for this review.

Proposals for Expanding Access to Financing

The limited financial deepening found in the Argentine economy results in a reduced supply of credit as well as its high costs and extremely short terms. It also causes financial market segmentation and credit concentration. This situation suggests that the public sector still has an important role to play in this area. It could, for example, undertake to arrange for an extension of the terms of credits, a task that cannot be initiated by the private banking sector because of the high risk involved. The public sector could also provide credit assistance to

Table 2.17. Three-Year Program to Promote and Develop Small and Medium-Sized Enterprise
(Goal: To facilitate access by these enterprises to credit through competitive interest rates, with subsidies from the Federal Government)

	Purchase of capital goods A	For working capital B	Purchase of technologies C	For working capital	Investment and/or production retooling projects	Export of capital goods
Available credits	US$1,000,000,000	US$200,000,000	US$100,000,000	US$600,000 000	US$100,000,000	US$180,000,000
Maximum amount per enterprise	80 percent of the value of the goods, maximum US$400,000	20 percent of what is extended in line A	10 percent of what is extended in line A	US$100,000 per enterprise or consortium	US$1,000,000	
Term	40 months (6 months grace period)	10 months	36 months	From 24 and up to 36 months (minimum 3 months grade period)	7 years (2 years grace period)	Minimum 4 years
Conditions		To have secured line A credit	To have secured line A credit	Social security and tax obligations up to date in pesos or US$		
Guarantee	Pledge on goods purchased or mortgage + supplemental guarantee if requested by Bank	Supplemental guarantee fund provided they have a chattel mortgage on other goods	Supplemental guarantee fund provided they have a chattel mortgage on other goods	To the financial institution's satisfaction	To the financial institution's satisfaction	To the financial institution's satisfaction

Source: Prepared using data from the Ministry of Economy.

those economic sectors whose size or location prevent them from being adequately served by the private banking sector.[29]

National Public Banking Sector

In light of the restructuring of the national public banking sector, only the Banco de la Nación remains as a first-tier nationwide financial institution. Its announced purpose is to serve primarily small and medium-sized enterprise, especially in the agricultural sector. There are also two wholesale banks, one dedicated to financing investment and foreign trade (BICE), and the other dedicated to funding housing construction (Banco Hipotecario Nacional).

In the case of the Banco de la Nación, its share of deposit receipts, although declining in recent years, still assures it a stable anchor and a major role. To reach its objectives, the Bank must continue its process of portfolio recovery still a high proportion of sunk cost), and intensify the current program to professionalize and depoliticize its management, thereby increasing its autonomy and efficiency.

Considering that a high proportion of the bank's lending is aimed at small and medium-sized agricultural enterprises, and that these funds will increase in the immediate future with the program that issues rural mortgage bonds, more attention will have to be paid to the quality of the credit assistance provided to this sector. Better and more complete assistance will be required to expand access for small and medium-sized agricultural enterprises to available financing. An alternative to consider is the establishment of accords with the Instituto Nacional de Tecnología Agropecuaria (INTA) to provide comprehensive assistance (business, technical, and financial) to these enterprises. Local offices of INTA could also someday be established within some of the branches of the Banco de la Nación.

In the cases of BICE and Banco Hipotecario, the availability of fresh funds depends chiefly on their access to credit lines abroad and placement of their bonds on the domestic capital market. With regard to external financing, funds from multilateral organizations are, on the one hand, already committed under various credit agreements concluded in recent years. On the other hand, a certain saturation of Latin American bonds has in recent months been noted. Accordingly, Argentine companies and banks are now finding it more difficult to attract private funds. With regard to the domestic capital market, it is still only in the early stage of development. Nonetheless, the number of issues of private securities has recently increased sharply.

---

[29] See Machinea (1990) and Rozenwurcel and Fernández (1993).

Aside from considerations about the current cycle of world capital markets, the phenomenon that needs to be emphasized is the potential instability that could make the financing capacity of these institutions exclusively dependent upon the availability of resources in international markets. Past experience clearly justifies the decision not to utilize discounts and advances from the Central Bank for this purpose. But in addition to external resources, these institutions should be adequately capitalized with resources explicitly included in the federal budget. Additionally, serious consideration should be given to more effective utilization of existing funds, such as those of the Fondo Nacional de la Vivienda (FONAVI).

Finally, once the reform of the public banking system is complete, no other first-tier bank will be specifically designed to serve small industrial enterprises; BICE, which focuses primarily on industry, will operate exclusively as a second-tier bank. This situation creates a serious obstacle to the financing of small and medium-sized industrial enterprises, since both domestic and international experience show that the private banking sector limits financing to this sector. In light of the need to finance new projects, this weakness is even more critical.

Although BICE's complementary role as a wholesale bank to the private banking sector seemed a reasonable criterion for distributing the external financing it secures, it would still be advisable in light of international experience to give serious study to the domestic feasibility of creating a first-tier bank to serve small and medium-sized industrial and mining enterprises. Such a bank, like the Banco de la Nación, could be financed with resources from domestic and international markets. Additionally, it could eventually even become eligible for budget allocations aimed explicitly at subsidizing the sector.

Such a bank could allow the effectiveness of these resources to be maximized. Experience shows that in many cases a significant portion of these subsidies are appropriated by the private banking sector when, as in the case of the three year program, the funds are intended to upgrade the quality of credit previously granted. This new institution could also become intensively active in serving small and medium-sized enterprise, working together with the National Institute of Industrial Technology (INTI) to support new projects as well as existing enterprises.

Provincial Public Banking Sector

Reforms are also being carried out at provincial banks that will allow contributions of private capital (in different proportions, depending on the case). This new influx of capital will help these banks to resolve problems in the area of net worth, portfolio, over-indebtedness to the Central Bank, and low levels of administrative efficiency. In general, however, the reforms implemented have not resulted in any major improvements, as may be seen indirectly from the current performance indicators for this group of institutions, discussed earlier in this chapter.

Provincial banks have a role to perform in the Argentine financial system. In addition to acting as financial agents of the provincial treasuries, these institutions (occasionally accompanied by small cooperative banks) are the only ones available to provide financial services in more remote regions. In fulfilling this function, the provincial public banking sector has some comparative advantages—a vast network of branches, customers, and information in the regions where it operates.

To capitalize on these advantages, the current restructuring process should proceed along the following lines: (a) deepen the rationalization process of structures and costs; (b) make greater efforts to improve portfolio recovery, (c) establish, in their charters, precise limits and adequate guarantees for loans to the public sector, (d) eliminate the implicit guarantee of the provincial governments to these institutions and submit them fully to the authority of the Central Bank, making all necessary constitutional changes, and, when possible, reorganizing them as corporations, (e) encourage agreements with the Central Bank under conditions that promote the paying off of debts with that institution upon the successful implementation of the rationalization and portfolio recovery programs, and (f) facilitate access to international financing by using a portion of the external resources intermediated by BICE for these institutions.

More importantly, the activities of the national and provincial public banking should be closely coordinated. In many cases, such coordination might appear to cause an irrational superposition of branches and functions. In fact, proper coordination will permit the banking structure to be optimized and will significantly reduce operating expenses. One example of this is the policy recently followed in issuing mortgage bonds following signature of an accord between the Banco de la Nación and the provincial banks. Additionally, consideration should also be given to merging smaller provincial banks with larger regional institutions.

Private Banking Sector

Other measures aimed at improving the quality of assistance to small and medium-sized enterprise should be included in those credit programs involving the private banking sector. In this connection, minimum requirements should exist in the areas of advertising, information, and advice. The establishment of procedures for proper supervision and performance evaluation at each institution in the program is also of great importance. The performance evaluation could also include a survey of the recipients of the line of credit.

Consideration should also be given to the feasibility of establishing an appeal procedure whereby the claims of those entrepreneurs whose credit requirements were found insufficient by private banking could be reviewed.

Guarantee Fund

To complement public banking programs and other assistance measures for small and medium-sized enterprise, it would be advisable to set up a system of guarantees designed to reduce the high cost of the surety bonds required of these enterprises.

Taking as a basis a study conducted in Argentina in 1989 within the framework of a technical assistance program financed by the World Bank, as well as the vast and, in many cases, successful international experience in this area, we would like to cite a few of the principal points that such a system should take into consideration.[30]

- The basic objective of the system would be to prevent small and medium-sized enterprises from being forced to post guarantees in amounts greater than the credit they receive. To avoid phenomena such as "subjective risk" by the enterprises, and in order for the banks to assume part of the credit risk, the guarantees offered by the system would be partial and involve the payment of fees.
- Because legal and technical restrictions of credit insurance have frustrated attempts to implement the three-year program, the new system should be based on the commercial bond procedure. This would assure the shared assumption of the risk of noncompliance by financial institutions and would force them to evaluate applications for credit thoroughly. This is vitally important to prevent the system from ever becoming an implicit subsidy for inefficient or insolvent enterprises.
- The system should be structured on two levels. Lending institutions that provide direct guarantees for private or mixed property would operate in the first level. In the second level, a state-run lending institution would provide counter-guarantees for property owned predominately by the state.
- Together with the established net worth requirements, the direct lenders would be requested to set up liquid guarantee funds to back their operations. The counter-guarantee fund would be integrated with an initial government contribution.
- The role of the guarantee funds would be to cover a portion of the performance bonds granted, much in a manner similar to bank reserves. This would confer a great potential for expansion of the system, although the fixing of reserve ratios should also contemplate the solidity of the system in light of the risk of non-performance.
- For the same reason, in addition to a charge for the service, small enterprises should contribute a refundable premium based on the amount of

[30] See Imperatore (1989) and Harm (1992).

the performance bond which could then be used as a fund for uncollectible credit.

- In the first stage and until the direct lenders are organized, the second level state-run institution could grant direct guarantees to small enterprises through banks that wish to become accredited as agents of the system.

Bibliography

Baek, N. 1993. "Desarrollo e incentivos para las pequeñas y medianas empresas coreanas." *Revista comercio exterior.* Mexico City.

Calvo, G., L. Leiderman, and C. Reinhart. 1992. "Capital Inflows and Real Exchange Rate Appreciation in Latin America: the Role of External Factors." Working Paper Series 92/62. Washington, D.C.: International Monetary Fund.

Chen, Tain Jy. 1993. "Las empresas pequeñas y medianas de Taiwan." *Revista comercio exterior.* Mexico City.

Fanelli, J.M., R. Frenkel, and G. Rozenwurcel. 1992. "Transformación estructural, estabilización y reforma del estado en Argentina." CEDES Document 82. Buenos Aires, Argentina.

Gatto, Francisco, and G. Yoguel. 1993. "Las PYMEs argentinas en una etapa de transición productiva y tecnológica." In *Desafío de la competitividad. La industria argentina en transformación* (Chap. IV). Argentina: CEPAL/Alianza Editorial.

Giorgio, L. 1988. "El sistema financiero argentino. Evolución y estructura actual." Monetaria. XI (71), January–March. Centro de Estudios Monetarios Latinoamericanos.

Harm, Christian. 1992. "The Financing of Small Firms in Germany." Working Paper Series 899. Financial Policy and Systems, Country Economics Department, World Bank, Washington, D.C.

Imperatore, R. 1989. "Fundamentos e instrumentación de un sistema de garantías para el PYMEs en Argentina." World Bank Program 2712 AR, SME Subcomponent. Buenos Aires, Argentina. Mimeo.

Katz, Jorge. 1993. "Una interpretación global del proyecto de desarrollo industrial de la República Argentina." Working Paper No. 9. Buenos Aires, Argentina: Instituto para el Desarrollo Industrial (IDI) - Fundación Industrial Argentina (FUIA).

Layne, Donald. 1993. "Políticas financieras para el desarrollo de la pequeña empresa." *Revista comercio exterior.* Mexico City.

Machinea, J.L. 1990. "Reformas estructurales en el sector financiero." Inter-American Development Bank, Washington, D.C. Mimeo.

McKinnon, R.I. 1989. "Financial Liberalization and Economic Development: A Reassessment of Interest-Rate Policies in Asia and Latin America." *Oxford Review of Economic Policy* 6(4).

_______. 1991. "The Order of Economic Liberalization." *Financial Control in the Transition to a Market Economy.* Baltimore: The Johns Hopkins University Press.

Rozenwurcel, G., and R. Fernández. 1993. "El fortalecimiento del sector financiero en el proceso de ajuste. El caso argentino." Working Paper Series 141. Washington, D.C.: Inter-American Development Bank.

Stiglitz, J.E. 1993. "The Role of the State in Financial Markets." Annual Bank Conference on Development Economics, World Bank, Washington, D.C.

Zahler, R. 1988. "Estrategias financieras latinoamericanas: la experiencia del Cono Sur." *Colección Estudios CIEPLAN No. 23*. Santiago, Chile.

APPENDIX

Financial System Performance Indicators

a. Cost structure and efficiency indicators

a.1	Average cost of financial intermediation	*Administration Expenses* Total deposits
a.2	Yield on capital	*Net result of ordinary and extraordinary operations* Net worth
a.3	Productivity	*Income per service-expense per service*[31] Personnel employed
a.4	Share of labor costs in total costs	*Labor costs* Total costs
a.5	Real financial yield per deposit account	*Total financial income—total financial expenses—charges for uncollectible accounts + monetary results* Total deposits
a.6	Receipt of deposits per bank office	*Total deposits* Number of bank offices
a.7	Receipt of deposits per bank employee	*Total deposits* Number of bank employees

b. Asset structure and liquidity indicators

b.1	Sunk cost of capital	*Sunk cost* Net worth
b.2	Immediate deposit liquidity	*Availability + public securities in listed foreign currency* Total deposits
b.3	Sunk cost of liquid capital	*Public securities in domestic currency* Net worth - sunk cost
b.4	Share of deposits in foreign currency	*Deposits in foreign currency* Total deposits

[31] At variance with the net result owing to regular and special operations; this does not include capital gains or losses resulting from the holding of financial assets.

c. Financial portfolio quality and solvency indicators

c.1	Quality of financial portfolio	*Delinquent loans, with insolvency risk, in receivership, bankruptcy, or liquidation* / Total gross loans from funds
c.2	Share of the public sector in asset portfolio	*Nonfinancial public sector loans* / Total loans
c.3	BCRA financing to the financial system	*Total Central Bank loans* / Total deposits

CHAPTER THREE

CHILE: IMPROVING MARKET MECHANISMS

Miguel Basch H.*

Macroeconomic Developments in Chile since 1973

Liberalization of the Financial System and the Crisis Period, 1973–85

Financial systems in developing countries are usually "repressed systems" (McKinnon, 1973 and Shaw, 1973). Two decades ago, Chile certainly fit that description: financial repression was the main feature of the capital market. At that time private financial savings basically consisted of currency in circulation and deposits.

To finance the budget, the government used a series of financial mechanisms: (i) very high reserve requirements for checking and savings accounts (above 50 percent); (ii) fixed interest rates (after correction for inflation, real interest rates were negative); (iii) selective allocation of credit, thus subsidizing particular economic sectors; and (iv) restrictions on foreign debt. Finally, if these methods failed to finance the fiscal deficit, an inflation tax was levied.

The consequences of such financial repression were soon apparent. Those who had access to official credit continued to obtain it, while others could get credit only at a very high real interest rate through the informal market. Financial resources dwindled, and heavy distortions in resource allocation, due to negative real interest rates, were reflected in the poor quality of projects. Eventually financial repression reduced domestic savings and created pressure to compensate for that lack with foreign savings (Held, 1989).

---

* The author is especially grateful for the help provided by Mario Chamorro, Luis Felipe Jiménez, and Camilo Morales. He also appreciates the comments, suggestions, and time of many financial system executives and government officials, such as Rodrigo Azócar, Nélida San Martin, Francisco Donoso, Guillermo Geisse, Oscar González, Gonzalo Jara, José Mena, José Rojas, and Enrique Román. Finally, research assistants Vicente Pérez and Rodrigo Caputo deserve thanks for their help.

To correct this situation, the government decided to carry out a complete and profound liberalization of the capital market. But this was undertaken only after reorganization of the real sector of the economy, through restructuring the state apparatus and policy reforms. The steps taken in that direction were as follows (Arellano, 1983; Barandiarán, 1983; Held, 1989; Le-Fort, 1993; De la Cuadra and Valdés, 1989)

- Interest rates were liberalized and credit restrictions were eliminated. (Credit controls had been completely lifted in 1974, but that effort failed until the necessary fiscal adjustment was undertaken.)
- Reserve requirements were lowered to 4 percent for savings deposits (for 30 days or more) and 10 percent for checking accounts. This entire process was carried out gradually between 1976 and 1980, along with efforts to reduce inflation.
- Tax reform limited taxes on savings deposits to the positive portion of the real interest rate.

Liberalization of Chile's financial market was one pillar of the neo-liberal economic model applied to the economy. These financial reforms, which caused a kind of *laissez-faire* in the capital market, were intended to increase savings and investment, and to lead to an optimum allocation of investment. Savings and investment decisions were to be governed exclusively by supply and demand, which in turn were to be determined by the interest rate. The government would return to its role of assuring that the newly introduced norms were applied.

For a capital market liberalization process to succeed, according to McKinnon (1982), fiscal deficit and government-subsidized credit must first be eliminated. Another important element of the process is the existence of a high real interest rate (McKinnon, 1973). If the interest rate depositors receive is greater than the yield from productive activity, producers will have incentives to replace old technology with new, and so raise their yield rate. Increased yield from investment has a direct impact on the rate of economic growth.

Let us now examine the results of financial liberalization in Chile.

- Between 1975 and 1982 the real interest rate was extremely high, averaging above 30 percent a year.
- Total bank credit rose from 5.6 percent of GDP to over 77 percent during the same period.
- If M2 is used to measure the financial deepening caused by monetization, it grew from 6 percent of GDP to 26 percent.
- Despite the prevailing high real interest rates, gross national savings declined on average from 16.3 percent of GDP in the 1960s (during "financial repression") to 12.4 percent in the 1975–81 period.

- Even taking into account the rise in (domestic and external) credit, investment declined 5 percentage points of GDP during the 1975–82 period in comparison to the 1960s. That was due not only to a sharp decline in public investment, but also to lower private investment (Arellano, 1983).
- During this period, resources were poorly allocated for investment, if we take the portfolio write-offs of commercial banks as an indicator. Between 1981 and 1983, a total of 22 financial institutions, which together held 60 percent of private bank holdings, were liquidated or taken over by the government. By December 1984, total losses were around 200 percent of capital and reserves, which equalled 18 percent of GDP.
- Finally, due to the high interest rate paid for 30-day deposits, the deposit period for a significant sector of the capital market was cut considerably (Meller and Solimano, 1984).[1]

As indicated, the first symptoms of the financial crisis became apparent when the banks were left holding a significant amount of unpaid debt. The severe 1981 recession caused banks not under government control to become more insolvent, and these failures had major repercussions.

The crisis was the product of an unsustainable economic policy and an extremely vulnerable financial system. Among the conditions that caused the crisis was the existence of implicit deposit insurance, which completely distorted the relationship between risk and yield in bank holdings. This became clear in 1976 when the government backed the credits issued by Banco Osorno, a private foreign bank. Despite the crisis, the government was not exercising preventive oversight over banking, since it was practicing laissez-faire in the financial market as in other markets.

There was excessive optimism about the potential for growth in the economy. Financial problems were regarded as temporary, and banks continued to refinance their borrowers at extremely high interest rates. However, at this point the banks were not risking their own capital, but that of their insurers and creditors. The most significant banks were part of the so-called "economic groups," whose capital was marginal within the conglomerate, so that companies in the "group" were rescued with credits that were quite disadvantageous for the bank. The Central Bank clearly lacked adequate mechanisms to monitor conflicts of interest that arose through loans made within the "economic groups" (Le-Fort, 1993; Ramírez, 1989; and Held, 1989).

---

[1] For analysis of these results, see Arellano, 1983; De la Cuadra and Valdés, 1989; Ramírez, 1989; and Le-Fort, 1993.

Banking Regulation Reforms, 1985–93

Faced with the severe financial crisis that struck Chile in the early 1980s, the government moved to rescue the financial system. The Central Bank intervened by purchasing the "bad" portfolios held by the banks. That restored the financial system and also allowed companies that could not pay their debts to continue operating normally (Basch and Maquieira, 1993). Government assistance was now, in effect, backing foreign private debt.

The Central Bank bought the "bad" portfolios from banks at face value with its own notes, thus notably improving the quality of banking assets on the books. Banks were forced to repurchase this failed portfolio with a fraction of whatever future profits they might generate. However, considering the volume of assets and the expected profitability of the banks, in practice the arrangement meant that a significant part of these credits was lost forever. The banks currently owe the Central Bank approximately US$4 billion, and only US$2.5 billion is likely to be recovered (Basch and Maquieira, 1993).

This bailout strategy created many distortions that still exist (Basch and Maquieira, 1993).

- As the arrangement with the Central Bank did not specify clear time-limits for canceling the debt, debtors were allowed to postpone paying their obligations until better times.
- Since it was difficult to evaluate how solvent banks were, the conditions for repurchasing the "bad" portfolios were too easy, thus creating expectations of a sweeping "forgiveness" of the debt involved.
- The conditions under which the government stepped in entailed handing over a large amount of state resources in a discretionary fashion, benefiting only a few debtors, thus naturally producing a major political problem at the time.
- Finance companies with negative net worth were allowed to continue receiving financing, thus distorting proper resource allocation.
- Finally, all the transactions caused a serious cash flow problem for the Central Bank, due to purchase of the banks' failed portfolios and the subsidies thus entailed, and because debt was refinanced in local currency. Benefiting from this last program were companies, mortgage holders, and a variety of consumers with debts in dollars.

All of this created a significant quasi-fiscal deficit. The resulting annual Central Bank losses reached 0.5 percent of GDP (Eyzaguirre, 1992). This deficit was financed primarily by issuing domestic bonds and, secondly, by levying the inflation tax. The total accumulated cost of the bailout programs is estimated to be approximately US$8 billion (Eyzaguirre and Larrañaga, 1990).

As noted, the lack of adequate regulation and oversight of Chile's banking and financial system allowed the conditions that led to the financial crisis. The 1986 reform of the General Banking Law established a body of regulations to deal with the problems that produce a financial crisis.

Subsequent Events

After reforms were introduced to the financial system, new kinds of financial services entered the market, and traditional banks consequently had less market share, a process termed "financial disintermediation." These new mechanisms have comparative advantages over the banks since they are less strictly regulated. Given these new competitors, the banks have been authorized to engage in new businesses such as financial leasing, brokerage services, and investment banking primarily in the area of advising, mutual fund management, and financial consulting. A bill before the Chilean Congress would allow them to have branches outside the country and to engage in insurance, securities brokerage, factoring, and bond issues.

Banks have also increasingly moved toward financing individuals, thus leading to the creation of consumer credit divisions and taking advantage of their economies of scale and scope. The other market toward which they are increasingly directing their offers of credit is that of small and medium-sized business, which represents 75 percent of employment but only 20 percent of total market sales, mainly in the commercial sector.

One problem facing officials is the speed with which these intermediaries have appeared. Competition is thus stimulated to the direct benefit of depositors and investors, but these developments have so much momentum that regulatory agencies have often been overwhelmed. The challenge, therefore, is to adjust current legislation to avoid financial instability without constraining the sector's development.

One of the main accomplishments over these past decades in the Chilean capital market is the establishment of the AFP (*administradoras de fondos de pensiones*) system for administering pension funds. The pension system was reformed in 1981, when it shifted from its traditional function of simply making payments to becoming a system based on obligatory capitalization. Funds deposited to the AFPs by contributors are taken and invested in instruments such as securities, government-backed bonds, bank deposits, and so forth. Currently the AFPs have holdings that amount to 35 percent of GDP and are expected to reach 100 percent by the end of the decade. These institutions have played a fundamental role in deepening the Chilean financial system.

Financial Deepening and the Behavior of the Financial System

A positive correlation between the development of financial markets and economic growth is widely acknowledged (Goldsmith, 1969; McKinnon, 1973; Shaw,

1973; Díaz-Alejandro, 1985; De Gregorio and Guidotti, 1992; Fry, 1989). Some studies nonetheless point to a negative correlation between financial development and growth, especially in Latin American countries (De Gregorio and Guidotti, 1992). This apparent contradiction may be due to lack of adequate regulation of the financial system when liberalization efforts go into effect. Eliminating "financial repression" is clearly not enough: establishing oversight procedures for the whole banking and financial system is absolutely necessary (Díaz-Alejandro, 1985; Baltensperger and Dermine, 1987).

Even though many studies suggest that there is a positive relationship between the various indicators of financial intermediation and growth, it is not clear how to measure the degree of intermediation that exists. McKinnon and Shaw think it is reflected in the real interest rate, which indicates the degree of financial repression. Thus, a high real interest rate would discourage consumption and encourage greater financial savings—and greater use of bank intermediation. This would increase the credit supply, which in turn would stimulate investment and growth. A number of studies support that idea (see Fry, 1989; the World Bank, 1989; and Roubini *et al.*, 1991).

Other interpretations are proposed, however. Dornbusch (1990) demonstrates that despite the positive relationship between the real interest rate and growth, there is no relationship between financial savings and the real interest rate and that, moreover, the effect of the interest rate on growth does not derive from its impact on investment level. This suggests that the real interest rate acts as a variable and replaces the productivity of investment rather than financial repression. As happens with the real interest rate, traditional ways of measuring the degree of financial development, that is, money supplies, also present problems. According to the hypothesis of McKinnon and Shaw, a highly monetized economy should also reflect a highly developed financial market. However, banking not only serves as an intermediary between depositors and investors, but also supplies liquidity to the market—two functions not necessarily related. Hence money supplies such as M1 or M2 may send the wrong signals.

Financial Intensification in Chile (Money Supply)

Although measuring financial development by money supplies entails a series of problems, by examining M1, M2, and M7 one may analyze the process of financial intensification. This latter indicator is less liquid and hence is a better reflection of the degree of financial intensification (Gelb, 1989). In Table 3.1 we see that M2 grew from 10 percent of GDP in 1975 to 30 percent in 1992, and that the M7 grew from 28 percent of GDP in 1980 to 73 percent in 1992. Another measure used for these purposes is to subtract M1 from M7 and observe the development of that sum. In Chile, M7—M1 increased 45 percentage points of GDP

Table 3.1. Money Supplies

Year	GDP balance	M7/GDP	M1A/GDP	M2/GDP	(M7-M1A/GDP)
1980	23,830.9	0.28	0.07	0.19	0.21
1981	25,785.9	0.34	0.07	0.24	0.27
1982	20,765.7	0.39	0.07	0.26	0.32
1983	21,207.4	0.38	0.06	0.19	0.32
1984	20,950.3	0.41	0.06	0.21	0.34
1985	22,552.8	0.45	0.06	0.20	0.40
1986	28,412.5	0.48	0.06	0.20	0.42
1987	31,024.7	0.52	0.06	0.23	0.46
1988	33,228.7	0.52	0.08	0.25	0.44
1989	36,946.4	0.60	0.08	0.25	0.52
1990	38,054.4	0.68	0.07	0.26	0.61
1991	38,563.6	0.71	0.08	0.29	0.64
1992	40,819.5	0.73	0.08	0.30	0.65

Note: M7 includes M2A + private sector time deposits + time deposits (inc. housing) + Central Bank notes in hands of public + Treasury bills in hands of public + letters of credit in hands of public + private sector deposits in foreign currency.
GDP: In millions of 1993 dollars.
M1A: Year average.
M2, M7: Balance as of December in each year.
Source: Banco Central, *Boletín Mensual.*

between 1980 and 1992, confirming that the country's financial system had advanced significantly.

Financial Deepening (Credit)

The first part presented some evidence of the significant increase in financial system deepening during the last twelve years. We may ask whether this growth is also observable in the intermediation activity of banks.

In order to answer this question we must follow the evolution over time of bank placements and of their investments, for these latter include the acquisition of fixed-income instruments (basically bonds issued by both the Treasury and the private sector), which also constitute credits. Tables 3.2 and 3.3 indicate how placements and investments are divided between the State Bank, the national banks, foreign banks, and finance companies (so named because they do not handle checking accounts). If the ratio of holdings and investments over GDP is taken as an indicator of the deepening of bank intermediation, the latter has clearly declined since 1985. Only in the past year were there signs of recovery. If absolute amounts are considered, a downward pattern clearly begins around 1987–88.

Several reasons help account for the decline in deepening. First, at the moment when the intermediation function began to decline, a process of growing "disintermediation" started. Pension funds increased to become the main institu-

Table 3.2. Placements in National and Foreign Currency
(Ratios)

Year	National banks/ GDP[1]	State Bank/ GDP	Foreign banks/ GDP	Financial institutions/ GDP	Total/ GDP
1985	0.43	0.14	0.07	0.01	0.65
1986	0.33	0.10	0.07	0.01	0.51
1987	0.34	0.09	0.07	0.01	0.51
1988	0.31	0.09	0.06	0.01	0.47
1989	0.33	0.09	0.08	0.01	0.51
1990	0.30	0.09	0.07	0.01	0.47
1991	0.28	0.07	0.07	0.01	0.43
1992	0.31	0.06	0.08	0.02	0.47

[1] National banks do not include the State Bank.
Note: Values in December of each year, in millions of 1993 dollars. Placements are understood to be those denominated in national and foreign currency.
Source: Banco Central, *Boletín Mensual.*

Table 3.3. Placements and Investments in Relation to GDP
(Ratios)

Year	National banks/ GDP[1]	State Bank/ GDP	Foreign banks/ GDP	Financial institutions/ GDP	Total/ GDP
1985	0.73	0.29	0.13	0.02	1.16
1986	0.63	0.23	0.13	0.01	1.00
1987	0.59	0.20	0.14	0.01	0.94
1988	0.48	0.17	0.13	0.01	0.79
1989	0.46	0.15	0.13	0.01	0.75
1990	0.44	0.14	0.15	0.01	0.75
1991	0.40	0.13	0.13	0.02	0.67
1992	0.41	0.12	0.14	0.02	0.68

[1] Investments are understood to be financial investments in both national and foreign currency.
Source: Banco Central, *Boletín Mensual.*

tional investors; from 1985 to 1992 pension fund assets grew 25 percentage points of GDP. The sum total of funds managed by institutional investors has reached 49 percent of GDP.

The 1994 changes to the 1986 General Banking Law significantly stimulated the support banking can provide for the small business sector through factoring. These operations make it possible to provide liquidity with a small discount on the basis of accounts payable. Only small and medium-sized businesses are intended to be the major clientele.

Table 3.4. Gross and Net Differential
(Percentages)

Year	National Banks Differential		State Bank Differential		Foreign banks Differential		Finance companies Differential		Financial system Differential	
	Gross	Net	Gross	Net	Gross	Net	Gross	Net	Gross	Net
1985	4.7	1.7	7.8	6.9	9.0	5.2	8.9	2.2	6.0	3.3
1986	4.5	3.0	4.8	2.6	5.5	2.4	11.1	4.2	4.8	2.9
1987	5.4	2.8	5.1	2.8	6.1	2.9	11.8	4.2	5.5	2.8
1988	5.6	3.0	6.1	4.2	5.5	2.9	15.0	7.0	5.8	3.3
1989	7.1	3.9	6.8	4.2	7.0	3.8	16.9	7.9	7.2	4.0
1990	7.6	3.8	7.4	3.9	8.2	4.9	4.0	1.7	7.4	3.9
1991	6.2	1.9	7.6	3.5	5.4	2.2	16.1	5.8	6.5	2.4
1992	5.6	1.4	6.3	2.1	5.2	1.4	14.4	4.8	5.9	1.6

Lending rate: Operating revenue/(investment + placements)
Borrowing rate: Operating expense / (investment + placements)
Gross differential: Lending rate - borrowing rate
Net differential: Gross differential - (support expenses - provisional revenues from previous fiscal period + non-operating revenue)/(investment + placements)
Source: Información Financiera of the SBIF.

Costs of the Intermediation Process

It is interesting to know how much it costs the banks to intermediate their funds during this period. Table 3.4 indicates the gross and net spreads for placements and investments for the financial system as a whole and for its component parts: the State Bank, national banks, foreign banks, and finance companies. These spreads are partially determined by the reserves required on deposits in national currency along with the interest rates of funds attracted.[2] Just as important, spreads make it possible to judge the efficiency of the intermediation process.

The table indicates that the gross spreads of the financial system have remained relatively constant over the period, except in 1988, 1989, and 1991. Examination of the breakdown into the components of the financial system indicates that the State Bank has the greatest differentials and the finance companies have the least. Examining net spreads—in which overhead is subtracted from the work of intermediation—shows that the cost of placing money on the market has been decreasing. For the system as a whole, the net spread declined from 3.6 percent in 1985 to 2.2 percent in 1993. (Between 1988 and 1989 this cost was over 4.0 percent.)

[2] If the bank receives a unit of deposits, the required reserve is e, and the interest rate of placements is r, then its income from intermediation is $r\,(1–3)$. The spread would be zero if the interest rate on the placement were equal to this financial revenue.

Table 3.5. Profitability of the Banking Business and Its Breakdown
(In millions of 1993 dollars)

Year	Capital and reserves[1]	Net profit[2]	Payment of debts to Central Bank	Percentage of profitability
1985	374,646,41	21,544.68	6,286.59	7.43
1986	473,144,19	18,655.09	10,578.98	6.18
1987	449,715,35	20,210.05	41,243.74	13.67
1988	424,797,30	23,513.33	49,214.50	17.12
1989	435,204,12	39,462.29	53,006.01	21.25
1990	462,395,88	44,565.17	47,221.31	19.85
1991	470,509,82	36,577.98	35,406.42	15.30
1992	486,879,29	44,782.75	36,330.45	16.66

[1] December balances.
[2] Accumulated in December.
Profitability: = (i)/(ii)
(i) = Post-tax surplus (without paying subordinate debt to Central Bank
(ii) = Capital and reserves (without subordinate bonds)
Ex-post differential: (After tax surplus)/(placements + investment)
Leverage: (Investment)/(capital and reserves)
Profitability: (Ex-post differential) x (leverage)
Source: Boletín Mensual of the SBIF

Nevertheless, on the basis of Table 3.4 we are still not able to determine whether lower or higher spreads are due to a "price" effect or a "quantity" effect. To that end the profitability of capital and reserves derived from the banking intermediation business was calculated in a way that makes it possible to separate the latter into what is called "ex post margin" and "leverage."[3]

In Tables 3.5 and 3.6 we see that the profitability of the financial system has been very unstable over this period and has tended to decline since 1989. This decline coincides with the process of increasing disintermediation since that year. If the column for leverage is examined, it is clear that there is a sharp fall in the volume of financial intermediation in 1986, but that it remains more or less steady from that point onward. Thus it can be concluded that the decline in profitability is due to a "price" effect resulting from a decline in ex-post margin, which is due to an increase in bank placements and investments and to lower levels of surplus. It means, in other words, that the banks are able to distribute approximately 11 times their capital and reserves in placements whose surpluses are continually diminishing.

[3] Profitability of capital and reserves is defined as the ratio between post-tax surplus of the bank (before payment of the debt subordinated to the Central Bank) and its capital and reserves. The ex-post margin is the coefficient between that surplus and placements and investments; finally, leverage measures the volume of intermediation indicated by the ratio between the bank's holdings and investments and its capital and reserves.

Table 3.6. Breakdown of Banking Profitability

Year	Capital and tax reserves[1]	After-tax surplus[2]	Ex-post placements and investments[1]	Differential (in %)	Leverage effect No. of times	Profitability (in %)
1985	2,061.74	152.42	31,919.18	0.40	15.50	7.43
1986	2,207.96	136.43	26,467.27	0.52	11.99	6.18
1987	1,727.95	236.12	20,882.41	1.13	12.09	13.66
1988	1,448.48	247.99	17,707.88	1.40	12.23	17.12
1989	1,222.26	259.69	14,059.96	1.85	11.50	21.25
1990	1,019.58	202.45	10,793.12	1.88	10.58	19.85
1991	874.61	133.81	8,980.67	1.49	10.27	15.30
1992	803.94	133.93	8,898.50	1.51	11.07	16.66

[1] December balances in millions of 1993 dollars.
[2] Accumulated in December in millions of 1993 dollars.
Source: Boletín Mensual of the SBIF.

Table 3.7. Evolution of Indicators of Concentration of Placements and Investments

Period	No. of companies	Herfindahl[1]	C4 (Percentage)
1985	43	0.115	57.4
1986	41	0.115	58.5
1987	41	0.106	55.1
1988	41	0.101	54.3
1989	41	0.092	51.4
1990	41	0.090	50.2
1991	40	0.086	49.0
1992	40	0.078	46.3
1993	38	0.079	45.7

[1] The Herfindahl-Hirschman index is defined as the sum of the individual market share of each company squared. It looks at the portfolio sold to the Central Bank.
C4: Sum of the four principal relative shares.
Source: Prepared using company balance sheets.

The foregoing is a sign that banking is increasingly competing with other sources of financial intermediation. This will become clearer when we examine how the process of disintermediation has advanced in the Chilean capital market.

Another explanation for an ever "tighter" intermediation market could be that placements and investment have increased—that is, that during this period more competitors entered, diluting profits. Table 3.7 shows that is not the case, however: Both the Herfindahl and C4 indices, which indicate concentration for placements and investments, remain relatively steady over time.[4] Nevertheless

[4] For the definition of these indices of concentration, see Maddala and Miller (1989).

Table 3.8. Distribution of Financial Institutions

Year	State Bank	National banks		Foreign banks		Finance companies		Total of financial institutions	Total No. of branch offices
	No. of branch offices	No. of banks	No. of branch offices	No. of banks	No. of branch offices	No. of finance companies	No. of branch offices		
1985	185	12	432	20	150	3	51	36	818
1986	190	12	496	20	153	3	52	36	891
1987	190	13	519	21	158	3	58	38	25
1988	191	13	545	22	163	3	65	39	964
1989	190	13	614	22	166	3	71	39	1,041
1990	194	13	639	22	161	4	86	40	1,080
1991	201	13	677	22	169	4	100	40	1,147
1992	208	13	674	22	179	4	113	40	1,174

Note 1: Includes headquarters, branch offices, auxiliary and exchange offices, agencies, and payment stations.
Note 2: Data are as of October for each year.
Source: *Boletín Mensual* of SBIF.

Table 3.9. Assets of Institutional Investors in Relation to GDP

Year	Pension fund/GDP	Foreign capital fund/GDP	Mutual funds/GDP	Total/GDP	Stock ownership/GDP
1985	0.109	0.000	0.008	0.163	0.143
1986	0.113	0.000	0.011	0.169	0.217
1987	0.127	0.000	0.013	0.179	0.244
1988	0.145	0.000	0.015	0.203	0.281
1989	0.161	0.003	0.012	0.223	0.340
1990	0.207	0.014	0.013	0.292	0.423
1991	0.289	0.027	0.024	0.401	0.794
1992	0.334	0.029	0.025	0.472	0.802

Source: Boletín Mensual, Central Bank.

one could argue that the financial system has become more competitive due to the appearance of competitors that are not formal financial institutions, which the Herfindahl index would not reflect.

Diversification of Financial Services

As the financial system has deepened, both the kind of financial institutions (national and foreign banks, and finance companies) and the services they provide have diversified.

Table 3.8 shows how financial institutions and branch offices have grown throughout the country. The most dynamic sectors are the finance companies, whose branch offices almost tripled between 1985 and 1993. Banking is exploring new markets, probably small enterprise, which is likely to be an increasingly important market for financial institutions in general.

Disintermediation of Monetary Liabilities

Perhaps the most interesting development in recent years is the change in the composition of the liability portfolios of companies. Table 3.9, for example, shows assets in the hands of institutional investors. Pension funds alone increased their investment portfolio from 10.9 percent of GDP in 1985 to 33.4 percent in 1992. Total resources of institutional investors increased from 27 percent of GDP in 1985 to almost 50 percent.

To see further changes in the financing structure of companies, one can examine to what extent the assets of public corporations finance their long-term liabilities. Table 3.10 shows that for the 1985–86 period this averaged 36.8 percent, while from 1987–92, it declined to an average of 19.4 percent.[5] The banks' share in company financing—measured as the ratio between their debts to banks and financial

Table 3.10. Debt Indicators of Public Corporations
(Percentages)

Year	No. of companies	LTL/TA	BFI/(LTL + CL)	DP/(LTL + CL)
1985	250	36.2	71.7	1.7
1986	253	37.4	73.4	2.1
1987	249	23.7	62.0	4.4
1988	253	18.3	55.3	9.1
1989	271	18.3	43.4	14.6
1990	273	19.5	44.5	18.7
1991	287	18.8	42.6	24.5
1992	304	17.7	40.6	21.8

Note: LTL: long term liabilities; TA: total assets; CL: current liabilities; BFI: debts to banks and financial institutions; DP: debts to the public.
Source: Superintendency of Securities and Insurance.

institutions and cash and long-term liabilities—has fallen steadily from 73.4 percent in 1986 to 40.6 percent in 1992. This table, in contrast to the previous one, indicates a significant growth in public debts as a way of financing: they have risen from 1.7 percent in 1985 to 21.8 percent in 1992. With regard to publicly offered instruments, bond issues and commercial securities increased from 1.4 percent of the financial system's loans in 1986 to 10.8 percent in 1991.

With regard to financial disintermediation, the Bill on Capital Market Reform recently approved by Congress encourages investing in instruments that are only occasionally traded on the securities market. This could mean a growing market for shares, and perhaps even for some small businesses. Nevertheless, such a deepening of the capital market depends on Chile's economic stability and respect for the established rules of the game.

Efficiency in the Banking Industry

In economic theory, efficiency and competitiveness are closely connected. A market functions efficiently when it produces at the lowest average cost, and at that point an industry operating under conditions of perfect competition attains long-term equilibrium with stability. If the banking market is to function efficiently, the requirements for a competitive structure must be fulfilled. According to this theory, the banking industry would be efficient when it is producing at the lowest average long-run cost. In practice, however, the classic microeconomic

[5] This change cannot be explained by an increase in financing through short-term liabilities, since these varied at most between 15.4 percent in 1985 and 19.7 percent in 1991.

method of analysis for a competitive market does not fit the banking system, because entry into this market is not free. To measure the efficiency and competitiveness of the banking system, one must take other features into account.

Efficiency is a relative concept, measured in relation to a specific end. Banking may be evaluated in terms of social efficiency, for example—that is, how efficiently it meets the objectives assigned by the community. Another is private efficiency, that is, how well bank management meets the objectives of bank owners.

Efficiency from a Social Standpoint

Banking will have more or fewer functions to fulfill depending on the role the community assigns to it, as reflected in each country's laws and regulations. In the extreme case of a highly regulated context in which banks are solely devoted to providing government lines of credit for predefined uses, banks function as administrative and accounting facilitators for the transfer of funds. It may be concluded that in such an arrangement, the banks are efficient insofar as this transfer takes place at lowest cost.

According to Fama (1983), the functions of banking are the transfer of wealth between economic actors and the management of an asset portfolio for the depositors and the bank owners. Efficiency in the transfer of wealth is compatible with the traditional approach to measurement, to measure the costs of operation. The problem arises with the second function.

In portfolio management, three groups interact in the credit process: shareholders, depositors, and borrowers. Shareholders will be satisfied to the extent that their shares produce yields, which when adjusted for risk are at least similar to those that they would obtain if those same resources had been placed in other investments. The depositors will be content if their deposits (when adjusted for risk) perform at least equally to what they would obtain had they bought other financial instruments. The borrowers are content to the extent that the cost of the debt that they assume is no more than what they would have to pay if they had gone to other lenders. The objectives these different actors seek to maximize are seemingly at odds. Indeed, they are not only at odds with one another, but also with other concerns relevant for determining the social efficiency of banking.

From the standpoint of bank owners, the business management must seek to achieve the greatest yield for each peso invested. Such a yield comes from comparing revenues and costs, broadly understood—costs incurred in obtaining funds, business operating costs, and those incurred to compensate for losses resulting from poor lending decisions. Achieving the greatest possible yield requires both the highest revenues and the lowest costs.

Revenues consist of the interest rate charged on the total of the various kinds of credit granted. An increase in the rate applied to loans may be favorable to bank owners and depositors insofar as it increases expected yield. According to

Goldsmith's hypothesis (1963), the relationship between banking performance and a country's economic welfare results from the quantity and quality of the allocation of intermediated resources. Although a higher interest rate benefits bank owners, it rules out a series of investment projects that would be profitable at lower rates, thereby diminishing the amount of intermediation. Obviously some combinations of interest rates and amounts of intermediation would maximize the yield for bank owners, but would not necessarily constitute the best option in social terms.

Expenditures fall into three main categories: those made to obtain funds to intermediate (interest rate paid on deposits), overhead, and those assumed to compensate risk incurred through poor loan decisions (reserves).

If depositors believe that the bank instruments they hold are producing insufficient yields, funds will be shifted from the banking sector toward other intermediating agents, or spending will be greater, thus reducing funds available for lending and thereby levels of intermediation. Hence, high interest rates favor depositors and hurt borrowers. Low interest rates, on the other hand, favor the borrower but harm the depositor.

The interest rate should therefore remain in the middle so as to maximize the volume of resources handled. High interest rates are detrimental to welfare because they lower the level of investment and consumption. Low interest rates have similar consequences, by diverting financial savings toward other ends.

The difference between the rates charged and those paid is called a differential. This spread must be enough to make up for the cost of overhead and risk provisions. To the extent that the relative importance of these expenditures declines, the lending rate can be reduced to the benefit of investment, without lowering the rate for attracting funds, thus serving to generate financial savings.

Losses due to poor lending decisions affect bank investors, since they are tantamount to a volume of actual loans less than those on the books or to lower interest rates for such loans. Indeed, credits wrongly issued not only impact on yield to investors but they are also resources poorly allocated from a social standpoint. In such circumstances, and leaving aside externalities, the safeguards put into place by banking companies to deal with losses of capital (reserves) represent a measure of social loss as well. In this instance, private and social interests are alike.

If social efficiency is the impetus the banking system gives to savings and investment, certain indicators would suggest that the social role of banking is improving. A decline in the interest rate for loans would reduce pressure on borrowers and lead away from the process of disintermediation. An increase in the amount of funds attracted, and a concomitant rise in levels of intermediation would reflect that depositors regard the reward they receive to be in line with the risk they took. The lowering of risk would reflect high quality in decisions about who may borrow; and a reduction in operational expenses would indicate efficient credit management in the banks. This vision is consistent with the viewpoint that regards banking as a less than optimal decision, since it amounts to lowering the transaction costs involved in the banking system. Based on these observations, the social efficiency of banking is evaluated with four indicators: the active rate of interest; overhead; risk; and levels of intermediation.

Banking is more socially efficient when the interest rate for borrowing is lower, overhead is down, risk declines, and the levels of intermediation rise. The period measured extends from 1980 to 1993, and the results can be seen in Table 3.11.

Based on the indices, three periods can be distinguished: 1980–83, 1984–86, and 1987–93. These periods approximately represent the end of the boom and the crisis of the Chilean economy; recovery and consolidation; and normalization.

During 1980–83, the "social efficiency" indicators—lower overhead and expanding levels of intermediation—seem to indicate improvement. However, both rising interest rates and the growing risk to assets worsened the banks' performance in terms of serving social needs.

During the next period, the indicators shifted in a positive direction. Borrowing interest rates and overhead costs declined; risk increased sharply at first but then fell, while levels of intermediation gradually adjusted to the direction taken by the economy.

Since 1987, behavior has fluctuated. The interest rate for borrowers continued to fall; then it rose and remained around 3.5 percent for the past two years, an acceptable figure given the country's level of development. Overhead has continued to rise, primarily due to changes in the composition of banking assets and liabilities. In short, banks have favored customers whose operations are more profitable (at a higher lending rate), and therefore more spending-intensive.

Efficiency from a Private Standpoint

From the owner's perspective, banking is efficient insofar as it maximizes the yield of each peso invested by its owners. Achieving maximum success entails managing various aspects of banking activity efficiently. Based on those goals, different concepts of efficiency can be defined.

When assessing a past period, a bank's profit can be divided into at least four factors: *operational yield,* or how efficiently the institution maximized the difference between the rates of placing and attracting funds; overhead, or how efficiently the institution handled the expenses of providing credit and attracting funds; *reserves and write-offs,* or how efficiently the bank invested the funds attracted; and lastly, *other net revenues,* those related to the non-operational part of activity, and revenues and outlays originating in previous fiscal years.

A bank's profitability is affected by a number of variables although it aims to attain efficiency in operational yield, management expenses, reserves and write-offs, these are still not sufficient requirements for reaching maximum benefit. Only by reaching maximum efficiency in all the different criteria can an optimal final result be attained.

Table 3.11. Evolution of Indicators of Social Efficiency

	1980	1981	1982	1983	1984	1985	1986	1987	1988	1989	1990	1991	1992	1993
Lending rate[1]	−1.1	16.8	31.0	5.5	11.3	7.4	4.6	3.7	4.4	−1.0	0.6	2.5	3.5	3.7
Overhead[2]	4.6	4.2	3.5	3.0	2.3	2.1	1.9	2.1	2.2	2.7	3.0	3.2	3.3	3.3
Risk[3]	1.6	1.8	3.2	3.2	4.0	3.2	0.9	0.9	1.1	1.3	1.5	1.1	0.8	0.6
Level of intermediation[4]		38.9	12.8	23.9	−2.2	15.8	6.8	1.3	2.1	2.9	−2.4	0.1	3.9	9.6

[1] Measured as a percentage, this is the real average yield of placements and financial investments. Contingencies and mortgages are discounted, the former because they produce a commission without committing resources, while for the latter the reason is the lack of evidence for the entire period.
[2] Measured as a percentage of average assets.
[3] Equals provisions maintained plus the deficit of such provisions measured against average assets.
[4] Equals annual real percentage variation of assets, net of accounting duplications and net of duplications that arise due to the adoption of measures to support banking and borrowers.
Source: Prepared on the basis of data from the year-end balance sheets of financial institutions.

If a bank's objective is to maximize profit, it will be more efficient if it makes capital more profitable. Such efficiency is in turn the result of efficiency in three different aspects: the difference between lending rates and deposit rates (known as operational efficiency), management of overhead (administrative efficiency), and reserves and write-offs (allocative efficiency).

Table 3.12 indicates measures of private efficiency within the Chilean bank system from 1980 to 1993. To analyze this, the earnings statement was broken down by identifying the results according to the concepts of efficiency listed above.

The main kinds of efficiency illustrated in Table 3.11 show how results have varied with the economy's performance during the periods considered. The economic context is especially important for explaining the evolution of operational efficiency and allocative efficiency.

Operational efficiency is the difference between revenues and operational expenses. Since 1980 the operational spread has shown a persistent decline, which in the early years may have been due to greater competitiveness. Subsequently this margin declined because of the lower quality of borrowers. Once measures were adopted to reorganize matters, the margin grew as poor quality assets were replaced by Central Bank bonds and as some borrowers managed to recover.

The idea of allocative efficiency is connected to the sum of reserves and write-offs. Hence it reflects the quality of the assets in which institutions have invested their deposits and fluctuates with the level of economic activity. Hence, a good portion of the reserves and write-offs recorded in 1984 and 1986 correspond to losses in 1982 and 1983. Only in 1987 did reserves and write-offs reach levels consistent with a normally functioning system.

Overall efficiency is the combination of the various ideas of efficiency found in the statement of results. The negative figure for 1982 and 1983 reflected the increase in reserves, the most obvious sign of deterioration in the quality of assets. Efficiency was initially influenced by the mechanisms for supporting banks and borrowers, and then by the recovery of the economy, until the figure became positive again. It remained that way until 1993, because a significant part of banks' liabilities were calculated at a value higher than the economic value (foreign debt).

Access of Small Enterprise to Financial Credit

Arguments for Promoting the Role of Small Enterprise

Small businesses are often said to be key agents of progress and fairness. Many features of small businesses are basic to economic development, such as creating jobs, adapting new technologies, making foreign exchange available through exports and import substitution, and channeling of family savings and initiatives into investment.

Table 3.12. Chilean Banks' Earnings, Breakdown of Results
(Percentage of average assets)

	1980	1981	1982	1983	1984	1985	1986	1987	1988	1989	1990	1991	1992	1993
Operational efficiency[1]	8.3	7.2	6.1	3.7	3.6	6.2	4.2	4.8	4.8	5.7	6.1	5.2	4.8	5.2
Administrative efficiency[2]	4.6	4.2	3.5	3.0	2.3	2.1	1.9	2.1	2.2	2.7	3.0	3.2	3.3	3.3
Net operating margin	3.7	3.0	2.6	0.7	1.3	4.1	2.3	2.7	2.6	3.0	3.1	2.0	1.5	1.9
Allocative efficiency[3]	1.6	1.8	3.2	3.2	4.0	3.2	0.9	0.9	1.1	1.3	1.5	1.1	0.8	0.6
Margin after reserves	2.1	1.2	–0.6	–2.5	–2.7	0.9	1.4	1.8	1.5	1.7	1.6	0.9	0.7	1.3
Other net revenues	–0.1	–0.2	1.0	0.8	1.2	0.5	–0.4	–0.4	0.1	0.1	0.4	0.6	0.6	0.3
Pre-tax efficiency[4]	2.0	1.0	0.3	–1.7	–1.5	1.4	1.0	1.4	1.6	1.8	2.0	1.5	1.3	1.6
Tax on income	0.7	0.3	0.2	0.1	0.2	0.4	0.2	0.1	0.2	0.2	0.3	0.2	0.1	0.1
Total efficiency[5]	1.3	0.7	0.1	–1.8	–1.7	1.0	0.8	1.3	1.4	1.6	1.7	1.3	1.2	1.5
Assets/capital[6]	9.1	11.0	11.1	12.9	14.8	16.8	13.5	13.7	14.4	12.6	11.3	11.6	12.2	13.3
Surplus/capital	19.1	10.4	3.5	–21.7	–22.2	22.2	13.5	19.4	23.0	23.6	22.9	17.6	16.5	20.9

[1] Revenues less operating expenses.
[2] Overhead for managing credit.
[3] Reserves and write-offs.
[4] Pre-tax surplus
[5] Use of surplus in: repurchase of portfolio, accelerated creation of reserves, absorption of deferred losses, division of preferred dividends, and acceleration of reserve creation in compliance with Law No. 18.304.
[6] Broadly defined as encompassing the debt of all those portions of assets that have some effect on the results.
Source: Prepared on the basis of information presented by the financial institutions themselves at the end of each year.

The employment creation capability of these companies is one of the reasons justifying support for this sector. Because it leans toward highly labor-intensive activities and is more widely dispersed throughout regions, small business is a vehicle for avoiding concentration both in income levels and geographically. The small enterprise sector plays a significant role in employment creation in Chile—36.5 percent—and the figure goes up to 80 percent when microenterprise is included (Tables 3.13 and 3.14).[6]

The share of small business in production is considerably less than its share in employment. As illustrated in Table 3.15, smaller-sized enterprises (micro-, small and medium) had only a 24 percent share of gross sales between 1990 and 1992. This divergence between the share in employment and in production may be explained by other production factors, such as the greater labor intensity of small businesses. Table 3.16, which shows the distribution of businesses in each layer by types of economic activity, corroborates this hypothesis. Except in a few instances, the sectoral distribution of small and medium-sized enterprises is not notably different from that of large companies. The divergence must therefore be due primarily to differences in the intensity and endowment of production factors, which give rise to differing levels of productivity.

Besides providing employment, small businesses may be supporting growth in the region. Entrepreneurial ability is a scarce resource in the region, and it is precisely in small enterprises that new entrepreneurs are formed. Due to their flexible organization, these enterprises are more capable of innovation and adaptation, making imported technologies fit domestic circumstances. Small companies would thus be functional to economic growth due to their positive effects on the conditions of aggregate supply.

Similarly, the activity of this group of companies would also help reduce the restrictions that seriously affected growth during the 1980s. Thus, more often than might be expected, small companies have recently been exporting. The greater organizational flexibility mentioned above would seem to allow them to deal with changes in external demand patterns. This export activity is not necessarily carried out directly, but may also take place through distributors that market the production of a number of small companies. They are also involved as significant indirect exporters, because as subcontractors small companies often act as suppliers to other companies that export directly. Given the characteristic shortage of outside resources in the regional economies, this can strengthen external

[6] The Chilean government groups companies by annual sales volumes, rating them as microenterprises (up to US$60,000); small (up to US$625,000); medium-sized (up to US$1,250,000); and large enterprises. If we instead classify companies by number of employees, the intensity of factor use varies within segments that would be obtained by using different economic sizes of companies. Thus for our purposes, annual sales volumes are more important in analyzing financial policies for small and medium-sized businesses.

Table 3.13. Estimated Share in Employment by Size of Enterprises, 1992
(Percentage of national employment in each branch)

	Microenterprise	Small and medium-sized enterprises	Large enterprises	Percentage of whole country
Agriculture and fishing	61.5	25.5	13.0	18.1
Mining and quarries	19.1	22.8	58.1	1.8
Industry	36.5	39.5	24.0	17.1
Construction	39.4	41.9	18.7	7.2
Commerce	68.1	23.2	8.7	17.9
Municipal services	23.7	51.8	24.5	25.7
Financial services	25.0	40.0	35.0	5.1
Transportation	45.2	30.4	24.4	7.1

Source: Rojas and Román, 1993.

Table 3.14. Composition of Employment by Type of Activity, 1992
(Percentage of national total in each segment)

	Microenterprise	Small and medium-sized enterprises	Large enterprises
Agriculture and fishing	25.7	12.7	11.6
Mining and quarries	0.8	1.1	5.2
Industry	14.4	18.5	20.3
Construction	6.6	8.3	6.7
Commerce	28.1	11.4	7.7
Municipal services	14.1	36.5	31.1
Financial services	3.0	5.6	8.9
Transportation	7.4	5.9	8.5
Percentage of national total	43.3	36.5	20.2

Source: Rojas and Román, 1993.

Table 3.15. Share of Gross Sales
(Percentages)

	1990	1991	1992
Microenterprises	5.5	4.9	4.9
Small enterprises	14.1	13.3	13.9
Medium enterprises	6.1	5.8	6.0
Large enterprises	74.4	76.0	75.2
Total	100.0	100.0	100.0

Source: Rojas and Román, 1993.

Table 3.16. Distribution of Enterprises by Type of Economic Activity, 1992
(Percentage of total number of enterprises in each segment)

	Microenterprises	Small enterprises	Medium-sized enterprises	Large enterprises
Agriculture and livestock	13.6	12.5	5.9	3.2
Agricultural services	0.3	0.5	0.4	0.4
Hunting	0.0	0.0	0.0	0.0
Forestry	0.5	1.2	1.0	1.0
Fishing	0.3	0.6	0.7	1.4
Mines, petroleum, and quarries	0.2	0.6	0.8	1.6
Manufacturing industry	5.2	12.6	18.6	23.9
Electricity, gas, and water	0.2	0.1	0.2	1.0
Construction	1.8	4.7	8.1	8.3
Commerce	37.3	35.2	40.3	39.7
Restaurants and related services	5.2	3.5	2.8	1.2
Transportation	6.8	8.3	6.1	4.7
Technical and professional services	3.7	5.8	5.2	4.3
Various services and recreation	0.5	0.2	0.2	0.1
Personal and household services	7.1	4.0	1.8	1.1
Other	17.5	10.2	8.0	8.1
Total	100.0	100.0	100.0	100.0

Source: Rojas and Román, 1993.

balances and make higher growth rates possible. In addition to the supply effects mentioned earlier, there are those that flow from greater involvement by small business in producing tradable goods, thus allowing aggregate demand to expand more rapidly.

Small enterprises may also make a significant contribution to financing development. This is especially important for countries whose financial system is not sufficiently developed to channel the savings efforts of medium and low income groups efficiently. Most small and medium-sized businesses are family-owned and are the embodiment of family efforts to save and invest. This investment capability could be frustrated by the lack of access to financial resources from outside sources. Access to the formal financial system to spur their development would mobilize the savings potential of these families, having a positive effect on investment and growth.

Restricted access to financial resources also introduces a distortion into factor markets, significantly affecting how intensely they are used and the level of investment in small enterprise. For their financial needs, small enterprises must use the informal loan market, where interest rates are far higher than in the formal market. The upshot is that large enterprises have an incentive to use more capital per unit of labor than would be desirable. For their part, smaller enterprises find that their access to financial resources becomes very expensive, and the result is underinvestment in that sector. Thus, small-business projects or activities with high profit potential remain outside the market, unable to develop or grow, thereby hindering efficient allocation of investment resources.

From another angle, small enterprises would seem to be playing a new role in the technological paradigm that is now expanding (Medeiros, 1993). One feature of this new arrangement is a new division of labor between different-sized companies, manifested in the growing use of subcontracting and franchising arrangements. By such procedures large companies can decentralize their operations of large companies, having smaller companies supply inputs and services, including final sales. Strengthening the small business sector would then help improve overall productive efficiency.

Despite these positive features, certain negative aspects must also be kept in mind in the promotion of small and medium-sized enterprise. To begin with, as Medeiros argues (1993), while they are more labor intensive, the employment that these companies create is less stable, especially during economic downturns. Contractions in aggregate demand lead to a high failure rate of small businesses and the consequent loss of employment, while the opposite takes place during periods of expansion. Such fluctuation in employment may be partly explained by the greater informality in this stratum, as manifested in lower compliance with labor legislation, including pension provisions, thus making hiring and firing cheaper. This informality extends to tax obligations with the familiar fiscal effects. Some have argued that the apparent competitiveness of small businesses is based primarily on their failure to comply with labor and tax laws.

The quality of employment small companies offer is likewise said to be inferior to that of large companies, since the latter grant additional benefits such as uniforms and vouchers for food and transportation, and are more inclined to upgrade their employees through training.

In short, a number of factors indicate the importance of supporting small and medium-sized enterprise within a development strategy. Their contribution in terms of employment, the funnelling of savings and investment efforts, improved productive capacity and their impact on redistribution and decongestion would justify this support. On the other hand, possible counterproductive effects connected to the quality of the employment that these companies provide and their tax behavior have also been noted. Such undesirable types of behavior are connected to the low degree of formalization found in a significant number of small companies. However, eliminating factors that constrain their development, such as financing restrictions, might raise their level of formalization, thereby moderating such behavior.

Bases for a New Direction in Policies for Supporting Small and Medium-Sized Enterprise in Chile

Recently there has been increasing interest in studying the financing constraints on small business development in order to formulate policies to counteract them. This accent on the financial aspects is not accidental since various experiences point to the lack of adequate access to financial resources as one of the main obstacles facing small and medium-sized businesses.[7]

As the financial system deepens and expands, it gradually covers the needs of larger groups of the population. Nevertheless, as the formal financial system continually expands, some gaps remain and certain needs for financial services are not met. Even in developed countries, small enterprises may find it difficult to gain access to the resources of the financial system.

Factors Restricting the Access of Small Enterprises to Financial Resources

In a number of countries, even individual borrowers have had easier access to financial resources than small companies. The reason lies in the different risks to the financial system represented by both kinds of borrowers. Information on the creditworthiness of a potential borrower is one of the most important factors to the lender. This information, which is obtained at a cost, may be shared by a number of those seeking it. A dilemma may ensue over who will incur the initial cost and risk of trusting a potential borrower, while other lenders wait to assess the result. Larger companies, however, by virtue of their reputation within the market, can provide such information almost like a free good that costs nothing to obtain. Indeed, large companies often devote resources to producing information on how well they are doing, because it improves their access to the financial system. The management of the companies themselves, in the course of assessing their own performance, evaluate the market and their own projects, and continually monitor their revenues and outlays. Hence the marginal cost of the information for assessing the potential risks of larger enterprises is low compared to the benefits that financial institutions obtain by granting them credit. Much of the information is a byproduct of the activity of the company applying for the loan (Table 3.17).

The situation of individuals as borrowers is different. In each case, risk is a matter of their ability to pay, which is relatively easy for a modern financial system to assess. Since the individual's main income source is labor, salary and length of employment provide a substantial portion of the information needed.

Compared to such cases, small businesses generate less free information since their presence in the market is relatively minor. Moreover, they generally

---

[7] See Levy (1991).

Table 3.17. Share in Placements of the Financial System by Segments of Enterprises
(Percentages)

	1991	1992	1993
Large	63.5	67.0	67.7
Medium	6.9	7.1	6.0
Small	18.7	15.8	16.3
Microenterprises	10.9	10.1	9.9
Total	100.0	100.0	100.0

Note: As of April 30 each year.
Source: Domestic Tax Service and Superintendency of Banks and Financial Institutions.

do not have internal monitoring and project assessment. Their ability to pay depends on factors that are hard to judge, including some that are subjective, such as the management ability of the proprietor. Since competitors can also benefit from the information obtained for credit purposes, financial agencies are loathe to make loans or do so under extremely restrictive conditions.

Table 3.18 presents estimates made by Azócar (1990) of the lending transaction costs of two financial institutions. As can be seen, the administrative costs, including the cost of information, are substantially higher for small business. Likewise, costs arising from arrangements to protect the solvency of financial institutions, including those entailed in the reserve requirements, are also greater in dealing with small businesses. That situation may be explained by the problems supervisors have in evaluating the risk of the loan portfolios involved with smaller companies.

When the financial system grants credits to these companies, it often does so at rates and with guarantees that exceed the standards applied to larger companies, as confirmed by a study carried out by Azócar (1990) (see Table 3.19). In the sample examined, loans to small and medium-sized business are protected by demanding greater guarantees than for large companies. Thus two tendencies limiting the financial system's coverage of small and medium-sized businesses are aggravated. The number of potential loan candidates is thus restricted insofar as smaller companies generally have fewer real guarantees to offer as backing for their commitments. Moreover, higher interest rates may diminish the quality of the borrowers: this selection gives the lending process a bias toward higher risk borrowers, thus creating a vicious circle that tightens financial restrictions on such companies.

General Guidelines for the Small Enterprise Support Program

Like other countries,[8] Chile has supported small enterprise with direct assistance and with loans directly provided by state institutions, often with refinancings at

[8] See Camacho (1993) and López (1993).

Table 3.18. Transaction Costs in Financing Credit
(Percentage of placement)

	Institution 1		Institution 2	
	Large companies	Small and medium-sized companies	Large companies	Small and medium-sized companies
Administrative costs[1]	1.0	3.7	0.3	5.7
Loss risk[2]	2.8	4.2	2.0	3.6
Total	3.8	7.9	2.3	9.3

[1] Costs of evaluating, granting, and recovering loans.
[2] Reserves for risks from losses and write-offs.
Source: Azócar, 1990.

Table 3.19. Coverage of Guarantee Required
(Percentage of cases)

	Scope of guarantee (%)	Large companies	Small and medium-sized companies
No guarantee	0	54	38
Partial guarantee	15-95	24	19
Total guarantee	100	22	43

Source: Azócar, 1990.

rates subsidized by the Central Bank. Important changes are underway in the region in this regard. Greater emphasis has gradually been given to market mechanisms as preferred instruments for allocating credit. Moreover, the scarcity of public funds has made it necessary to make greater use of the private financial system's ability to generate funds. Here the state acts as a "second level" financial agent, promoting the development of financial instruments adapted to the financing needs of small businesses, and establishing transitory policies aimed at making these companies creditworthy.

Experiences of direct financing in the region can possibly be explained by the lack of development of financial systems, and the interventionist conceptions that were a part of development thinking. That led to loan portfolios showing a high level of delinquency, but also to: a gradual exhaustion of public resources available for that purpose, and hence considerable losses for those financial institutions involved; the granting of subsidized loans to a small number of small and medium-sized businesspeople with good connections or to major business figures; diversion of resources for purposes other than those originally proposed; and finally, the dependence of beneficiaries on continuing public sector financial support.[9]

[9] See Camacho (1993), Levitsky (1987), López (1993), Rojas and Román (1993), and World Bank (1989).

This experience also indicates that while promoting greater access to financing, it is also necessary to provide a certain level of basic business training along with technical assistance in order to make possible proper use of the funds provided as well as their recovery.

As reforms have been applied to this sector, the private financial system has become the main agent channeling credit resources. The preferred provider of funds for small business should be private financial institutions that are actively involved in assessing and taking risks in this market segment. For its part, the public sector provides financing for these institutions, which assume responsibility for their actions. Incentive mechanisms are also used to draw such institutions into this segment.

The aim is to create conditions conducive for transforming small and medium-sized businesses into true borrowers who may be regarded as such by the private financial system, without permanent public subsidy. Success will be determined not by how many companies have taken advantage of resources from the public sector, but rather how many ceased receiving support from these programs and remained creditworthy. For that to happen, the problems discussed above must be resolved: the lack of sufficient information about these companies' ability to pay and the lack of guarantees or appropriate safety mechanisms. The tools used for that purpose generally do not discriminate between sector uses and aim at improving and developing market mechanisms rather than selectivity and supplanting the financial system in allocating credit.

Not only this sector benefits from the encouragement for its financing. The current tendency of large companies toward financial disintermediation has gradually forced financial institutions to seek new markets. That partly explains the growing dynamism of credit for individuals, which is often for consumption purposes. Therefore, promoting the development of financing for small enterprises, in addition to giving them support, will direct financial resources toward investment and productive activities rather than consumption.

Principal Financial Support Programs for Small Businesses

Within the guidelines mentioned above, programs for supporting small business financially aim at overcoming the problems of information and risk coverage. The main aspects of these programs are now described.

Credit Support Mechanisms Aimed at Small Businesses

SUAF *(Subsidio a la Asistencia Crediticia,* Credit Assistance Subsidy)

SUAF seeks to lower the information costs that financial institutions incur in evaluating the creditworthiness of small businesses, which typically lack bookkeeping records and properly evaluated projects. The program grants subsidies to small business owners to hire the services of specialists.

Credit applicants must satisfy basic conditions of being "bankable," such as not being delinquent in payments owed to the state and financial institutions, and requesting an appropriate amount of credit. Under this plan, 75 percent of the cost of financial assistance services is covered by CORFO (*Corporación de Fomento,* Corporation for Development) and the rest by the businessperson. The amount of subsidy is subject to limits, which as of July 1994 were set at 50 and 75 development units (UF, *unidades de fomento*) for short- and long-term credits, respectively (around US$1,230 and US$1,845).

The financial consultants must be certified by CORFO, which has established a consultant list. Their task is to collect the information required for credit requests or for financial leasing operations, by preparing standardized reports. For short-term credits and financial leasing operations they must prepare balance sheets, income statements, and cash budgets; for investment projects to be financed, an evaluation is required. The report or evaluation is then analyzed by the bank making the loan. Consultants work with the business owner in negotiating with the financial institution, in managing the company, and in monitoring the investment.

The importance of preparing standardized reports must be emphasized. In the absence of competition to use such information, the standardization of reports makes it possible gradually to create a basic data bank available to any financial institution interested in serving this sector's needs. This will reduce the asymmetry of information between small and large companies, that is, the lack of adequate bookkeeping records and properly evaluated projects. This mechanism counteracts the low level of information on the financial viability of this stratum of companies.

The quality of these standardized reports must be high enough not only to win the trust of financial institutions, but also to delegate a share of credit evaluation to others.

CUBOS (Cupones de bonificación aplicables a las primas de seguro de crédito, Bonus coupons applicable to credit insurance premiums)

As mentioned above, the lack of collateral to cover the risks of small business bankruptcy is one factor limiting their access to credit. Insurance for credit and financial leasing are mechanisms that help reduce the use of collateral, but they are only now being developed. To encourage mechanisms for overcoming such problems, a system of subsidies for contracting this insurance has been put into practice.

In keeping with the "second story" thrust of the policy established by CORFO, interested financial institutions offer coupons for bidding. These coupons can be used to pay the insurance premiums for credits granted to small business. Each coupon obliges CORFO to pay the sum of 1 UF (approximately US$25), but since the price is set in each bidding, the difference between the two figures constitutes the implicit subsidy. On average, the bidding price has fluctuated around 30 percent, and hence the subsidy for credit insurance premiums is around 70 percent.

The advantage of this system is that it establishes the size of the fiscal impact by anticipation. By setting in advance the sum of the coupons to be bid, CORFO limits the amount of resources that it will commit in this fashion for supporting this sector, in contrast to other state guarantee mechanisms whose impact on spending is very difficult to anticipate. Moreover, the partial coverage offered by credit insurance maintains the incentives for financial institutions to evaluate the primary source of payment. Finally, state involvement is focused on the bidding and subsequent supervision of the operation. The work of analyzing and assuming risk is carried out by specialized institutions, thus making it possible to serve small and medium-sized businesses more rapidly.

Credit Cards for Production

Credit cards are widely used by small businesses for working capital. They apply the familiar system of credit cards for individuals, except that use is restricted to the purchase of inputs. Although this operation is carried out entirely by the private sector, it has been the result of a joint effort on the part of the Technical Cooperation Service and a commercial bank.

As a form of revolving credit, credit cards lower transaction costs. Moreover, small amounts of credit suit the needs of these companies and allow financial institutions to spread the risks over time in accordance with the cardholder's payment performance.

Support of Non-Governmental Organizations (NGOs)

Many NGOs are now providing credits to microenterprises. At the same time, these institutions provide financial guidance (especially in bookkeeping), training, and development. Notable among these NGOs are the Fundación Contigo [With You Foundation], the Fundación Trabajo para un Hermano [Work for a Brother Foundation], and FUNDES. Focusing primarily on medium-sized enterprise, FUNDES grants credit insurance for up to 50 percent of credit obtained in the formal financial sector, and also provides financial and accounting advice.

Fundación Contigo provides loans to groups of jointly liable borrowers. These are small groups composed of three to seven microenterprise owners, who constitute a system of mutual endorsements in which each one oversees the others. The members of each group establish a guarantee fund equal to 10 percent of the

Table 3.20. Credit Assistance Subsidy (SUAF) Operations

	1992			
	No. of companies	Sum Percentage	Committed (US$)	Percentage
Microenterprises	64	37.0	63,140	34.5
Small business	109	63.0	119,840	65.5
Total	173	100.0	182,980	100.0
	1993[a]			
	No. of companies	Sum Percentage	Committed (US$)	Percentage
Unclassified	55	38.2	61,940	39.5
Microenterprises	43	29.9	43,460	27.8
Small business	46	31.9	51,210	32.7
Total	144	100.0	156,610	100.0

[a] Figures as of August 1993.
Source: CORFO, Management of Investment Development.

amounts requested. Every group has a permanent advisor who works with the foundation. In order to obtain a loan, one must have been involved in the work for at least six months and not have had any financial disputes with the formal system. The maximum loan granted is approximately US$2,350 at market rates for a year, and payments are weekly.

Functioning of Credit Support Mechanisms

Functioning of SUAF Operations

Table 3.20 shows that the impact of the SUAF is still limited, perhaps because the policy is relatively new. But since the State Bank, a major promoter of credit programs for small business, has decided to use SUAF in its operations with that sector, the use of this mechanism is likely to increase.

Analyses of the SUAFs have noted certain problems, some of which have been overcome as the program has been implemented. At first, the amounts offered to the financial consultants were too low to make such work attractive. That also prompted financial institutions to refuse to base their decisions on the analyses made. This was later changed and higher limits were set for aid provided.

Moreover, payment of most of the honoraria for advisory service initially depended on whether the small or medium-sized businessperson received the loan, thus distorting the program's purpose. SUAF's aim was to help reduce the information disparities between larger and smaller companies by preparing a body of financial reports that would make it possible to assess the applicant's ability to pay. Such information, combined with that from other analyses, would make it possible gradually to create a uniform data bank for estimating the risk of small businesses. This is therefore not a system designed for having loans approved, but one for proceeding as efficiently as possible while respecting the nature of financial activity in a market economy.

If a loan request is denied because upon examination it becomes clear that the company is not solid enough at a particular moment, the market is thereby further developed, and that is a desirable outcome in terms of the suitable allocation of credit resources. This is especially the case if the potential borrower later shows that he or she is now better able to make payment, in which case the consultants would recommend that the loan be approved. Thus, the system has demonstrated its ability to select potential borrowers and to promote the development of the market by improving the quality of its customers. In other words, the activity of the consultants must be judged and rewarded according to the quality of their assessments of a particular applicant's ability to pay, whether negative or positive, and not by loans obtained. Recently, the proportion of honoraria paid to the consultants upon signing a contract with the applicant has increased.

At the beginning of the program, loans for less than six months were excluded. However, for small businesses such operations are the most necessary, and are usually the first step taken by financial institutions in establishing a business relationship with a new client. That exclusion has recently been lifted.

Moreover, the annual sales ceiling on businesses choosing this program has been raised from 15,000 UF (US$370,000) to 25,000 UF (US$615,000). This change, together with the inclusion of operations of less than six months, should lead to greater use of SUAF operations.

The excessive administrative zeal manifested in the limits placed on remuneration, (involving ex ante control over those who may serve as consultants), and the conditions under which honoraria must be paid, seem to show an exaggerated precaution for public resources. Rather than establishing adequate supervisory and monitoring systems during and beyond the period of advisory service, bureaucratic zeal is said to have been one factor initially hobbling this mechanism.

Certain problems still persist: CORFO does not yet seem to have established a mechanism for monitoring the system. For this tool to be applied more widely, such a mechanism will be absolutely necessary to assure the quality of the financial services.

Some analysts (e.g., Geisse, 1993) question whether financial institutions should delegate risk evaluation of small businesses to outside consultants, who may be identified with the clients' aims, particularly because evaluating and taking risks are essential to financial services. Furthermore, while standardized reports and project evaluations are important starting points, the financial institutions must continually monitor their customers, especially the newer ones. This should go beyond the initial operation, since new clients have a special motive for paying well during the first borrowing period. Hence, these bodies must develop the necessary staff to continually monitor credits to small businesses, since the initial report is not enough. SUAF will have a lasting effect only if it significantly improves the information, management, and oversight activities within small businesses. This will require training staff in financial institutions to specialize in handling the needs of small enterprises, which has not yet been adequately considered.

Functioning of CUBOS

Table 3.21 provides information on CUBOS, an instrument first used in December 1991. During the first two years, only financial leasing companies participated in bidding for CUBOS. In 1993 they were joined by a commercial bank and the State Bank, which intends to use CUBOS widely in its small-business credit programs. Hence use of CUBOS is going to increase significantly in the future.

One reason given for the limited development of CUBOS operations is that to obtain credit insurance for placing a particular loan, the financial institution must first examine whether the borrower qualifies for the insurance. In other words, these institutions must incur information preparation costs before obtaining the benefit of insurance coverage. The fact that the CUBOS mechanism amounts to a partial subsidy for credit insurance premiums assures that the financial institutions will pay attention to how payment of credit to small and medium-sized companies progresses. Risk of default is thus shared jointly by CORFO—representing the government—and the commercial bank. The CUBOS will consequently tend to be used by institutions that have a prior inclination to handle operations with small businesses, such as financial leasing institutions. Other institutions aimed at different parts of the market would not be inclined to use CUBOS in their operations, and would prefer to wait until the small business segment with "bankable" features develops enough to become an attractive target.

In defense of this instrument, while its volume of operations is still low, the unit cost of credit available through CUBOS has been substantially lower than that of credit operations granted directly by the public sector.

Functioning of NGOs

The success achieved by the different NGO support programs, especially those for microenterprises, must be emphasized. These efforts have demonstrated a low index of delinquency and losses. For example, Fundación Contigo recovers 99 percent of loans granted, and delinquency varies between 5 and 8 percent. This orga-

Table 3.21. Bonus Coupons Applicable to Credit Insurance Premiums (CUBOS)

	No. of companies	Percentage	Sum (US$)	Percentage
1991				
Microenterprise	1	10.0	2,140	15.3
Small business	8	80.0	11,360	80.9
Medium-sized business	1	10.0	540	3.8
Total	10	100.0	14,040	100.0
1992				
Microenterprise	41	19.2	36,600	16.1
Small business	173	80.8	190,800	83.9
Medium-sized business	214	100.0		100.0
Total				
1993[a]				
Microenterprise	26	17.7	19,190	15.1
Small business	98	66.7	88,700	69.7
Medium-sized business	2	1.4	1,280	1.0
Unclassified	21	14.3	18,030	14.2
Total	147	100.0	127,200	100.0

[a]Figures as of August 1993.
Source: CORFO, Investment Development Management Office

nization began operation in 1989 and has grown steadily since then. It placed 639 loans in 1992, a total of 1,010 in 1993, and an estimated 1,800 in 1994.

The successful experience of Fundación Contigo is not isolated, and many similar cases of other NGOs could be cited.

Provision of Funds to the Financial System and Credit from State Financial Institutions

Financial Intermediation by CORFO

In order to supply the financial system with long range funds, CORFO's Financial Intermediation Program operates by accepting bids on funds obtained from international financing agencies, such as the IDB. While this program is not specifically aimed at developing small enterprise, the support provided to the financial leasing industry represents an advance, since it is well-suited to satisfying the demands for resources from smaller-sized businesses and investment initiatives. Financial leasing can be a tool to overcome the smaller business sector's

Table 3.22. CORFO Financial Intermediation Program, 1992

	I. Placements through banks			
	No. of companies	Percentage	Contribution in millions of (US$)	Percentage
Unclassified	10	14.5	11.2	13.8
Microenterprise	6	8.7	1.3	1.7
Small business	17	24.6	15.7	19.4
Medium-sized business	6	8.7	1.2	1.6
Large business	30	43.5	51.5	63.6
Total	69	100.0	80.9	100.0
	II. Placements through financial leasing institutions			
	No. of companies	Percentage	Contribution in millions of (US$)	Percentage
Unclassified	92	8.1	8.0	5.4
Microenterprise	81	7.1	4.1	2.8
Small business	279	24.6	24.9	16.8
Medium-sized business	144	12.7	12.3	8.3
Large business	538	47.4	99.1	66.7
Total	1,134	100.0	148.4	100.0

Source: CORFO, Financial Intermediation Management Office

lack of collateral, because ownership of the leased good remains in the hands of the financial institution until the borrower's obligations have been met.

Table 3.22 shows placements made in this program by business classification. Obviously, big business has taken the largest portion of resources.

The State Bank Program to Support Small and Medium-Sized Businesses

The Program to Support Small and Medium-Sized Business, which was established two years ago by the State Bank, is currently the largest in terms of resources. The program has five lines of credit covering the main needs of these businesses. These lines are described below:

- **Non-readjustable development credit for small businesses**

This is a special line for small businesses intended to finance working capital and investments in fixed assets. The amounts vary according to ability to pay, with a ceiling of 1,000 UF (US$24,600); the principal is not subject to readjustment. The nominal interest rate is fixed and is set every twelve months.

Servicing is monthly and payment periods are variable up to a maximum of 48 months; there may be a grace period of up to six months. It is interesting to note that a flexible guarantee system is used in this line. For qualified cases of known customers, and depending on the quality of the project or operation, no special guarantees are required. When customers do not have a prior record, the guarantee must cover up to 80 percent of the credit. That figure is considerably lower than the practice in other banks, and may be provided in various ways through pledges, endorsements, and mortgages. Again, the composition of the guarantees depends on the evaluation of the project or operation, for which specialized consultants and more recently SUAFs are used. The more favorably the project is evaluated, the less collateral will be required.

- **Credit to finance working capital**

This credit is intended to finance working capital for small and medium-sized enterprise and is expressed in readjustable units (UFs, or development units). The amount varies depending on the ability to pay and what is owed to the financial system. The interest rate may be adjusted every three months and amounts to over a 9 percent real annual rate. The time period is variable up to two years. Guarantees are required in a flexible manner in the form of mortgages, pledges, endorsements, or certificates of deposit.

- **Credit to finance investments**

This credit is intended for purchasing machinery and equipment and for financing investment projects. It is expressed in readjustable units (UFs) and its payment period varies from three to ten years, in accordance with the technical evaluation made by the bank. The interest rate is variable and is adjusted every three months; recently it has held steady at a 9 percent real annual rate.

- **Credits for importing**

These are credits expressed in dollars with a variable term up to one year, guaranteed by means of a mortgage, pledge, or certificate of deposit.

- **Credits for exporting**

The conditions are similar to those of import credits. For pre-shipping financing, the amount varies according to ability to pay. For financing after shipment, the amount of credit covers up to 85 percent of the FOB export value.

The objectives of credits allocated for this program have been more than attained. Tables 3.23 and 3.24 provide the figures for new loan flows, and it is clear that small agricultural entrepreneurs receive a high proportion of the credits granted. This is the case for two reasons. First, this bank has traditionally played an important role in financing agricultural projects in general. Secondly, a portion of the credits granted within this program have been given to old bank customers who are now being served by a new program. Among its positive features are the high proportion of small (as compared to medium-sized) businesspeople and the fact that those directly involved in production are receiving credit.

Table 3.23. State Bank. Credits Granted Within the Program of Support for Small and Medium-Sized Business
(In millions of June 1993 dollars)

	1992			1993[a]		
	Small	Medium-sized	Total	Small	Medium-sized	Total
Agriculture	100.05	13.15	113.20	69.16	6.74	75.90
Industry	23.85	18.07	41.92	16.85	20.16	37.01
Commerce and services	39.21	12.54	51.75	31.11	9.76	40.87
Transportation	19.16	1.69	20.85	13.22	0.87	14.10
Other	30.95	17.39	48.34	30.36	12.68	43.03
Total	213.23	62.84	276.07	160.70	50.21	210.90

[a]For 1993 only the January to June period was taken into account.
Source: Small and Medium-Sized Enterprise Management Office, State Bank.

Table 3.24. State Bank. Sector Composition of Credits Granted to Small and Medium-Sized Business.
(Percentages)

	1992			1993[a]		
	Small	Medium-sized	Total	Small	Medium-sized	Total
Agriculture	46.9	20.9	41.0	43.0	13.4	36.0
Industry	11.2	28.9	15.2	10.5	40.2	17.5
Commerce and services	18.4	20.0	18.7	19.4	19.4	19.4
Transportation	9.0	2.7	7.6	8.2	1.7	6.7
Other	14.5	27.7	17.5	18.9	25.2	20.4
Total	100.0	100.0	100.0	100.0	100.0	100.0

[a]Provisional estimate.
Source: State Bank.

Other Mechanisms

Financial Leasing

Financial leasing has been one of the most important mechanisms allowing small and medium-sized enterprise greater access to investment resources. Financial leasing suffered the consequences of the sharp economic fluctuations of the 1980s, but it has advanced significantly since 1985. Table 3.25 shows the advance of the financial leasing market in real terms. As the table indicates, the growth in the real value of the contract stock is higher than the variation in the product and in the placements of the financial system, thus proving how dynamic this instrument has

Table 3.25. Financial Leasing Market in Chile
(Percentages)

Year	Contract stock (US$ millions)[1]	Variation	GDP growth	Growth stock of placements in the financial system
1989	290.3	35.8	10.0	10.1
1990	333.3	14.8	2.1	–8.5
1991	444.8	33.5	6.0	3.9
1992	707.8	59.1	10.4	18.3

[1]In December 1992 US$.
Source: Geisse (1993) and Rojas (1993).

become. Table 3.26 shows the relative importance of financial leasing. The nominal value of the flows of new contracts has increased considerably during the last four years. As a percentage of gross domestic investment and of the import of capital goods, financial leasing has become increasingly significant, although still quite below the level of developed countries, and should continue to increase.

Several factors help explain the expansion of financial leasing. First, since 1986 Chile has been stable and has grown steadily, thereby encouraging investment, which in 1993 reached almost 27.5 percent of GDP. Second, in combination with the corrections introduced after the 1982–83 financial crisis, the reform of the financial system has brought about a vigorous development, modernization, and sophistication of that sector. As a result, the system is highly professional and is able to evaluate and take risks and to move into new financing alternatives, including financial leasing. Third, the reform of the pension system has given rise to the creation of various institutional investors (pension fund management companies and insurance companies), which have a great ability to generate long-term resources and which require long-term financial assets. These are the very funds financial leasing companies need for financing their operations. Fourth, Chile has been the only country in the region that has systematically practiced indexation of financial assets, continually improved the methods used, and generally maintained a high respect for the conditions established in indexation clauses and the quality of the price indexes used. Fifth, the legal system has encouraged expansion of financial leasing. Finally, of lesser import but still significant is that bank branch offices are able to carry out financial leasing operations. Consequently, the portion of long-term funds within total funds is substantially higher in Chile than in other countries.[10] The foregoing is valid for both public and private bonds, including long-term debt bonds issued by financial leasing companies.

[10] See Morandé (1993) and Jiménez (1993).

Table 3.26. Relative Importance of Financial Leasing in Chile

Year	Contract flow (1)	Gross domestic investment (2)	Capital goods imported (3)	(1)/(2) (%)	(1)/(3) (%)
1989	163	4,681	1,950	3.5	8.4
1990	182	5,414	2,320	3.4	7.8
1991	295	5,701	2,041	5.2	14.5
1992	408	7,503	2,774	5.4	14.7

Source: Geisse (1993) and Rojas (1993).

This instrument has features that make it possible to overcome some of the obstacles to the long-term financing of small and medium-sized business.[11] First, the legal device of financial leasing contractually separates ownership of the goods leased from their use, thus allowing finance institutions to better manage risk. When financial leasing is used instead of conventional credit to finance investment in equipment, the financing agent reduces its risk because the leased good remains its property, with no need for additional guarantees. Moreover, since financial leasing institutions generally establish close ties with suppliers of equipment and capital goods, they know more than commercial banks about how to place them on the secondary market if necessary to implement the guarantees. In this manner, financial leasing helps overcome the scarcity of guarantees of small and medium-sized business and improves their quality.

Secondly, because financial leasing is not granted for general uses (such as working capital or financing investments in general) but for the acquisition of specific goods, the financial institution has better control over the use of the resources provided. Because the financial leasing institution retains ownership, guarantees are improved and legal costs are lower, which lowers transaction costs.

There are no figures available regarding the portion of small and medium-sized businesses in financial leasing placements, but managers in these companies calculate that the share is at least 40 percent, which is higher than the figure for the banking system.

Factoring

Among the new alternatives, factoring has recently taken on major importance. The features of this instrument lead to the hope that its development will increase the financial resources available to small and medium-sized businesses.

---

[11] See Rojas (1991).

In general terms, factoring is the discount on invoices to be paid that one firm has received in return for its sales to another. Under one option, the factoring company can discount the entire value of the invoice, charging a certain commission and completely assuming the risk of nonfulfillment by the company issuing the invoice. Under the other option, the factoring company advances cash funds equal to only a portion of the invoice's value, retaining it as a guarantee, and the risk of nonpayment remains with the party that originally received the invoice. The remainder of the value is credited to the company once the issuer of the invoice has collected the full amount due.

The first modality suits the needs of small enterprises, especially when they are suppliers for large companies. Since financial institutions are generally familiar with the risks offered by large companies, the discount on invoices that they allow should not present further problems. Thus the credit capacity of large companies could be utilized in favor of small businesses, providing them with working capital based on their accounts receivable.

The second modality is better suited to situations in which small businesses are suppliers to others of similar size. The discount is partial and the risk of nonpayment remains with the company that accepts the invoice. Thus, the factoring company takes advantage of, and motivates, the risk assessment evaluation and knowledge that businesspeople have of their customers.

It should be noted that in both modalities, payment is made to the factoring companies, which have greater experience in collecting, thus simplifying administration for smaller companies.

Factoring has been included among the proposed changes to the General Banking Law, which is currently being discussed in Congress. In view of that change, a number of bank investment companies have set up factoring companies which thus far have devoted themselves to granting advances of liquid resources on the basis of check discounts. In one year the volume of operations has reached almost US$25 million. Laws now in effect do not expressly provide for endorsement of bills nor their transformation into a document that creates obligations between the parties. Changes in these restrictions, which seem relatively easy to overcome, are part of the proposed legislation.

Secondary Securities Market Circle

In order to provide capital resources to this segment of businesses, proposals have been made to create a secondary securities market suited to the nature of medium-sized businesses. Securities markets in Latin America have traditionally grown up around government bonds and shares in large companies. The demands for ongoing stability, volume of business, and accounting information required in such exchanges generally exceed both the financial needs as well as the administrative ability of medium-sized businesses. Hence, it has been proposed that a specialized exchange with fewer requirements in those areas, along with an initiative to allow the bond issues, would make it possible to create a market for securities issued by medium-sized businesses. Because the vast majority of small businesses are family-owned, however, they are unlikely to be willing to change the structure of their capital.

Additional Mechanisms

Other current alternatives for supplying capital resources to medium-sized companies include investment funds and venture capital companies. Five investment funds plan to have shares in the capital of closed corporations; three venture capital companies intend to hold capital shares of companies for specific periods. Both are only beginning to develop.

Guarantee funds are also still at a low level of development, probably due to unhappy experiences in this area. Excessive bureaucracy surrounds the operation of some of these funds, and risk is concentrated in the transportation sector. Due to these and other financial problems, credit institutions are not using them much.

Conclusions

Financial support for small businesses is based on information about their financial viability and transaction costs, which are higher than those of larger enterprises. Information problems are aggravated by inadequate management (especially among small entrepreneurs) and lack of knowledge of how the financial system operates. For risk coverage it has traditionally relied on demanding collateral. That worsens the situation of credit rationing affecting small businesses, since the availability of such guarantees is generally in short supply.

Moreover, financial institutions incur heavy costs in evaluating the ability of small customers to pay given their managerial shortcomings, the low level of their operations, and the requirements to make provisions for expected losses. In short, the picture is one in which the small business sector is largely excluded from access to the resources of the formal financial system.

Chile's programs have attempted to resolve these restrictions at their source, by strengthening the management capability of small businesspeople and subsidizing premiums for credit insurance. This has been done through "second level" policies, by which the public sector intervenes indirectly by complementing and striving to improve market mechanisms where shortcomings in their development become apparent.

As can be seen in Table 3.27, the number of companies that have had access to the placements of the financial system has continued to increase. The composition of these companies, however, has not changed very much, as shown in

Table 3.27. Number of Companies Owing the Financial System[1]

	1991	1992	1993[a]
Large	4,260	5,076	5,698
Medium-sized	3,388	4,080	4,468
Small	30,452	36,431	42,500
Microenterprises	73,265	95,429	115,510
Total	111,365	141,016	168,176

[1]Current and due.
[a]Figures as of August.
Source: Domestic Tax Service and Superintendency of Banks and Financial Institutions.

Table 3.28. Distribution of the Number of Companies Owing the Financial System
(Percentages)

	1991	1992	1993
Large	3.8	3.6	3.4
Medium-sized	3.0	2.9	2.7
Small	27.3	25.8	25.3
Microenterprises	65.8	67.7	68.7
Total	100.0	100.0	100.0

Source: Domestic Tax Service and Superintendency of Banks and Financial Institutions.

Table 3.28. From the standpoint of borrower behavior, it is clear that indicators of delinquency have declined among all strata of businesses, as Tables 3.29 to 3.31 indicate. Despite the improvement shown by micro-, small, and medium-sized enterprises, the former continue to show relatively higher levels of delinquency. Chile's economic progress during the past six years has allowed businesses from all strata greater access to the financial system, and delinquency indicators have declined. As noted, the effect of the new financial instruments is still slight, primarily because the programs began only recently. It is too early to issue a final judgment on the experience, even though in each case critical comments were made on use of the new instruments. Nevertheless, two general observations are appropriate concerning the new approach to supporting smaller-sized businesses.

First, there is a reasonable doubt about how interested the financial system might be in small and medium-sized business, particularly smaller businesses, even apart from the problems of information, management, and risk coverage. Analysts point out that the low volume and minimally diversified operations of small business might not profitably sustain a specialized commercial platform.[12]

[12] See Medeiros (1993).

Table 3.29. Borrower Behavior
(Percentage of companies with payment overdue in comparison to total in each stratum)

	1991	1992	1993
Large	2.9	1.6	1.9
Medium-sized	4.7	3.5	2.7
Small	8.3	5.7	4.8
Microenterprises	13.3	9.4	7.5
Total	11.3	8.0	6.5

Source: Domestic Tax Service and Superintendency of Banks and Financial Institutions.

Table 3.30. Share of Past-due Loans in Total Loans by Size of Company
(In percentages)

	1991	1992	1993
Large	0.7	0.3	0.4
Medium-sized	3.4	3.6	0.9
Small	5.6	4.5	2.4
Microenterprises	9.2	6.2	3.4
Total	2.7	1.8	1.1

Source: Domestic Tax Service and Superintendency of Banks and Financial Institutions.

Table 3.31. Distribution of Companies' Past-due Loans by Size
(In percentages)

	1991	1992	1993
Large	16.3	10.1	25.6
Medium-sized	8.6	14.3	5.3
Small	38.2	35.4	37.5
Microenterprises	36.8	35.4	31.6
Total	100.0	100.0	100.0

Source: Prepared on the basis of figures from the Domestic Tax Service and Superintendency of Banks and Financial Institutions.

Similarly, when a particular market segment becomes potentially attractive, private institutions carry out research and training efforts to exploit it. For example, credit to individuals, despite its losses in the 1980s, has boomed in recent years. Even without special incentives, private financial institutions have established the most appropriate methods for handling this sector.

We thus come to our second observation. Financial institution officers have pointed out that the formal system will probably never cover the needs of small companies to the same extent that it does for larger and medium-sized businesses. First, credit from suppliers is more functional for smaller enterprises than that provided by the banks; and second, the larger supply companies have a personal knowledge of their customers unlikely to be equalled by credit institutions.

Credit from suppliers may be more suitable to the needs of small businesses for various reasons. The main financing need of small companies is for working capital, which is generally provided by their suppliers. This credit is often connected with technical assistance in specialized aspects. A number of analysts regard this as crucial to the success of small businesses, and the businesspeople seem to appreciate it greatly.

Furthermore, financing activity is only one part of the productive interrelationship between different-sized units. This is true both for supplier credit and for a large company acquiring inputs from small businesses and granting them advances in liquid resources. In practice, there is a relationship of interdependence between such companies, though one may be the dominant partner. Thus, the small business entrepreneur obtains credit from someone who knows him or her personally, and the larger company assures that its production will move forward and that it will be adequately supplied with inputs. In short, relationships of mutual convenience are established, which facilitate granting credit at this level instead of shifting it toward the formal financial system. For small businesspeople, dealing with the formal financial system often means meeting someone with a different socioeconomic background, who is difficult to understand and has no connection with their production and work environment. By contrast, their relationships with suppliers or large customers are closer and friendlier. Thus one alternative is to encourage larger companies to provide financial support to suppliers and smaller customers, thus improving their ability to channel working capital toward their production partners. Doing so would probably require special lines of credit granted to big business under certain conditions. With their existing knowledge regarding the production and creditworthiness of the companies with which they interact, larger companies would be better able than formal financial institutions to take risks on some specific segments of the market.

However, the instruments currently being applied can also assist new entrepreneurs or others who are not yet seeking credit. Other segments of the financial system should develop, such as credit insurance—an important part of modern approaches to financing in developed countries. Nevertheless, given the information gathered on the problems that small businesses encounter in obtaining access to credit, the results would be notably better if these instruments were offered together as a "package" of measures for small businesses. Hence, arrangements such as a properly monitored guarantee fund (for example, through solidarity endorsements of some kind), credit insurance, subsidized finance consulting, and training and development activities could accomplish much more for developing small business than each of these instruments would do by itself.

The many efforts mentioned above aimed at making it easier for small businesses to obtain credit have left some segments clearly underserved. Some small businesses have no access to programs that help microenterprises, because the credits are less than their needs; others cannot meet the requirements of the formal financial system). Taking note of this fact, the government soon intends to remedy this deficiency.

Bibliography

Arellano, J.P. 1983. "De la liberalización a la intervención: el mercado de capitales en Chile, 1974–1983." Colección Estudios CIEPLAN 11. Santiago.

Baltensperger, E. and J. Dermine. 1987. "The Role of Public Policy in Ensuring Financial Stability: A Cross-Country, Comparative Perspective." In *Threats to International Financial Stability,* R. Portes and A. Swoboda, eds., Cambridge University Press.

Barandiarán, E. 1983. "Nuestra crisis financiera," *Estudios Públicos* No. 12.

Basch, M. and C. Maquieira. 1993. "Evolución del Mercado de Capitales," in "Comentarios sobre la Situación Económica." Departamento de Economía, Facultad de Ciencias Económicas y Administrativas, Universidad de Chile.

Camacho, Arnold. 1993. La experiencia en el financiamiento de la pequeña y mediana empresa en Costa Rica. (Mimeo). Proyecto Políticas Financieras para el Desarrollo, CEPAL/PNUD.

Chamorro, M.C. and Budnevich. 1987. "Concentración en el mercado bancario chileno." Mimeographed document presented at the Encuentro Anual de Economistas.

Chamorro, Mario. 1987. "Eficiencia bancaria: Concepto y medición." In *Tecnificación y eficiencia del sistema bancario.* Colección Economía y Finanzas Volumen IV. Instituto de Estudios Bancarios Guillermo Subercaseaux.

De Gregorio J. and P. Guidotti. 1992. "Notas sobre Intermediación Financiera y Crecimiento Económico." *Cuadernos de Economía,* 29 (87), Universidad Católica de Chile.

De la Cuadra, S. and S. Valdés. 1989. "Myths and Facts About Instability in Financial Liberalization in Chile: 1974–1983." Mimeographed draft document, De la Cuadra and Hachette, Instituto de Economía, Universidad Católica de Chile.

Demsetz, Harold. 1973. "Industry Structure, Market Rivalry, and Public Policy." *Journal of Law and Economics.*

Díaz-Alejandro, C. 1985. "Good-bye Financial Repression, Hello Financial Crash," *Journal of Development Economics* 19(1).

Dornbusch, R. 1990. "Policies to Move from Stabilization to Growth." Proceedings of the World Bank Annual Conference on Development Economics.

Edwards, Franklin. 1977. "Managerial Objectives in Regulated Industries: Expense Preference Behavior in Banking." *Journal of Political Economy.*

Eyzaguirre, N. and O. Larrañaga. 1990. "Macroeconomia de las operaciones cuasifiscales en Chile." Serie de Investigación No. 31, ILADES-Georgetown University.

Eyzaguirre, N. 1992. "Financial Crisis, Reform and Stabilization: The Chilean Experience." Presented at the Seminar on Financial Sector Reforms in Asian and Latin American Countries organized by the World Bank in Santiago.

Fama, Eugene. 1980. "Banking in the Theory of Finance." *Journal of Monetary Economics* 6.

Fry, M. 1989. *Money, Interest and Banking in Economic Development.* Johns Hopkins University Press.

Geisse, Guillermo. 1993. La industria del leasing en países desarrollados y América Latina. Mimeo.

Gelb, A. 1989. "Financial Policies, Growth, and Efficiency." World Bank, Working Paper WPS No. 202.

Goldsmith, Raymond. 1963. "La estructura financiera y el crecimiento económico." CEMLA.

Goldsmith, R. 1969. *Financial Structure and Development.* New Haven: Yale University Press.

Gramley, Lyle. 1969. "Scale Economies in Banking." Federal Reserve Bank of Kansas City.

Hannan, Timothy. 1979. "Limit Pricing and the Banking Industry." *Journal of Money, Credit and Banking.*

Held, G. 1989. "Regulación y supervisión de la banca en la experiencia de liberalización financiera en Chile (1974–1988)." ECLAC, Santiago, Chile.

Jiménez, Luis Felipe. 1993. "La indización de activos financieros en cinco países latinoamericanos. Síntesis de la experiencia." In L. Felipe Jiménez (ed.) *Indización de Activos Financieros. Experiencias Latinoamericanas* ECLAC/ Government of The Netherlands. SRV Impresores, Santiago.

Larraín, Mauricio. 1980. "Regulación financiera y riesgos bancario." Banco Central de Chile.

Le-Fort, G. 1993. "The Financial System and Macroeconomic Stability: The Chilean Experience." Paper presented at the Seminar on Financial Sector Reforms and Liberalization, Bali, Indonesia.

Levitsky, Jacob. 1986. *World Bank Lending to Small Enterprises. A review.* Industry and Finance Series, Volume 16. World Bank, Washington, D.C.

Levitsky, Jacob and Ranga N. Prasad. 1987. "Credit Guarantee Schemes for Small and Medium Enterprises." World Bank Technical Paper No. 58. Industry and Finance Series. World Bank, Washington, D.C.

Levy, Brian. 1991. "Obstacles to Developing Small and Medium-Sized Enterprises. An Empirical Assessment." Policy, Research, and External Affairs. Working Papers. Country Economics Department. The World Bank. Washington, D.C.

López, Mario. 1993. El financiamiento de la pequeña y mediana empresa en América Latina. La experiencia de México. Mimeo. Proyecto Políticas Financieras para el Desarrollo CEPAL/PNUD.

Maddala, G.S., and E. Miller. 1989. *Microeconomics: Theory and Applications.* McGraw-Hill.

McKinnon, R. 1973. *Money and Capital in Economic Development.* The Brookings Institution, Washington D.C.

_______. 1982. "The Order of Economic Liberalization: Lessons from Chile and Argentina." K. Brunner and A.H. Meltzer, eds., *Economic Policy in a World of Change,* in Carulfil-Rockerter Conference Series on public policy, Vol 17.

Medieros, César Manoel. 1933. Empresas de menor porte. Algumas Características do caso brasileiro. Mimeo. Proyecto Políticas financiera para el Desarrollo CEPAL/PNUD.

Meller, P. and A. Solimano. 1984. "El Mercado de capitales chileno: Laissez Faire, inestabilidad financiera y burbujas especulativas." CIEPLAN.

Morandé, Felipe. 1983. "Indización financiera, ahorro privado e inercia inflacionaria. El caso de Chile." In L. Felipe Jiménez, ed., *Indización de Activos financerios. Experiencias Latinoamericanas.* ECLAC/Government of The Netherlands. SRV Impresores, Santiago.

Ramírez, Guillermo. 1989. "Política Bancaria y Legislación Financiera: La Experiencia Chilena de los Años 1980." *Revista Información Financiera.* Superintendencia de Bancos e Instituciones Financieras.

Revell, Jack. 1980. "Cost and Margins in Banking. An International Survey." OECD.

Rojas, José A. 1991. "El leasing como instrumento para facilitar el financiamiento de la inversion en la pequeña y mediana empresa en América Latina." Serie Financiamiento del Desarrollo 7, CEPAL, Naciones Unidas. Santiago.

Rojas, J.A. and Román, E. 1993. "El acceso de las pequeñas y medianas empresas al financiamiento. El programa de apoyo a la PYME del Gobierno chileno. Análisis de una experiencia." Mimeo. Proyecto Políticas Financieras para el Desarrollo CEPAL/PNUD.

Shaw, E. 1973. *Financial Deepening in Economic Development.* Oxford University Press.

TASC. 1992. "Pequeña y Mediana Empresa: Acceso al Mercado de Créditos." ILADES. Santiago, Chile.

Tobin, James. 1984. "On the Efficiency of the Financial System." *Lloyds Banks Review.*

World Bank. 1989. "World Bank Lending for Small and Medium Enterprises: Fifteen Years of Experience." Industry and Energy Department. Working Paper. Industry Series No. 20. Washington, D.C.

_______. 1989. *World Development Report.* New York: Oxford University Press.

CHAPTER FOUR

GUATEMALA: LIBERALIZING THE FORMAL FINANCIAL SYSTEM

Lizardo Sosa López*

From the 1970s until the early 1980s, Guatemala modelled its development on an import substitution strategy. Import substitution stimulated industrial sector growth within the framework of the Central American Common Market and contributed to Guatemala's economic vitality, especially in the 1970s. Nonetheless, the country's domestic market experienced slow growth not only in the supply of goods, but also in employment and income (ASIES, 1990).

Guatemala's economic, political, and social crises after the late seventies caused its productive capacity to contract and impoverished much of its population. Average real per capita income fell by about 14 percent between 1980 and 1986. Beginning in 1986, the economy showed positive growth rates again, although they were slow compared to an annual population growth rate of approximately 2.9 percent (Table 4.1).

Against this backdrop, and with the peace initiatives launched across Central America since 1987, Guatemala has worked hard to adjust to the demands of the international economy. A number of economic and social programs supported by international financial organizations such as the World Bank, the International Monetary Fund (IMF), and the Inter-American Development Bank (IDB) have been attempted, but did not generally succeed in achieving their objectives. This lack of success was due either to the absence of political will or to the virtual impossibility of implementing these programs. For years Guatemala's economic policy was limited to adopting isolated measures, with neither international financial support nor the prerequisite conditions for macroeconomic stability. Such an erratic, incongruent policy doomed these programs to failure, due to the resulting fiscal and monetary disequilibrium.

* The author wishes to thank the following for their assistance: Ranferi Alfaro, Isabel Ibarra de Cálix, Carlos González Arévalo, Stefan Hartleben, Mariano Rayo, Otto Samayoa, Ana Silvia Escobar de Segura, Jorge Tello, and Edin Velásquez.

Table 4.1. Major Macroeconomic Indicators, 1979–93

	(1)	(2)	(3)	(4)	(5)	(6)	(7)	(8)
1979	8,348.9	9.3	6,726.3	1,241.2	2.6	0.0	660.0	1.0
1980	8,639.4	7.3	6,916.8	1,249.0	4.7	0.0	348.6	1.0
1981	8,570.4	8.1	7,113.4	1,204.8	0.7	0.0	70.0	1.0
1982	8,635.9	8.3	7,315.5	1,180.5	4.7	0.0	−28.5	1.0
1983	8,495.8	6.7	7,523.9	1,129.2	3.3	0.0	−85.0	1.0
1984	8,683.7	7.5	7,739.6	1,122.0	3.8	0.4	−67.2	1.5
1985	8,609.6	31.4	7,963.3	1,081.2	1.8	3.0	−112.4	3.0
1986	9,188.8	25.7	8,195.1	1,121.3	1.5	1.5	−3.2	2.8
1987	9,266.5	10.0	8,434.3	1,098.7	1.3	1.4	−363.6	2.7
1988	9,745.6	11.1	8,681.1	1,122.6	1.4	1.6	−385.8	2.6
1989	9,947.3	17.8	8,935.4	1,113.2	2.9	1.3	−284.9	2.8
1990	10,219.5	60.6	9,197.3	1,111.1	2.1	2.1	−232.7	4.5
1991	10,421.7	9.0	9,467.0	1,100.8	0.0	1.6	383.2	5.0
1992	10,786.7	13.9	9,744.6	1,106.9	0.0	1.2	436.3	5.2
1993	11,210.4	11.6	10,029.8	1,117.7	1.7	1.3	582.3	5.7

(1) Real GDP (millions of US$, base 1993)
(2) Cumulative annual inflation (rate)
(3) Population (thousands)
(4) Real per capita income (US$, base 1993)
(5) Fiscal deficit/GDP (percentage)
(6) Quasi-fiscal deficit/GDP (percentage)
(7) Net international reserves (millions of US$)
(8) Banking market exchange rate, quetzal per US$ (annual average)
Source: Bank of Guatemala. *Estudios Económicos y Memorias de Labores*, 1979–92. Guatemala City: BANGUAT, 1980–93; Bank of Guatemala. *Boletines Estadísticos*, 1979–92. Guatemala City: BANGUAT, 1980–1993; General Secretariat of the National Economic Planning Council. *Proyecciones de Población Urbana y Rural por Región y Departamento*, 1980–2000. Guatemala City: SEGEPLAN, 1988.

At the time this study was prepared, Guatemala was experiencing the macroeconomic consequences of the May 1993[1] political and institutional crisis. The government was trying to implement a joint economic program agreed upon with the IMF, and to achieve the objectives of a structural adjustment program signed with the IBRD in November 1992 (a US$120 million credit for economic and social modernization). Nonetheless, with the support of the IDB, economic authorities were able to redefine the objectives of both programs and to adopt a program for modernizing the financial sector.[2]

---

[1] The country experienced political and institutional upheavals as a result of the coup attempt of former president Jorge Serrano on May 25, 1993. The consequences of this are still being felt, though some solutions were found through democratic channels and the naming of a new constitutional president.
[2] A sectoral loan to support the financial modernization program (US$132 million) was approved by the IDB Board of Executive Directors on November 24, 1993, and was signed on January 25, 1994. The first disbursement in the amount of US$62 million was made in early March 1994.

Recent Macroeconomic Trends

Guatemala's macroeconomic policy failed to overcome the crisis of the 1980s. Certain decisions that laid the groundwork for reforming economic policy[3] were made during the latter half of that decade. Yet the economy continued to suffer from serious fiscal and balance-of-payment crises. Given the narrow confines for maneuvering monetary policy, financial disequilibrium led to a rapid deterioration in the value of Guatemalan currency abroad and to domestic price increases, particularly in 1990 (Table 4.1).

With the start of a new term of constitutional government in 1991, fiscal revenues improved significantly, allowing equilibrium in public finances to be achieved. Monetary authorities[4] instituted a restrictive credit and monetary policy by raising the percentage of the minimum reserve ratio required for banks and by managing interest rates through open market operations (OMOs). Consequently, in 1991 and 1992, the inflation rate was down substantially, monetary reserves increased appreciably, and nominal exchange rates stabilized (Table 4.1). Monetary policy[5] caused interest rates on financial markets to remain high.[6] By early 1994, however, two important changes had taken place. First, on March 14, monetary authorities, by means of Resolution JM-204-94, ceased setting foreign exchange rates. Second, new amendments to the constitution prohibited the Central Bank from making loans to the government.

Recent Trends in the Financial System

The domestic financial system developed under legislation that dates back to the 1940s. Accordingly, the system has not adapted to new international economic conditions, particularly to conditions underlying modern financial markets. The restrictions placed on the regulated financial system prevented it from offering a variety of direct financial services (leasing, factoring, credit cards, deposit and lending operations in foreign currency). Parallel institutions and companies were then formed to meet the demand for these services. Eventually the country's financial sector began responding to current market conditions and demands. However, the market for

---

[3] The emergence of macroeconomic disequilibria demonstrated the need to modernize the economic system, which in turn forced monetary authorities to search within the legal framework for wider use of monetary regulation instruments, such as open-market operations.

[4] The Monetary Board, an autonomous entity, is the highest authority of the Bank of Guatemala (Central Bank).

[5] Monetary restrictions were increased in January 1993 when monetary authorities raised the minimum reserve ratio (legal reserve requirements) by 10 percentage points.

[6] At December 31, 1993, the weighted average interest rate was 25.7 percent for lending and 13.5 percent for deposits.

these new services, owing to a lack of information and widely varied interest rates, quickly became known for the diversity of its credit applicants.

To respond to this situation, Guatemalan monetary authorities, with the support of international financial organizations, approved the program for modernizing the domestic financial system. Measures in the program seek to further liberalize the financial system and to establish prudential supervision (see chapter appendix). The Monetary Board (discussed in the next section) oversees the structure and number of financial institutions, which in 1993 consisted of 30 banks, 11 finance corporations, and 12 bonded warehouses. As may be seen from Diagram 1, the number of banks and finance corporations has doubled over the last ten years.

Legal Framework of the Financial System

Under the Guatemalan Constitution, the state is obligated to protect capital formation, savings, and investment, as well as to foster conditions that will promote capital investment. In the area of rural development, the state also has an obligation to provide technical and economic assistance to farmers, craftsmen, and cooperatives (Art. 119). The constitution also provides for a central bank system, governed and managed by the Monetary Board (JM), under which all monetary, banking and financial activities, including the Bank of Guatemala (BANGUAT), are organized. Pursuant to Article 133, the Monetary Board is responsible for establishing the country's monetary, foreign exchange, and credit policies and for safeguarding the liquidity, solvency, and soundness of the financial system. Effective April 1994, this same article prohibits the Central Bank from granting loans to the government.

Article 132 of the Constitution states that the Monetary Board will be comprised of the Chairman of BANGUAT, the ministers of finance, economy, and agriculture, one other member and one alternate. The latter two are selected from the Congress; nonfinancial business associations; chairmen of the boards of directors of private banks; and the Administrative Council of the University of San Carlos (an autonomous state university). The Superintendency of Banks is responsible for supervising, monitoring, and inspecting banks and other lending institutions, finance corporations, bonding and insurance companies, currency exchange agencies, and other institutions as stated by law.

In theory, financial legislation is supposedly drafted to protect the interests of the depositors and investors. In practice, however, it protects the intermediaries (as in the case of Decree No. 7–72).[7] Thus financial repression has resulted from setting and manipulating interest rates for the formal system and using monetary measures to correct previous economic imbalances.

---

[7] Legislative Decree 7–72 grants the JM discretionary power to provide financial assistance to banks that are financially insolvent. In such cases, the JM may also intervene in troubled financial institutions.

Diagram of Financial System, Showing Number of Institutions Operating or Awaiting Authorization, 1982 and 1993

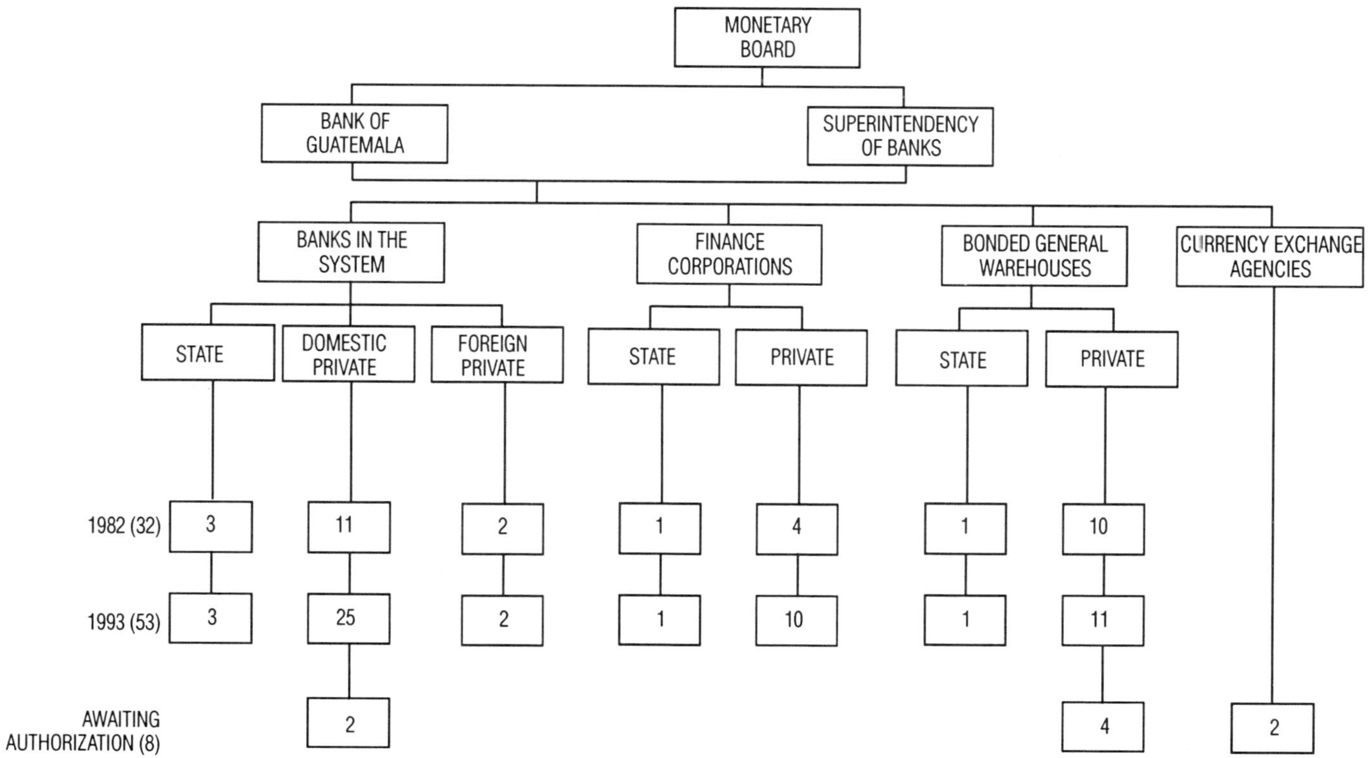

Organic Law of the Bank of Guatemala (Legislative Decree 215)

Enacted in 1946, this law defines the Bank of Guatemala as a state-owned, autonomous bank, which shall operate as the autonomous central bank, subject to provisions of the Monetary Law (Decree-Law 203). The organizational structure of BANGUAT, the functions and duties of the Superintendency of Banks, and the scope of central bank operations are established. The Central Bank is authorized to exercise direct regulation over the financial system by setting and modifying bank reserve requirements and interest rates, determining credit limits, and setting exchange rates.

Banking Law (Legislative Decree 315)

Like the Organic Law of the Bank of Guatemala, the Banking Law regulates a financial system that took shape under a paternalistic state directly responsible for developing the country. Although this system fostered stable economic development, it is today no longer applicable to the current situation. Under this law, banks, whose mains source of funds are deposits, may grant short-, medium- and long-term loans. By establishing minimum capital and reserves requirements, legal provisions on guarantees for loans, and intervention by the monetary authority and the Superintendency of Banks, the law in effect governs increases in intermediation costs and restricts wider access to credit.

Percentages for minimum capital and reserve requirements are set as follows: 5 percent of investments in government securities; 10 percent in other securities or in loans; and 50 percent in personal property, real estate, and other fixed assets. Rules governing guarantees require that loans not exceed 80 percent of the amount of collateral guarantee placed in government, public corporation, or public financial institution securities; 70 percent of other collateral guarantees; and 50 percent of mortgage guarantees. Unsecured loans theoretically may not be granted for a term of more than one year, but in reality they may be extended up to three years. The amount of loans to a single debtor is limited to 20 percent of the paid-in capital of the respective bank. As for rules and regulations, the banks were until recently encumbered by many restrictions, such as requiring prior approval to open branch offices or even to change hours of service to the public. This forced credit consumers to turn to unregulated financing sources and caused financial institutions to establish parallel financial companies.

Law Governing Private Finance Corporations (Decree-Law 208)

Finance corporations are defined as investment banking institutions dedicated to promoting productive enterprises that require medium- and long-term financing. Their deposit and lending rates have never been regulated. Their resources are derived chiefly from trading in bonds and notes, and they may not accept deposits. The Monetary Board's fund guarantee system for lending operations by finance corporations permits loans for up to 80 percent of the value of land; 50 percent of the value of buildings and plant; and 70 percent of the value of collateral securities. In comparison with the bank's fund guarantee system, the only difference refers to land. Generally speaking, the nature of guarantees is unrelated to the reserves required. If guarantees are insufficient or losses are identified, the finance corporations must deal with those that directly affect the performance of the fiscal year. The law does establish a system of minimum capital requirements with respect to the maturity date of the bonds: 35 percent for bonds with a term no longer than 30 thirty days, and 10 percent for those with longer terms.

Finance corporations are authorized to temporarily hold equity interests in the capital of the enterprise they finance (Art. 5). Lately, they have gained even greater importance as sources of investment capital as a result of the opening of securities exchanges on which they have placed their own debt instruments.

Law of General Warehouses (Decree 1746)

General warehouses are private enterprises that by their nature become auxiliary credit institutions. Their purpose is the deposit, maintenance, custody, handling, distribution, purchase, and sale of merchandise for third-party accounts. They may issue certificates of deposit and warehouse receipts on goods or products under their custody.

Many storage companies use warehouse receipts as instruments for securing working and investment capital from the banking system. With their lower cost, these investments are not subject to minimum bank capital requirements.[8]

Superintendency of Banks

Chapter IV of the Organic Law of the Bank of Guatemala contains some provisions regulating the Superintendency of Banks, as does the Banking Law. In most cases, however, the Monetary Board regulates the Superintendency of Banks. In its supervisory and monitoring role, the Superintendency does not conduct prudential supervision. Instead it acts only ex-post facto, conducting audits aimed more at ensuring compliance with fiscal and financial regulations and less at overseeing the soundness and solvency of the whole banking system. The effectiveness of the Superintendency of Banks, however, is greatly diminished by the appeals that may be filed by financial institutions with the Monetary Board against

---

[8] For the purpose of stimulating rural and warehouse credits, this law does not apply minimum capital requirements to bank investments guaranteed by certificates of deposit or security bonds (Article 28).

its resolutions. Additionally, it lacks the accounting standards required for prudential supervision as well as qualified personnel.

Modernization Measures to Expand Access to Financing Sources

In the past, macroeconomic policy, especially with regard to fiscal, monetary, and exchange matters, was noted for its direct controls and dedicated management. These features resulted in financial repression, which only by 1984 began to change.

Measures aimed at liberalizing the financial market were adopted with a view to better managing monetary, credit, and exchange policy. This gave rise to a proliferation of financial services parallel to the system regulated by the Monetary Board and the Superintendency of Banks. In many cases, however, these services were controlled by the same regulated financial institutions; they simply found legal devices to expand their range of services to financial operations not expressly authorized by the laws governing banking and finance.[9] The program[10] for modernizing Guatemala's financial system, approved by Monetary Board Resolution JM-647-93 and currently under way with financial support from the Inter-American Development Bank, addressed the need to make changes in the legislation.

Credit and Monetary Policy

Up to the mid-1980s, credit and monetary policy relied essentially on mechanisms like reserve requirements, credit ceilings, interest rate fixing, and advances and discounts as the means for exercising monetary control.

Beginning in 1986, the use of open market operations (OMOs) began to increase. Bank reserve requirements were gradually raised. Similarly, interest rates for deposits and lending operations were adjusted and eventually liberalized. The exchange rate was eased and certain changes in credit and monetary policy helped to control liquidity in the economy without causing a greater dispersion of credit.

Deregulation of the Financial Market and Modernization of Banking Supervision

Following approval of a World Bank credit for economic and social modernization, the government set about the task of modernizing its financial sector. In the

---

[9] On November 5, 1993, the Monetary Board issued Resolution JM-752-93, which approved a broader definition of deposit, lending, and confidential banking operations. According to the text of this resolution, banks may conduct the following operations: issue and transact business with credit cards; financial leasing; factoring; credits in monetary deposit accounts; deposit and lending swaps, including for third part accounts; creation of convertible debentures; deposits with financial investment options; and in general, other operations that do not violate any legal or regulatory provisions.

[10] A summary of this program is included in the chapter appendix.

second half of 1993, measures were adopted to promote monetary stability and diversify banking services, as well as to strengthen prudential standards, update financial supervision, and regulate money markets and securities exchanges.

Institutional and Community Development for Financing Small Enterprise

It may be safely stated that Guatemala's small business sector and community service groups have derived little or no benefit from services offered by the regulated financial system. Nonetheless, there are a few examples of cases in which institutions and communities have successfully provided financing to this sector.

Brief Description of the Sector

The parameters used for this study are those of the IDB (see note 8 of chapter one). Accordingly, a microenterprise is defined as a business that has no more than 10 employees, with assets totalling no more than US$10,000, and annual sales under US$45,000. The total assets of a small enterprise are less than US$50,000; its annual sales are under US$200,000; and its employees number no more than 20 persons. A medium-sized business employs a maximum of 50 workers and has assets under US$300,000.

Most enterprises in Guatemala are categorized as either micro- or small businesses. The former usually do not develop beyond the informal market. According to a 1987 USAID study, Guatemala then had an estimated 356,000 micro- and small enterprises, which generated approximately 800,000 jobs, especially in the production of clothing, footwear, wood and furniture, textiles and foodstuffs, but also in personal services.

According to the analysis conducted by the financial intermediaries consulted,[11] most loan applications were for working capital and the purchase of fixed assets. Parallel intermediaries saw increased demand for their services, because the minimum collateral requirements set by banks and finance corporations exceeded the ability of applicants from this sector. Thus, more bank disintermediation on the part of users from micro- and small enterprises took place. Other requirements also contributed to blocking these enterprises from access to credit: official registration, formal financial statements, at least two years in business, and a maximum of 50 employees. These requirements, combined with other factors such as policies on maximum interest rates and ceilings, caused a parallel system of financial intermediation to emerge. According to information furnished by the Federation of Small

---

[11] Three nongovernmental financial intermediation institutions that have shown the greatest impact in granting loans were visited.

and Microenterprise (FEPYME), this parallel system has largely succeeded in fulfilling the previously unmet demand.

There is no information that allows us to quantify the degree to which the informal market has met the demand for credit. Nonetheless, two estimates regarding specific cases may be considered. The first, based on a 1994 survey conducted by the newspaper *Diario Siglo Ventiuno,* covered loans to vendors in local community markets. Out of 400,000 vendors across the country, only 2.5 percent (10,000 sellers) ever obtain bank credit, according to the survey. The remainder secure credit from private lenders ("usurers") at interest rates of up to 25 percent per day or from NGOs at rates similar to those in the banking system. The second estimate was based on cash advances given by coffee exporters to growers for the purpose of working capital and indicated these loans were made at interest rates higher than those of the financial market.

Finally, the banking system itself admits that it has little incentive to grant loans to small enterprises. Such loans simply are not profitable, given the high administrative costs and legal obstacles raised by the insufficient collateral of the applicants. Nonetheless, private banks are now preparing initiatives for the sector, as described in the following section.

Credit Programs to Small and Medium-Sized Enterprises

Credit to the small enterprise sector has been the subject of programs promoted by state-run agencies, NGOs, cooperatives, and lately, even private banks.

Among government-run programs recently created are the Micro- and Small Enterprise Development Fund, the Guarantee Fund for Small and Medium-sized Enterprise, and the Guarantee Fund for Small Industry. The first of these funds was set up jointly by the National Bank for Agricultural Development and the Workers Bank for the purpose of granting unsecured loans. This fund has granted around 20,000 loans, totaling approximately Q74.0 million (roughly US$12.6 million), distributed among industry (74 percent), commerce (20 percent), and services (6 percent). The Micro- and Small Enterprise Development Fund estimated its delinquency rate in 1993 at 25 percent, despite financing at subsidized rates. This situation has of course limited its growth and capitalization.

The second fund (US$5.5 million), the Guarantee Fund for Small and Medium-sized Enterprise managed by BANGUAT, is designed to complement up to 50 percent of the collateral guarantees required by financial institutions. This fund has not worked well due to lack of credibility caused by the negative experiences of similar funds, excessive bureaucracy, and inadequate promotion. Inadequate analysis of credit applicants and failure to enforce collection procedures have produced poor results.

The third, the Guarantee Fund for Small Industry, was established with a contribution of US$1 million from the Central American Bank for Economic

Integration (CABEI) and the European Union (EU). The purpose of this fund is to guarantee loans granted by commercial banks to small industry with resources from the Program to Support Small and Medium-sized Industry in Central America (PAPIC). The Fund covers up to 65 percent of the total credit value of the loan and the end-user pays CABEI a 3 percent commission for its guarantee. Negotiations are currently underway for a line of credit for micro- and small enterprise to be financed by a US$10 million grant from the IDB and administered by BANGUAT. This credit line would be used to authorize loans up to US$5,000 for microenterprises and up to US$15,000 for small businesses.

In recent years a number of initiatives were launched to provide credit to small enterprises through NGOs. Using funds received from international programs, these resources were funneled through the Bank of Guatemala in order to obtain government guarantees and to cover exchange rate risks. NGOs dedicated to financial intermediation have successfully provided credit services to this sector. Although many NGOs have operated in the sector, only a small number of them has experienced a significant volume of operations.

Noteworthy among the NGOs is FUNTEC-Génesis Empresarial, which from 1988 through October 1993 had served a total of 14,726 owner-operators of microenterprises, granting nearly 29,000 loans for a total of Q128.5 million (US$22.7 million). Since 1990, this NGO's financing sources have come from 10 banks in the system, two finance corporations, and foundations that have granted credit for some Q12.0 million (US$2 million). Microenterprises may receive loans of up to Q15,000 (US$2,500) for working capital, machinery, and equipment under terms based on their business cycle. Loans of up to Q40,000 (US$6,780) are granted to small businesses for terms of up to 18 months at a 2.5 percent monthly interest rate. Promissory notes are used as legal instruments to formalize credits for operations involving fiduciary guarantees. Mortgage guarantees, which account for scarcely 1 percent of all credits, use a deed of acknowledgment of debt. Another innovation consists of providing on-site technical training and assistance, in addition to financing. Some ten NGOs are now working in this area.

The cooperative movement has also satisfied part of the demand for credit through its savings and loan cooperatives. Grouped under the National Federation of Savings and Loan Cooperatives (FENACOAC), these institutions play a vital role in financial intermediation for small and medium-sized agricultural producers. For example, at the end of 1992, FENACOAC had a loan portfolio of US$12.5 million, with the average credit granted ranging from US$400 to US$900. According to FENACOAC officials, the number of affiliated cooperatives has decreased, but the number of members has increased. In 1980, FENACOAC consisted of 76 cooperatives with 85,000 members; however, by 1993, it had 45 cooperatives and 93,388 members. Between 1980 and 1992, contributions by members in the cooperatives rose from Q10.4 million to Q42.9 million (US$7.3 million). Current savings increased from Q2.6 million to Q55.6 million (US$9.4

million), and credit to members went from Q18.0 million to Q74.3 million (US$12.6 million). Moreover, total liabilities of the affiliate cooperatives jumped from Q13.1 million in 1982 to Q67.3 million in 1992 (US$11.4 million). During the same period, the volume of credit granted to the affiliate cooperatives by FENACOAC dropped from Q9.3 million to Q5.5 million ($900,000). In some ways these changes reflect the efficient and self-supporting manner in which the affiliate savings and loan cooperatives operate.

The use of credit has not changed substantially. About 40 percent of the total credit still goes to agriculture. However, the credit used by small manufacturing enterprises has dropped from 36 to 22 percent of the total credit available. Loan minimums have also varied, from Q100 to Q500, while maximums have ranged from Q5,000 (US$848) to Q150,000 (US$25,425), compared with earlier averages of Q800 to Q1,000 in 1982 and Q5,000 to Q20,000 (US$3,390) in 1992. Deposit and lending rates applied by the cooperatives over the same period have increased substantially. Rates on FENACOAC credits to affiliate cooperatives went from 8 percent in 1980 to 18 to 21 percent in 1992, with terms of up to three years, requiring mortgage, collateral, and fiduciary guarantees.

A program started by a private bank, Banco Empresarial, S.A., provides financial resources to micro- and small enterprise at real interest rates above the average, with short terms and collections that could even be daily. Although it is premature to evaluate program results, this market is being considered by other intermediaries. A new bank (Banco Privado para el Desarrollo, S.A.) was recently authorized to grant loans to microenterprise.

The NGOs and private banks use mechanisms such as forming jointly liable groups with pooled securities, maintaining a stipulated amount of savings in accordance with the level of credit granted, and granting short-term credits with daily payments. The bank conducts collection and recovery operations (amortization, interest, and savings) on site. By the first half of 1993, these programs had provided financial assistance to approximately 500,000 individuals, excluding the cooperative sector, for some Q250 million (US$42.4 million). They also provided technical assistance, training, and consulting services to nearly 14,000 small entrepreneurs.

Community Credit Programs

Nearly 50 percent of Guatemala's population is of Mayan descent. Cultural traditions are preserved through customary laws rooted in indigenous customs[12] and in the presence of numerous cultural, social, economic, and political organi-

[12] See ASIES (1993).

zations and movements. These movements are beginning to play a role in community development and are conducting credit operations for their members. They utilize resources contributed by community members as well as by national and international assistance organizations. The Cooperative Association for Rural Development of the West (CEDRO)[13] promotes community development through work projects involving the participation of all levels of the community. From 1989 to 1993 CEDRO helped provide financing to member groups for a total of Q1.2 million (US$206,000) for productive projects (cloth, soaps, vegetables, canned fruit juices, ointments, teas, salves, natural medicines derived from plants, etc.).[14]

The Bank Intermediation Process in Guatemala

How banks and finance corporations operate in Guatemala's regulated system is discussed below. We describe the quantitative changes in the financial system during the period under study, and the factors that shape the framework for financial intermediation. The following indicators are used to measure the characteristics of the intermediation process: financial intensification or deepening; transaction costs; quality of the intermediation process; and the dispersion of credit and banking services.

Financial Intensification or Deepening[15]

Intensification or deepening indicators are related to the size of a country's financial sector and the development phase of its financial intermediation. An analysis thereof

[13] At the end of 1993, CEDRO consisted of 28 Maya-Quiché communities located in four municipalities. Data was taken from a special report published by the newspaper Siglo Ventiuno on October 28 and 29, 1993, and from information provided directly by CEDRO. Other community development organizations are operating in many locations throughout the country.

[14] Another example is Agua del Pueblo, a non-governmental, apolitical organization at work in nine departments. Six of these regions have a predominantly Mayan population and three a non-Mayan population; in all, 178 communities with a total of 88,000 inhabitants have built 16,000 drinking water connections. During the past five years, the organization has followed up successfully on work at the local level, so that after water connections are established, the communities themselves can continue sustainable development, under the motto *"water is a means, not an end."*

[15] The relationship between financial markets and economic growth of developing countries has been widely studied for the purpose of determining the degree to which deepening has contributed to improving growth rates. Overall results indicate a double effect: an increase in the efficiency of capital accumulation and an increase in savings and, therefore, the rate of investment. Unlike the first hypothesis that considered this growth endogenous to the system, it has been determined that macroeconomic policies played an important role in the intensity and efficiency of financial intermediation and that policies leading to financial repression had negative effects on the efficiency of this relationship.

may take either of two approaches: microeconomic, through which we try to determine the efficiency from the viewpoint of institutions like enterprises; or macroeconomic, which considers the relationship between financial intensification and economic growth.[16] We tried to determine the contribution to growth measured by the degree of participation of the regulated financial system in generating gross domestic product. Within the overall economic process, the role of financial institutions is defined as securing resources from savers, compiling and analyzing information, and funneling investment funds to those activities with the highest yield.

Economic analysis of the trend shown by indicators of financial intensification or deepening suggest that the formal financing system has become less important to the generation of gross domestic product and efficient development of intermediation. This diminishing importance, apparent since 1986, is due to the direct effect of demonetization on the sector. Economic measures aimed at demonetization have had a negative impact on intermediation levels through the relative reduction of growth in the volumes of monetary deposits and in the amount of credit granted to the private sector. Demonetization also affects the quality of the intermediation process, as reflected in cost increases and the reduced efficiency of operations. Furthermore, demonetization of the economy has aggravated the problem of credit concentration, since banks, in response to the reduction of liquidity, have greatly intensified their use of rationalization and selectivity criteria in credit operations.

Despite the downturn in the quantity and quality of the intermediation process, the size of the financial sector has experienced growth similar to the real sector of the economy, and in recent years the sector has shown extraordinary profit margins. This performance is due to the increase in other financial operations like bank commissions and, principally, the massive investments in securities issued by the Central Bank to reduce the money supply. Clearly a high degree of linkage exists between comprehensive economic policies, principally those of a monetary nature, and the degree of deepening and quality of the formal financial system. Thus monetary policies aimed at demonetization not only reduce the role of intermediation, but also contribute to the concentration of credit.

Money Supply

The analysis supports the hypothesis that a monetized economy reflects a market of developed money. Accordingly, a high level of monetization should be posi-

---

[16] Different authors have found negative correlations between financial development and economic growth in Latin America, results that are interpreted in light of the extreme cases of financial liberalization that occurred in the seventies and eighties. These results suggest that liberalization per se is not enough, since in the absence of adequate regulation, greater financial intermediation may be associated with less efficient investment.

tively related to growth. Some recently conducted studies, however, argue that the main role of the money supply in the economy is promoting liquidity or means of exchange, while financial intermediation's contribution to growth is directly linked to investment efficiency. Despite these limitations, the money supply continues to be used as an approximate indicator of financial deepening.[17] According to this analysis, after a period of growth that coincided with higher inflation rates (1985–90), the money supply (M1) has decreased slightly, indicating greater deepening (Table 4.2, columns 1 through 4). Other indicators, however, show a relative reduction in savings and time deposits, coinciding with a preference for government securities. This confirms that the reduction in means of payment is not due to greater financial deepening, but resulted from a policy of demonetization. Thus, the intermediation process is weakening, and that is further exacerbated by the high ratios established for bank reserves and mandatory bank investments (M3).

Financial Assets of Banks

This indicator can determine whether the size of the financial sector has increased in relation to real economic growth. Table 4.2 compares financial assets relative to GDP. Column 6 lists the net assets, excluding bank investments in government and Central Bank securities. Data in column 5 includes the value of said investments. During the first years of the period under study, the financial sector grew faster than the real sector of the economy. Only from 1986 onward, after the first monetary stabilization measures were introduced, did this trend stop. The financial sector began to decrease in relative size, although far less when government and Central Bank securities were included in the assets. This behavior suggests that although the sector tended to contract during the stabilization process, the effects of this were partly neutralized by bank investments in government and Central Bank securities.

---

[17] Table 4.2 lists the major indicators of financial deepening based on the money supply. The hypothesis assumes greater financial deepening when there is a reduction between the total means of payment (M1) and GDP, which would mean that more assets are available in the economy, allowing more operations to be conducted without using the money supply. Another hypothesis is that financial assets grow according to the degree of economic development, for which reason we would hope that with greater financial deepening, the M2/GDP ratio would increase, reflecting its effect on the growth of the real sector. The M3/GDP ratio indicates the effect of the level of bank reserve requirements and mandatory investments, for which the increase in the coefficient would indicate a reduction in the function of intermediation. Finally, the ratio with M4 would indicate the preference of economic actors for government and official entity securities, for which an increase in the coefficient represents a lower degree of intermediation.

Table 4.2. Indicators of Financial Deepening in Relation to GDP, 1979–93
(Percentages)

	(1)	(2)	(3)	(4)	(5)	(6)
1979	10.0	23.4	9.9	23.4	2.6	2.5
1980	9.0	22.8	8.2	22.8	2.6	2.5
1981	8.6	23.2	8.0	23.2	2.8	2.7
1982	8.6	26.2	9.2	26.2	3.3	3.1
1983	8.7	25.7	8.0	25.7	3.4	3.3
1984	8.9	27.7	8.3	27.7	3.7	3.6
1985	11.8	30.2	11.4	30.2	3.6	3.5
1986	9.9	25.6	9.8	25.6	3.0	2.8
1987	9.9	26.5	8.8	26.5	2.9	2.6
1988	9.7	25.3	9.3	25.3	2.8	2.7
1989	10.2	25.7	9.7	25.7	2.7	2.6
1990	9.4	21.5	8.9	25.4	2.2	2.1
1991	8.1	22.5	10.4	27.6	2.6	2.0
1992	7.6	23.9	11.6	27.5	2.9	2.4
1993	7.4	21.8	10.6	26.3	2.9	2.5

(1) M1 = Notes, coins, and demand deposits
(2) M2 = M1 + savings and time deposits
(3) M3 = Units of account + total cash reserve + mandatory investment
(4) M4 = M2 + government securities and other government-owned institutions' securities held by the non-bank private sector
(5) Financial system financial assets
(6) Financial system financial assets (less investments in government and Central Bank securities)
Source: Calculated on the basis of: Bank of Guatemala, *Boletines Estadísticos*, 1979–93 and Superintendency of Banks, *Boletines de Estadísticas Bancarias*.

Interest Rates

Studies of financial intermediation show a close correlation between financial repression and real effective interest rates, as well as between direct monetary control instruments and the regulatory framework. The hypothesis is that a positive real interest rate promotes financial savings and intermediation, thus increasing the supply of credit to the private sector.[18]

Until 1989, interest rate policy consisted of maintaining fixed rates set by monetary authorities within the maximum range for deposit and lending rates in the banking system. Table 4.2 (columns 1 through 3) tracks interest rate performance in the banking system and the effect of inflation on real rates. The maintenance of negative real rates up to 1990 does not seem to have strongly influenced

[18] International evidence is inconclusive regarding the relationship between savings and real interest rates, suggesting that interest rates are poor indicators of the degree of financial intermediation. Contradictory evidence indicates that low (and negative) real interest rates cause financial disintermediation, but high interest rates indicate inefficiency in investment and a lack of credibility in economic policies, thus resulting in lower investment.

domestic savings levels. The domestic savings/GDP ratio continuously decreased, reaching its lowest levels in 1990. Upward pressure on interest levels continued to be felt from that year onward, despite interest rate liberalization and the use of OMOs aimed at stabilization. This upward pressure, however, does not noticeably affect savings and investment rates because the resources neutralized through that channel are not included in banking or financial intermediation. Instead, these funds are funneled into the central bank in exchange for securities. The public's preference for high-yield central bank bonds effectively favored stabilization, but also made the sources of credit financing more expensive.

Obviously, interest rate liberalization alone is not sufficient to stimulate financial deepening or intermediation. Concurrent efforts should be made to eliminate the macroeconomic disequilibria existing in the economy and to issue suitable regulations.

Credit to the Private Sector

Wider use is made of the ratio between domestic credit to the private sector and GDP as an indicator of financial deepening (column 5, Table 4.3) because of its direct effect on investment and economic growth. With increased deepening, the ratio increases, indicating that a greater volume of credit generates more profits. Results, however, show that the ratio has steadily declined since 1985, confirming the reduction noted in the degree of financial deepening.

Interestingly, the private investment/GDP indicator (column 6, Table 4.3) shows a more dynamic growth of private investment. Econometric studies by ASIES on the Guatemalan economy's performance found that these two ratios show no relevant correlation between bank credit and GDP, but a positive, significant, longer-term relationship between private investment and GDP.[19]

Domestic and External Debt Levels

This indicator allows us to measure the degree to which the economy has developed with domestic and external resources. Indicators of the external and domestic debt-to-GDP ratio show that use of external resources began to intensify in 1985, but in recent years has slowed. According to data from the Bank of Guatemala's Department of Economic Studies, the domestic debt-to-GDP ratio reached a value of 23.3 in 1984, but by 1993, had dropped to 8.9; the external debt-to-GDP ratio reached 69.4 in 1985, but by 1993 had fallen to 18.9 (Table 4.3).

---

[19] The ASIES econometric model is a general equilibrium model in that private investment is treated as endogenous. If the volume of credit to the private sector is included as an exogenous variable, the results do not contribute to improvement of the statistical indicators.

Table 4.3. Interest, Savings, Credit, Investment, and Debt Rates, 1979–93
(Percentages)

	(1)	(2)	(3)	(4)	(5)	(6)	(7)	(8)
1979	11.0	7.3	–2.0	6.0	15.5	13.6	8.4	13.5
1980	10.8	6.7	–0.6	5.8	16.2	10.5	10.8	13.4
1981	11.5	8.0	–0.1	4.8	16.6	8.9	16.2	16.1
1982	13.9	8.2	–0.1	3.8	17.2	8.9	20.3	21.1
1983	11.7	6.7	0.0	3.0	19.9	6.6	21.9	23.7
1984	11.7	7.1	–0.4	3.1	21.3	6.7	23.3	39.9
1985	11.9	7.0	–24.4	2.1	18.9	8.8	21.6	69.4
1986	13.0	7.9	–17.8	1.5	14.8	8.1	16.8	47.8
1987	13.6	8.6	–1.4	1.8	16.1	9.7	16.5	40.4
1988	14.7	9.0	–2.1	1.5	15.9	10.5	15.8	33.8
1989	15.0	10.5	–7.3	1.3	15.2	10.6	15.4	32.6
1990	20.1	13.0	–47.6	1.0	11.7	10.3	11.9	34.1
1991	24.4	15.6	6.6	0.7	10.0	10.0	9.1	25.3
1992	26.0	14.8	0.1	0.7	12.0	12.6	8.6	21.4
1993	25.7	13.5	1.9	1.3	11.8	13.6	8.9	18.9

(1) Lending interest rate, based on the weighted average of new loans
(2) Deposit interest rate, equal to the interest paid on the annual average of savings and time deposits
(3) Real interest rate = (deposit rates) – (inflation)
(4) Domestic savings/GDP
(5) Bank credit/GDP
(6) Private investment/GDP
(7) Domestic debt/GDP
(8) External debt/GDP
Source: Calculated on the basis of: Bank of Guatemala, *Boletines Estadísticos 1979–93;* Superintendency of Banks, *Boletines de Estadísticas Bancarias 1980–93;* and Bank of Guatemala, *Estudios Económicos y Memorias de Labores 1979–92.*

Transaction Costs

Finding the cost to society for transferring resources from savers to investors, allows us to determine the economic efficiency of the financial system. These transaction costs and other indicators are evaluated below.

Intermediation Margin

The margin of financial intermediation reflects the cost associated with intermediation and its development over time. Table 4.4 shows nominal gross and net margin estimates as well as the real gross and net margin[20] for regulated financial institutions.

[20] In this context, the term 'nominal' is used to denote the difference resulting between prevailing deposit and lending rates. The term 'real' denotes the ex-post difference resulting from the amounts received and paid, as obtained from consolidated bank balance sheets. The difference between the gross and net margin is arrived at by deducting administrative costs, the cost of bank reserves, and mandatory investments.

Table 4.4. Financial System Financial Intermediation and Leveraging Margin, 1979–93
(Percentages)

	(1)	(2)	(3)	(4)	(5)	(6)	(7)	(8)	(9)
1979	3.7	9.3	5.6	1.8	0.0	7.4	–3.7	1.9	1.3
1980	4.1	9.0	6.4	1.7	0.0	8.1	–4.0	0.9	1.4
1981	3.5	9.3	6.4	1.7	0.0	8.1	–4.6	1.2	1.4
1982	5.7	11.8	5.8	2.1	0.0	7.9	–2.2	3.9	1.5
1983	5.0	8.8	5.3	1.8	0.0	7.1	–2.1	1.7	1.5
1984	4.6	8.5	5.0	1.8	0.0	6.8	–2.2	1.7	1.6
1985	4.9	9.4	4.5	1.8	0.0	6.3	–1.4	3.1	1.6
1986	5.1	10.8	4.4	2.6	0.0	7.0	–1.9	3.8	1.5
1987	5.0	10.4	4.8	2.7	0.0	7.5	–2.5	2.9	1.9
1988	5.7	10.8	4.9	2.9	0.0	7.8	–2.1	3.0	2.3
1989	4.5	11.9	5.1	3.2	0.0	8.3	–3.8	3.6	2.4
1990	7.1	16.0	6.1	4.2	0.0	10.3	–3.2	5.7	2.7
1991	8.8	24.5	5.2	5.1	0.3	10.6	–1.8	13.9	2.4
1992	12.0	19.5	6.0	5.2	0.5	11.7	0.3	7.8	2.9
1993	12.2	24.2	7.2	5.5	n.a.	12.7	–0.5	11.5	2.9

(1) Nominal gross margin = nominal lending rates—nominal deposit rates
(2) Real gross margin = interest and commissions charged—interest and commissions paid
(3) General administrative expenses/total deposits
(4) Cost of bank cash reserve/total deposits. For the cost estimate, the following formula was used: (((100–CR)*NLR)/100)–NLR, where: CR = computable reserve and NLR = nominal lending rate of banks
(5) Cost of mandatory investments of banks in the Central Bank/total deposits. The cost for banks is equal to the deposit rate less the cost refunded to banks by the Central Bank
(6) Total cost, sum of columns 3, 4 and 5
(7) Nominal net margin = nominal gross margin – total cost
(8) Real net margin = real gross margin – total cost
(9) Leveraging = (capital stock + reserves)/assets
n.a. Not available
Source: Calculated on the basis of Bank of Guatemala, *Boletines Estadísticos 1979–93;* and Office of the Superintendent of Banks, *Boletines de Estadísticas Bancarias, 1980–93.*

The nominal net margin (column 7) is negative throughout the period, except in 1992. However, the real net margin (column 8) is positive, increasing from 1985 and recording extraordinary values by the end of the period. This outcome indicates that real differential depends not only on nominal effective interest rates. Other factors such as bank reserve requirements,[21] number of operations, and commissions on (and interest received from) purchase of government securities also help establish a positive margin.

In the recent search for options to reduce the money supply, banks have been ordered to maintain high-yield investments at the Central Bank, resulting in a quasi-bank cash reserve ratio that as of 1994 amounted to 15 percent on deposits, in addition to the legally required 20 percent reserve. This provision costs banks

[21] Banks reserve rates have been decreasing on monetary deposits (which utilize checks), but they have increased on current savings deposits (passbook) and the term affecting the banks' preference for securing this type of savings.

an amount equal to the difference arrived at by subtracting deposit and lending rates from the earnings obtained.

Overhead costs also affect the net margin and fluctuate over time, due not only to the company's management efficiency, but also to such exogenous factors as the money supply and inflation. Nonetheless, a monetized economy still offers more liquidity to the financial system and therefore generates a larger volume of operations.

Financial System Leverage

This important indicator shows the ability of the system to use its own resources and those of third parties to cover liabilities. Table 4.4 (column 9) shows the leverage estimate in the Guatemalan financial system as reflected by the primary capital-to-asset ratio (share capital plus reserves, expressed as a percentage of assets). Even when the indicator has grown over time, primary capital represents a low proportion of the assets, showing a high degree of leverage.

Development and Composition of Deposits

The 1993 Annual Statistical Bulletin of the Financial System shows that deposits secured by the financial system were distributed as follows: 25.6 percent in demand deposits (withdrawable by check); 67.2 percent in passbook savings accounts; and 7.2 percent in term deposits. A slight strengthening occurred in savings deposits (at the expense of term operations) and, to a lesser degree, in demand deposits. In 1979, passbook savings deposits held a 58.4 percent share, while demand and term deposits held 27.8 and 13.8 percent shares, respectively. This trend may relate to the differentiated reserve requirements in effect until March 1990, and to the preference by savers for liquidity in times of financial uncertainty.

Intermediation Quality

This topic examines the development and characteristics of the financial sector in relation to the productive sector's requirements. It includes indicators on solvency, the yield from operations, the quality of assets, and the risks associated with operations.

Yield

The yield from operations is estimated by the rate of return on banking institution assets, taking into account the ratio between the results of the fiscal year and the productive assets, including loans, debt instruments, and equities. Table 4.5 (column 1) lists yield estimates, revealing relative stability during 1979–86 but

Table 4.5. Indicators of Administrative Efficiency and Aggregate Risk in the Banking System, 1979–93

	(1)[a]	(2)[a]	(3)[a]	(4)	(5)	(6)	(7)[a]	8[a]
1979	1.1	4.0	6.1	5.80	0.06	6.30	5.0	7.6
1980	1.2	4.5	6.1	6.39	0.07	6.41	8.3	11.9
1981	0.6	4.6	6.4	6.52	0.04	6.54	12.2	17.2
1982	0.4	4.4	6.4	7.02	0.03	7.77	10.3	14.9
1983	0.7	3.7	5.3	6.95	0.05	6.93	11.6	16.7
1984	0.8	3.5	5.0	7.47	0.06	7.54	10.6	15.2
1985	1.0	3.5	5.1	7.13	0.07	8.07	10.4	15.4
1986	1.1	3.4	5.2	6.15	0.07	7.19	6.9	10.5
1987	1.7	3.5	5.1	6.46	0.11	6.85	5.4	7.9
1988	1.9	3.6	5.4	6.11	0.11	6.68	6.3	9.5
1989	2.0	3.7	5.7	5.96	0.12	6.68	5.1	7.8
1990	3.2	4.5	6.7	4.95	0.16	5.37	3.9	5.8
1991	3.2	4.0	6.1	4.80	0.15	5.54	1.9	2.9
1992	2.8	4.6	7.1	4.69	0.13	5.52	1.6	2.5
1993	2.6	5.1	8.3	3.91	0.10	4.51	1.7	2.7

[a]Percentages
1 Fiscal year profit/earning assets
2 Overhead and administrative expenses/total assets
3 Overhead and administrative expenses/earning assets
4 Earning assets/number of main offices, branches and agencies
5 Fiscal year profit/number of main offices, branches and agencies
7 Deferred assets/total assets
8 Deferred assets/earning assets
Source: Calculated on the basis of Bank of Guatemala, *Boletines Estadísticos 1979–93;* Superintendency of Banks, *Boletines de Estadísticas;* Superintendency of Banks, Banking 1980–93.

rapid growth from 1.7 percent in 1987 to 3.2 percent in 1990 and 1991 before decreasing to 2.6 percent in 1993. This yield is rather high when compared with international indices. Comparing these indicators with those in the financial margin and their recovery since 1987 (when financial reform was introduced) demonstrates the relative importance of financial sector earnings derived from noncredit operations, such as foreign exchange transactions and the use of OMOs by the Central Bank to reduce money supplies.

Operations Efficiency

One indicator used to measure operations efficiency is the ratio between financial costs and the amount of total and productive assets. Based on information in columns 2 and 3 of Table 4.5, the degree of efficiency rose during the first years of the period, until 1986, when the trend was reversed. Another indicator is the ratio between selected headings on the balance sheet (productive assets, results, and deposits) and the number of offices open to the public (main offices, branches, subsidiaries, and agencies). This indicator shows similar results, with efficiency levels rising until the intermediate years of the period, then falling off sharply.

Table 4.6. Number of Banking Institutions and Finance Corporations, 1979–93

	(1)	(2)[a]	(3)	(4)	(5)
1979	3	14	218	72	146
1980	3	14	218	72	146
1981	4	15	218	72	146
1982	5	16	222	81	141
1983	5	16	230	79	151
1984	5	17	235	79	156
1985	5	18	230	81	149
1986	5	19	235	87	148
1987	5	19	250	87	163
1988	5	19	264	90	174
1989	5	19	269	93	176
1990	7	22	272	93	179
1991	7	23	320	119	201
1992	9	26	361	153	208
1993	11	30	428	176	252

[a] The entire period includes three state banks
(1) Finance corporations (investment banks)
(2) Commercial and mortgage banks
(3) Total banking agencies
(4) Agencies located in the Department of Guatemala
(5) Agencies located elsewhere in the country
Source: Superintendency of Banks, *Boletines de Estadísticas Bancarias, 1979–93.*

Performance during the last stage is associated with an increase in assets and a lesser increase in expenses. The last five years of the period show diminishing efficiency: operating costs rose due to the proliferation of main and branch offices, which grew by 60 percent between 1989 and 1993 (Table 4.5 [columns 4 to 6] and Table 4.6).

Overall Risk of the Financial System

Estimates of overall risk are based on deferred lending rates—the percentage ratio between loans whose principal and interest are unpaid for more than 90 days, and the amount of total and productive assets). Indicators in Table 4.5 (columns 7 and 8) show a considerable reduction in risk since 1986. Later, a restrictive monetary policy resulted in improved credit rationalization and selectivity.

Dispersion of Credit and Banking Services

Credit dispersion is used to measure access and service available to different economic actors, according to sectors and locations. Different dispersion indicators show the distribution of credit over time, as well as its amount, composition, and use. Starting in 1986, the number of banking institutions forming part of the financial system has grown steadily (see Table 4.6). Primary reasons for this

Table 4.7. Use of Financial System Credits According to Economic Sector, 1979–93
(Percentages)

	Agriculture	Manufacturing	Construction	Trade	Others	Total
1979	16.0	31.5	10.3	21.0	21.3	100.00
1980	21.6	34.1	8.8	19.0	16.5	100.00
1981	21.0	31.8	8.5	21.8	16.9	100.00
1982	19.2	32.9	7.6	22.1	18.2	100.00
1983	18.2	29.9	6.6	23.1	22.3	100.00
1984	15.6	30.1	6.9	23.3	24.2	100.00
1985	14.5	34.9	5.2	25.3	20.0	100.00
1986	13.7	30.5	6.0	31.2	18.7	100.00
1987	11.4	32.9	6.2	27.0	22.5	100.00
1988	11.9	33.5	8.6	25.9	20.1	100.00
1989	14.0	28.2	9.8	26.2	21.7	100.00
1990	12.8	26.5	7.1	27.6	26.1	100.00
1991	13.3	24.7	8.7	25.6	27.7	100.00
1992	14.0	21.0	11.3	28.9	24.8	100.00
1993	10.4	15.1	9.8	35.5	29.3	100.00

Source: Superintendency of Banks, *Boletines de Estadísticas Bancarias 1980–93.*

increase are greater liberalization of the procedures for authorizing new banks and finance corporations, low initial capital requirements for new institutions, and the financial sector's increased yield in recent years.

As to the use of credit from the financial system (Table 4.7), credit once directed toward financing agricultural and manufacturing activities has now shifted toward financing businesses and other activities, including consumer goods.

This behavior may be traced to the effects produced by liberalization of the economy and the availability of foreign exchange for increased imports.

An analysis of the guarantees (Table 4.8) indicates that the Guatemalan financial system operates chiefly with unsecured loans, followed by loans backed by mortgage guarantees and warehouse receipts. This pattern, reinforced since 1987, represents the selectivity and rationalization of credit among individuals and companies who are connected with financial institutions and whose collateral for loans is sufficient for these institutions. Companies and individual producers who lack these connections, however, not to mention the necessary mortgage guarantees, have little chance of securing credit, as the credit/collateral ratio clearly demonstrates.

The geographical distribution of credit is also a good indicator of credit dispersion in the financial system. Table 4.9 lists the percentage of credit granted in the Department of Guatemala, where more than 80 percent of all loans are concentrated. Credit assistance in the rest of a country is not available, a situation that has become more acute in recent years.

Credit distribution by totals is a basic indicator measuring the dispersion and contribution of the financial system to the operations of small businesses. Table 4.9 lists the percentage structure of the distribution of loans. Around 75 percent

Table 4.8. Types of Loan Collateral, 1979–93
(Percentages)

	Unsecured	Pledge	Mortgage	Warehouse lien	Others	Total
1979	45.8	8.6	29.4	9.5	6.7	100.0
1980	44.3	6.3	29.3	9.3	10.8	100.0
1981	35.6	6.7	30.6	13.2	13.9	100.0
1982	34.3	6.5	30.9	13.2	15.2	100.0
1983	37.1	6.7	29.3	13.8	13.0	100.0
1984	40.6	6.8	27.9	13.7	11.1	100.0
1985	43.1	6.7	25.8	15.2	9.3	100.0
1986	45.6	5.9	24.1	16.5	8.0	100.0
1987	50.1	5.5	22.4	18.1	3.9	100.0
1988	51.1	5.1	21.4	18.4	4.1	100.0
1989	50.6	4.5	23.6	17.2	4.2	100.0
1990	49.5	4.0	23.6	18.2	4.7	100.0
1991	54.3	3.9	22.8	15.5	3.4	100.0
1992	58.6	3.2	24.5	11.1	2.6	100.0
1993	60.2	2.7	25.3	9.0	2.7	100.0

Source: Superintendency of Banks, *Boletines de Estadísticas Bancarias,* 1980–93.

Table 4.9. Distribution of Credits by Geographic Destinations and Amounts, 1979–93
(Percentages)

	(1)	(2)	(3)	(4)	(5)
1979	81.6	18.4	100.0	35.0	65.0
1980	79.7	20.3	100.0	28.7	71.3
1981	80.7	19.3	100.0	27.6	72.4
1982	77.0	23.0	100.0	25.6	74.4
1983	82.7	17.3	100.0	22.4	77.6
1984	80.7	19.3	100.0	22.9	77.1
1985	86.5	13.5	100.0	22.1	77.9
1986	85.9	14.1	100.0	20.4	79.5
1987	82.4	17.6	100.0	22.8	77.2
1988	86.7	13.3	100.0	23.7	76.3
1989	81.7	18.3	100.0	24.6	75.4
1990	89.4	10.6	100.0	26.7	73.3
1991	84.0	16.0	100.0	27.5	72.6
1992	87.1	21.0	100.0	17.9	82.1
1993	85.3	14.7	100.0	14.3	85.7

(1) Loans for use in the Department of Guatemala
(2) Loans for use elsewhere in the country
(3) Total
(4) Percentage of credits under US$8,771.90
(5) Percentage of credits of US$8,771.90 or more
Source: Superintendency of Banks, *Boletines de Estadísticas Bancarias, 1980–93.*

Table 4.10. Distribution of Total Assets, Placements, and Deposits by Banks Grouped According to Size[1] in Selected Years, 1983–93
(Percentages)

	Assets			Loans and discounts			Deposits		
	1983	1988	1993	1983	1988	1993	1983	1988	1993
The three largest	31.03	33.30	30.33	31.95	33.08	29.85	34.20	35.10	32.49
The five largest[2]	47.49	45.85	42.29	49.85	44.92	41.89	51.55	49.39	44.77
The five smallest	18.58	11.62	3.07	16.15	12.33	2.57	13.91	8.82	2.85
All others	33.93	42.53	54.64	34.00	42.74	55.54	34.54	41.79	52.38

1 The size of the banks is determined on the basis of the total deposits at the end of each year. The 1993 figures do not include with the small banks two state banks in the process of liquidation, nor one private bank which, as of December 31, 1993, had been in business less than six months.
2 Except for the first three positions, held by the same banking institutions throughout the period, there is a great deal of movement in the ranking of banks according to size. For example, the banks in the fourth and fifth positions in 1983, subsequently lost them, one in the 1983–88 period and the other in 1988–93.
Source: Bank of Guatemala, *Boletines Anuales de Estadísticas del Sistema Financiero, 1983–93.*

of the total granted is made up of credits over 50,000 quetzales (US$8,800), leaving relatively little room for smaller credits. A study of credit dispersion reveals that it is excessively concentrated.[22] Over time this situation becomes even more acute and affects in particular the financing possibilities of micro-, small, and medium-sized enterprise, both for working capital as well as for investment in equipment and technology.

Structure of the Banking Industry

The indicators in Table 4.10 show that during the period under study further concentration did not occur in the banking industry. For example, the nation's three largest banks from 1983 have maintained their market share in 1993, although their importance over the last five years has diminished slightly. As a group, the five largest banks have steadily lost market share over the entire period, decreasing approximately 7 percentage points. The share of the five smallest banks in overall bank transactions fell drastically, primarily because those five banks had only recently entered the financial system (six months to two years earlier). The importance of the group of medium-sized banks is seen in their approximate 20 percent increase in market share. The number of medium-sized banking institutions rose from six in 1983, to ten in 1988, to twenty in 1993.

[22] Bank legislation does not define the concept of 'economic group.' Accordingly, credit concentration can only be measured by individuals or companies. The established limit is 20 percent of paid-in capital and bank reserves. Thus, to date, it has not been possible to determine credit concentration by consolidating the financing granted to economically related borrowers.

Disintermediation

As a result of the financial repression implicit not only in economic policy in general, but also in the regulations governing the transactions and procedures inherent in intermediation itself, the Guatemalan economy has experienced a process of bank disintermediation.[23]

To better understand this phenomenon, we have analyzed the methods used by the institutions and companies that arose during the process of bank disintermediation. Also considered are companies that conduct financial intermediation but were created under civil and commercial law,[24] and are therefore not approved, regulated, or authorized by the Monetary Board. The Superintendency of Banks neither inspects nor supervises these companies. Accordingly, they are known as unregulated finance institutions, or informal financiers. Their main features are few employees, low initial capital investment, and operations conducted with lower average amounts than the financial operations of banks. Above all, they are known for the speed, flexibility, and the ease with which they grant credit, setting only minimum requirements for real guarantees.

Interestingly, according to information provided by bank executives, a fair number of non-regulated financial companies have business relationships or ownership connections with banking institutions. They operate as parallel or "satellite" companies, providing financial services that banks were not authorized to offer until the Monetary Board's approval of Resolution No. 752-94. These unregulated credit intermediaries include commercial financiers, leasing companies (with the option to buy), financial leasing corporations, factoring and credit card companies, offshore banks, mutual funds companies,[25] and securities exchanges.

Commercial Financiers

Due to extremely low levels of financial intermediation in the regulated banking system, the demand for financial services generated commercial enterprises to finance consumer goods and small-scale investments. Besides granting credit under fiduciary guarantees, these enterprises also take mortgage guarantees and other collateral when providing financing. These enterprises are referred to as

---

[23] Bank disintermediation is the process by which financial institutions, regulated by banking laws, progressively lose significant financial market share.

[24] Unregulated financial institutions work as commercial companies provide financial intermediation services. Their legal bases are for the most part found in civil and commercial legislation, i.e., the Civil and Commercial codes, respectively.

[25] Article 2 of the Banking Law establishes the seldom used legal form of mutual funds companies that accept deposits only from members and invest them in securities or lend them to other members. These companies are exempt from the provisions of the Banking Law and have no specific legislation.

financiers to distinguish themselves from finance corporations, which are regulated and supervised by the Superintendency of Banks. Financiers attract funds through mutual debt contracts, establishing a debt by formal registration and issuing promissory notes. To a lesser extent, financiers also secure financing from domestic and foreign private sector banks. This source of funds, however, has diminished since a number of financiers began trading government bonds and debt instruments on local securities markets.

Financiers[26] grant credit from a minimum of Q1,000 (US$170) to a maximum of Q100,000 (US$16,950), depending on the collateral posted by the consumer. For unsecured loans, the general standard is to grant credit up to a certain number of times of the amount of salary or verifiable monthly income (as a rule, credits are for amounts equal to two months' salary) for terms of up to two years. For mortgage financing, the maximum credit amount is Q100,000 (US$16,950). Monthly interest rates fluctuate between 2 and 3.5 percent (October and November 1993). It should be noted that the monthly rate for mortgage financing is 2 to 2.5 percent less than the fiduciary guarantee.[27] Credit allocations are generally quite varied, although some financiers tend to specialize in consumer goods financing for the purchase of electrical home appliances, personal loans, foreign travel, personal vehicles, etc.

Financiers involved in lease/purchase and factoring operations usually work in close collaboration with one or more banks, acting as satellite companies in accord with regulations in force up to November 1993. Terms and financial conditions for leases and factoring tend to vary greatly. Longest terms generally have the lowest monthly interest rates, averaging 2.5 to 3.1 percent. Other financiers specialize in financing foreign exchange invoices, cargo and passenger transportation, and heavy and light equipment. Considering the conditions and maximum amounts used to finance small enterprises, financiers appear able to meet this sector's needs as well. The total volume of this financial intermediation (leasing and factoring) was expected to reach approximately Q500.0 million (US$84.4 million) in 1993, or 8 percent of the loan portfolio of the country's banks.

Credit Card Companies

Credit cards are an important instrument of financial intermediation,[28] a widespread method of payment that has grown remarkably in recent years. While

---

[26] Data included was calculated on the basis of interviews conducted with representatives from 14 financier companies.

[27] In recent years the inflation rate has moderated: 13.9 percent (1992) and 11.6 percent (1993), i.e., 1 percent per month.

[28] Article No. 757 of the Commercial Code defines credit cards as a contract falling under credit transactions.

credit cards are used for consumer goods, small enterprises evidently have not used them to purchase inputs. By November 1993, according to bank executives and credit card companies, three nonbank companies issued credit cards as affiliates of international banks. Twelve banks issued them in conjunction with two of the nonbank companies. Four other banks issued credit cards under direct contract with two international corporations. Thus, a total of 16 banking institutions were in the credit cards business. By October 1993, the total portfolio of all companies offering credit cards amounted to Q480 million (US$82 million), with one of the nonbank issuers establishing clear dominance by having captured more than 50 percent of the market share.

In recent years the credit card industry has grown dramatically. The number of transactions from 1989 to 1990 increased by approximately 6 percent annually. However, during the 1991–1993 period, the number shot up to an annual rate of 35 percent. The number of credit cards issued rose from 16,000 in 1982 to nearly 400,000 by 1992. Currently, there are about 700,000 transactions each month and the average credit card balance is Q1,200 (US$203). Additionally, sales through credit cards in some commercial sectors have jumped from 5 percent in 1982 to 60 percent by 1992.

"Offshore" Banks

Offshore banks, financial institutions that represent nonresident banks, are established by individuals or companies from countries that restrict foreign currency deposit and lending operations. These banks are set up in countries where tax benefits are available for their operations or where certain operations restricted by one government's monetary laws are permitted by another. Operating outside the jurisdiction of banking supervision, they can offer services in foreign currency (e.g., demand deposits, savings accounts, time deposits, and credits in foreign currency) that are prohibited to local banks by existing financial legislation. At present, most banks in the system have ownership interests in the offshore institutions, which form part of business operations of these financial groups or their corporations. Offshore bank services have been offered by foreign banks in Guatemala for several years now.

Although all the offshore banks surveyed readily acknowledged rapid growth in 1993, we were unable to obtain information on the volume of their transactions in Guatemala, chiefly because of the discretion and confidentiality under which their services are provided.

Export Companies

Export companies conduct financial intermediation operations by granting working capital to small and medium-sized growers of products like coffee, cardamon, and sugarcane. The exporter grants these credits to ensure purchase of the exportable harvest. The National Coffee Association estimates that exporters fulfill around 87 percent of the producers' financing needs (Q823.2 million, or US$142 million).

Securities Exchanges

Guatemala has three securities exchanges:[29] the Bolsa de Valores Nacional (The National Securities Exchange), which opened in 1987; the Bolsa Agrícola Nacional (the National Agricultural Exchange), established in 1992; and the Bolsa Global (Global Exchange) since 1993.[30] There are about 90 brokerage offices that trade securities on the market. Up to now, however, this market has traded exclusively with debt instruments. The operations of Guatemalan financial markets are concentrated in the following areas: (a) the primary market, (b) the secondary market, and (c) the repurchase market. Gilt-edge securities, as rated by the Securities Regulation Fund of the Bank of Guatemala, are traded on these exchanges. Other securities of lesser quality, not rated by the Securities Regulation Fund, are also traded. These securities, however, carry the implicit rights and obligations of the corporations that issue them for sale through stockbrokers. The issuing companies are seeking financing under terms more attractive than those offered by the banking sector. Unregistered securities such as promissory notes and warehouse are also traded.

The repurchase market represents 70 percent of all exchange transactions. Repurchase agreements are arrangements allowing the owner of debt securities to borrow money by selling these securities to a buyer under the promise to repurchase them on a specified date, usually within 30 days or less. The primary and secondary markets for private securities are comprised mainly of notes issued by private companies that find a "window of opportunity" on the exchange, to secure the resources needed for their investments. The terms of these issues range from 3 to 120 months, although 6 to 12 months are usual for most transactions.

Securities exchange operations have increased significantly in recent years. They have caused bank disintermediation to increase because they can offer to borrowers and investors alike more attractive interest rates and more flexible operations. Borrowers in fact were able to secure funds at a cost of three or four

---

[29] Authorities from Agrícola Nacional and Bolsa Global exchanges have announced a merger that will take effect in the first half of 1994.

[30] A law has been proposed to regulate the securities market. In the meantime, the Ministry of Economy has authorized, on the basis of the Commercial Code, the operation of the three securities exchanges. The Ministry has approved the internal regulations and the independent auditors whose reports and other information may be required for submission. It would appear that up to now that self-regulation has worked reasonably well and has been sufficient.

points below the average bank lending rate (30 percent in November 1993). Investors, on the other hand, received a rate up to twelve points higher than that offered by banks (13 percent in November 1993). During the 1993–93 fiscal period, for example, 90 companies secured funds of around Q441.0 million (US$75 million) on the primary market. Those funds represent 4 percent of all securities traded on the country's principal exchanges and approximately 25 percent of all credits granted by the banking system during the same period.

Clearly, securities exchanges have become a strong force in the process of bank disintermediation. They have reduced the demand for credit from the regulated financial system, especially banks. Accordingly, banks will now be forced to find new consumers of credit. Micro-, small, and medium-sized businesses could very well become an important sector for funds at banks.

Conclusions and Policy Recommendations

Guatemala's macroeconomic policies during the period of serious monetary and fiscal disequilibria assigned monetary policy an excessive role in correcting these imbalances. The same policies had a negative impact on the formal financial sector, which became far less important in generating gross domestic product. Monetary restrictions reduced the volume of bank deposits and drove up the cost of intermediation, making operations less efficient and intensifying the concentration of credit.

Against the backdrop of the macroeconomic policies of recent decades and legislation governing them, the financial system has operated under severe financial repression. On the one hand, this repression led to banking disintermediation: many transactions and operations not permitted to banks were conducted by companies and institutions that emerged in the unregulated market. On the other hand, financial repression caused the services of the formal system to be absorbed by fewer economic sectors. Accordingly, the formal system was hindered in reaching groups of small producers, that were unable to take advantage of its financial services.

The Guatemalan financial market clearly suffers from a number of distortions in the cost and nature of its financial services. Generally speaking, cost levels in the formal system are substantially lower than those in informal market. Nonetheless, strict requirements in the formal market make credit more expensive and impede financial assistance to sectors that lack real collateral. Thus, the formal financial system has had no meaningful role in providing financial services to small enterprise. A number of state-run programs and other efforts to provide financial assistance to these enterprises have also failed, due to administrative incompetence or to financial and contractual conditions out of line with market standards. Loan delinquencies were common and delays in the recovery of credits were experienced. Furthermore, the credit distribution structure of banks and finance corporations is highly concentrated around a small percentage of consumers whose credit requirements far exceed that of the average amount granted by the system.

The most recent phenomenon in financial markets is the emergence of secu rities exchanges. Large companies now satisfy their financing demands by placing securities on these exchanges. This new development is now a major cause of large-scale bank disintermediation. To replace the demand that has now shifted to the securities exchanges, banks will need to adapt their loan portfolios to the size of the consumer.

Finally, the Guatemalan financial system is undergoing modernization to update its regulatory framework, increase market transparency, and streamline the conditions for cash inflows and outflows. The aims of this modernization are to diversify the products and services offered by financial institutions, promote competition, and develop forms of supervision that will strengthen the liquidity, solvency, and soundness of the system's institutions.

Recommendations

Our policy recommendations fall into three groups. The first group, general in nature, is aimed at managing macroeconomic policy. The second group sets forth specific recommendations related to further liberalization of the formal financial system, with favorable implications for the dispersion of financial services. The third group comprises policies aimed at expanding the access of small, enterprises to the services of the financial system.

The goal of these recommendations is to initiate a process to liberalize the formal financial system and greatly increase its services to the currently underserved small enterprise sector. The recommendations are also intended to stimulate organization of the informal market and promote its participation in the Guatemalan financial market with a view to expanding access to financial services.

General Recommendations

- Measures designed to expand access to financial services need the support of a coherent and constant economic policy aimed at controlling or eliminating the causes of macroeconomic disequilibria, especially those of a monetary or fiscal origin. Such a policy would contribute to creating an environment of stability and making market forces more transparent. The price system would become competitive and operate in a depersonalized environment. Higher standards of competency and a regulatory framework that allocates resources on the basis of price, risk, and nature of projects would be established, with professional supervision, to promote the financial system's solvency, soundness, and liquidity.

- The connections of small entrepreneurs to institutions in the regulated financial system are ineffective or nonexistent at present. We believe that the services of these institutions should be tailored to the characteristics of this demand in order to facilitate access to formal financial services. Monetary authorities as well as the financial system should launch a campaign to advertise the requirements and procedures needed to access their services.
- Capital and money markets (securities exchanges) should continue to be developed and strengthened. Placement of debt securities on this market by big business reduces demand for bank financing and forces regulated institutions to look for new customers, including smaller entrepreneurs. As for the Guatemalan securities exchanges, we recommend promulgation of the Securities Market Law to ensure better and more orderly development of the market.

Specific Recommendations Related to the Financial System

- Efforts to modernize the financial system and to liberalize it both domestically and externally should continue. Accordingly, we recommend abolishing the bank classification system established under current legislation (commercial bank, mortgage bank, or investment bank, and a commercial and mortgage bank) and paving the way legally to a full banking system. Regional financial integration should be accelerated, as a mechanism to develop and increase competition. Authorizing banks to conduct operations in foreign currency will reduce or eliminate the unsupervised activities of offshore banks.
- The role of the Central Bank and the composition of the monetary authorities should be reexamined in order to allow those authorities to become autonomous and independent. Additionally, the Superintendency of Banks' functions should be clearly defined with a view to strengthening its supervisory duties.
- Policies aimed at strengthening financial institutions' freedom to diversify the financial services they offer to the public should continue to be applied within a supervisory framework that will maintain the solvency, soundness, and liquidity of the entire financial system. For example, attention should be called to the advantages that could be gained by allowing banks in the system to ease restrictions on credit amounts based on a percentage of the collateral offered.
- The legislation governing financial institutions should be amended to reduce or eliminate the paternalistic spirit contained in current legislation

concerning the responsibility for maintaining the solvency and soundness of financial institutions. The legislation enabling the monetary authorities to bail out ailing institutions should be repealed and a deposit insurance system should instituted. Financial supervisors should also draw up clear and concise regulations for classifying portfolios and analyzing risks. Warning mechanisms that allow self-regulation and timely intervention by the supervisory authority should be established. Above all, no financial service or institution involved in financial intermediation should be allowed to go unsupervised. Supervisory authorities, however, should refrain from acquiring repressive characteristics that would stimulate the informal market.

Specific Recommendations for Financial Market Access by Small Businesses

- In view of the unmet demand for financial services by micro, small, and medium-sized enterprise, we recommend that (within the framework of the subsidiary role of the State) the public sector restructure and reorganize its financial institutions in order to redefine its function in the context of a modern financial system. It should also work to establish equality of operating conditions among these institutions and those of the private sector.
- Mechanisms for funnelling domestic savings from the formal system to smaller entrepreneurs need to be designed and put into place. Additionally, those institutions that have emerged to provide credit to small, enterprises should be brought into the formal financial system. Accordingly, we recommend the drafting of a body of legislation that would define administrative and accounting procedures, rules, and standards for financial supervision, as well as other requirements by which future institutions will be regulated.

Informal financial organizations, like NGOs, cooperatives, and community credit associations, which have channeled credit to small enterprises, could constitute a stratum within the financial system whose operations would be excluded from the direct supervision of the Superintendency of Banks. Instead, these organizations, along with new credit intermediaries that may later emerge (e.g., community banks, rural funds, savings and loan associations, mutual insurance associations or companies, mutual funds, etc.) could be governed by special financial supervisory regulations and procedures that would ensure the financial soundness of their operations.

For these reasons, the participation of NGOs, as well as regional, local, or community organizations dedicated to providing credit services (as well as regional, local, and community organizations) should be encouraged to act as credit intermediaries. Financial institutions in the system should act as second-tier banks, arranging resources for those credit intermediaries that would assume the operational risks vis-à-vis the banks, and in turn provide financial services to small users.

- Some NGOs have been quite successful in channeling credit to micro-, small, and medium-sized entrepreneurs. Encouraging the formation of more such organizations and promoting financial intermediation by regional, local, and indigenous community associations, would build on this success.
- The small business sector's demand for financial services and the credit it receives, should continue to be analyzed in greater detail. Existing legislation should be revised to improve the opportunities for small entrepreneurs to become eligible credit recipients.
- Finally, we propose the design of an organization that could issue reciprocal financial guarantees through contributions from its members and consumers. These users' organizations could post bonds or collateral to back operations for which they wish to receive credit. Such guarantees would foster greater trust between small credit consumers and financial institutions.

Bibliography

ALIDE. 1989. *Las Perspectivas para el Desarrollo Económico de América Latina y el Papel de sus Instituciones Financieras de Fomento.* Brazil ALIDE.

Alonzo M., and A. Bonilla. 1990. *La Política Monetaria como Mecanismo de Ajuste de la Balanza de Pagos de Guatemala.* Guatemala City.

Asociación de Investigación y Estudios Sociales (ASIES). 1990. *Compartiendo Costos y Beneficios, Lineamientos de Estrategia para el Desarrollo Social y Económico 1991–1995.* Guatemala City: ASIES, pp. 51 et seq.

_______. 1993. *Investigación Básica sobre Derecho Consuetudinario en tres Comunidades Mayahablantes de Guatemala, Informe final.* Guatemala City: ASIES, January.

_______. 1992. *Modelo Econométrico de la Economía de Guatemala.* Guatemala City: ASIES.

Bank of Guatemala. *Boletín Estadístico.* Various Issues 1979–1992. Guatemala City: BANGUAT.

_______. *Boletín Informativo.* Various Issues 1979–1992. Guatemala City: BANGUAT.

_______. *Estudio Económico y Memoria de Labores.* Various Issues 1979–1992. Guatemala City: BANGUAT.

_______. 1992. *El Sistema Financiero Guatemalteco: Propuestas para su Modernización.* Guatemala City: BANGUAT.

_______. 1981. *Leyes Bancarias y Financieras de Guatemala,* 8th Edition. Guatemala City: BANGUAT.

Botrán Díaz, Alejandro. 1993. *Banca Privada Especializada en el Desarrollo del Microempresario.* Guatemala City: Universidad Francisco Marroquín.

CIEN. 1990. *Propuesta de Reforma del Sistema Financiero Nacional.* Guatemala City: CIEN.

De Gregorio, J. 1992."Economic Growth in Latin America." *Journal of Economic Development.*

de Melo J., and J. Tybout. 1985. *The Effect of Financial Liberation on Saving and Investment in Uruguay. Economic Development and Cultural Change,* Vol. 34.

_______. 1994. *Suplemento Económico PULSO,* Tuesday, February 15, 1994, pp. 10–11. Guatemala City.

Diario Siglo Veintiuno. 1993. *Informe Especial,* October 28–29, 1993. Guatemala City.

Díaz, Alejandro C.F. 1985."Good-Bye Financial Repression, Hello Financial Crash." *Journal of Development Economics* 19:1–24.

Dornbush, R. 1990. "Policies to Move from Stabilization to Growth," *Proceedings of the World Bank Annual Conference on Development Economics:* 19–48.

Federación de la Pequeña y Mediana Empresa Guatemalteca (FEPYME). 1992. *"La Pequeña Empresa en Guatemala."* Guatemala City. Mimeo.

Fundación para el Desarrollo Integral de Programas Socioeconómicos (FUNDAP)/ Asistencia Técnica Internacional (AT Internacional). 1993. *Reunión Consultiva Iniciativa para los Productores de Pequeña Escala en Centroamérica (IPECA).* Antigua, Guatemala: FUNDAP/AT Internacional.

GENESIS Empresarial. 1992. *Evolución y Resultados. Reporte 1988/1992.* Guatemala City: GENESIS Empresarial.

Goldsmith, R. 1969. *Financial Structure and Development.* New Haven: Yale University Press.

International Monetary Fund. 1991. *Financial Liberalization, Money Demand and Monetary Policy in Asian Countries.* Washington, D.C.: IMF.

_______. 1990. *Recent Developments in Financial Regulation and Market Structure.* Washington, D.C.: IMF.

King, R., and R. Levine. 1992. "Financial Indicators and Growth in a Cross Section of Countries." WPS 819 Working Paper. Washington, D.C.: World Bank.

Long, Millard, and Eirik Evenhouse. 1989. "La Reestructuración de Sistemas Financieros en Dificultades." In *Finanzas y Desarrollo.*

Lorente, Miguel A. 1980. *El Marco Económico del Sistema Financiero.* Ed. Hispano Europea.

Lüders, Rolf. 1979. "La Regulación Financiera: Concentración, Economías de Escala y la Multibanca en Chile." Revista FELABAN No. 36.

McKinnon, R. 1973. *Money and Capital in Economic Development.* Washington, D.C.: Brookings Institution.

Marshall, Enrique. 1991. *El Sistema Financiero y El Mercado de Valores en Chile.* Mexico City: Ed. CEMLA.

Martínez Neira, Nestor H. 1992. "Reforma Financiera de la Post-Crisis en América Latina: De las libertades y la Regulación Prudencial." Estudio presentado en el Seminario Hacia un Mercado Común en las Américas: Retos y Oportunidades para las Instituciones Financieras, organizado por la FIBA y FELABAN. Miami, Fla., USA.

Morris, Felipe. 1989. "Ajuste Estructural en América Latina y Reforma a los Sistemas Financieros: La Regulación y Supervisión de las Filiales Bancarias." Washington, D.C.: World Bank. Mimeo.

Recinos, R. 1992. "La Política Monetaria en Guatemala: Un Análisis de su Impacto Interno y Externo." *Banca Central* No. 15, Year IV.

Secretaría General del Consejo Nacional de Planificación Económica. 1988. *Proyecciones de Población Urbana y Rural por Región y Departamento 1980–2000.* Guatemala City: SEGEPLAN.

Secretaría Técnica del Programa Nacional de Microempresa y Pequeña Empresa (SIMME). 1992. *Resultados de la Evaluación de las Microempresas y Pequeñas Empresas atendidas en 1992 por las ONGs que participan en el Programa Nacional de Microempresas y Pequeñas Empresas.* Guatemala City: SIMME.

_______. 1991. *Reglamento de crédito para el fondo de préstamo a las ONGs.* Guatemala City: SIMME.

Shaw, E. 1973. *Financial Deepening in Economic Development.* New York: Oxford University Press.

Sistema Nacional de Garantía Crediticia y Corporación de Retrogarantía de Ecuador. 1989. *Sistema Nacional de Garantía Crediticia.* Quito.

Superintendencia de Bancos de Guatemala. *Memoria de Labores.* Various issues, 1979–1992. Guatemala City.

_______. *Boletín de Estadísticas Bancarias.* Various Issues, 1979–1992. Guatemala City.

Villegas, Boneo et al. 1984. *Contratos Bancarios Modernos.* Buenos Aires: Editorial Abeledo Perrot.

World Bank. *Informe sobre el Desarrollo Mundial 1989. Los Sistemas Financieros y el Desarrollo.* Washington, D.C: World Bank.

APPENDIX

MODERNIZATION PROGRAM FOR THE DOMESTIC FINANCIAL SYSTEM

Summary of policies, objectives and measures pursuant to JM Resolution 647–93 of September 22, 1993.

OBJECTIVES

—Establish legal and regulatory framework and implement a financial policy that promotes growth and development in an environment of monetary and price stability.

—Implement a financial supervision policy that allows banking institutions to diversify their products and services, thereby increasing their opportunities in the market and allowing greater domestic and international competition.

—Develop instruments and mechanisms through prudential regulations, with institutions having a preventive and self-regulatory focus for monitoring the solvency and soundness of the financial system.

—Ensure a legal, regulatory, and policy framework of financial supervision that modernizes and strengthens the capacity of the Superintendency of Banks to participate, prevent, and intervene in a timely manner to remedy situations or practices that may endanger the liquidity, solvency, or soundness of financial institutions.

		RESOLUTION No.	DATE
1.	**MONETARY STABILITY**		
1.1	**Macroeconomic policy**		
	—Maintain economic growth with monetary stability		
1.2	Monetary policy		
	—Approve legislation on liberalizing interest rates		
	—Establish market terms and interest rates for credit provided to the government		Nov.[31] 1993
	—Gradually reduce bank reserve requirements in order to promote financial intermediation		
	—The Time Certificates of Deposit of the Central Bank may be traded on the securities market	JM 482	Oct. 1992
	—Weekly report on bank deposit & lending rates	JM 572-92	Dec. 1992
1.3	**Credit policy**		
	—Limit or prohibit Central Bank credit operations		Nov. 1993
	—Swap of central government domestic debt for Central Bank external debt		
	—Market interest rates for state-owned financial institutions and trusts	MF 694-93	Nov.[32] 1993
1.4	**Exchange policy**		
	—Improve the market orientation of the legal mechanism now in force (public sales of foreign exchange)	JM 202, 203, 204, 205, 206-94	March 1994
	—Eliminate the principle of concentrating foreign exchange at the Central Bank		
	—Regulate financial intermediation in foreign currency		
1.5	**Central Bank autonomy and restructuring**		
	—Strengthen the autonomy of the central bank system and financial supervision		
	—Restructure the Central Bank		
2.	**FINANCIAL LIBERALIZATION AND DIVERSIFICATION OF BANK PRODUCTS AND SERVICES**		
2.1	**Banking operations**		
	—Banks may conduct operations not expressly provided by legislation in order to diversify its products and services	JM 752-93	Nov. 1993
	—Work for legal reform of other prohibited operations		
	—Facilitate acquisition of company shares by banking institutions	JM 715-93	Oct. 1993
	—Modernize interbank compensation procedures		
	—Encourage transition to full service banking		

[31] Central Bank credit operations will remain restricted until the constitutional reforms approved by referendum enter into force in January 1994.

[32] Government resolution issued through the Ministry of Public Finance.

		RESOLUTION No.	DATE
	—Authorize interest payments on cash deposit accounts	JM 500-92	Oct. 1992
	—Expand the schedule of service hours to the public at banks		
	—Facilitate mergers between banking institutions	JM 703-93	Oct. 1993
	—Encourage acquisition of shares between banking institutions	JM 715-93	Oct. 1993
	—Expedite approval of the establishment of agencies of banks already established	JM 703-93	Oct. 1993
2.2	**Conditions for entry**		
	—Simplify and streamline the authorization process for new banking institutions		
	—Define minimum amounts of capital	JM 737-93	Oct. 1993
	needed to begin operations	JM 738-03	Oct. 1993
2.3	**External liberalization**		
	—Support, through symmetrical and harmonious criteria, signing of the Central American Financial Integration Agreement		
	—Establish conditions that allow and favor the opening of Guatemalan bank branches and agencies outside Central America		
3.	**STRENGTHENING OF PRUDENTIAL STANDARDS**		
3.1	**Credit risk, solvency, and bank soundness**		
	—Regulate minimum capital requirements in accordance with risk level	JM 176-94	Feb. 1994
	—Regulate valuation of credit assets and determination and classification of doubtful recovery assets	SB 20-92[33]	Dec. 1992
	—Prohibit, limit, or regulate operations with directors, officials, and employees or with connected individuals in order to avoid favoritism		
	—Regulate operations with accounts of foreign origin and trust operations		
	—Streamline banking investment rules	JM 122-94	Jan. 1994
3.2	**Ailing bank institutions**		
	—Set strict deadline limits for replacement of equity in banks with insufficient capital	JM 768-93	Nov. 1993
	—Revoke Decree 7-72 that authorizes to the Monetary		
	—Board to recapitalize insolvent financial institutions		
	—Draft legislation to insure the funds of small depositors		

---

[33] Regulations issued by the Superintendency of Banks.

		RESOLUTION No.	DATE
4.	**MODERNIZATION OF FINANCIAL SUPERVISION**		
4.1	**Information and supervision**		
	—Determine the financial and credit portfolio information that banks should disseminate	JM 567-92	Dec. 1992
	—Introduce a basis for a bank accounting system with internationally acceptable standards that include accounting treatment of delinquency, refinancing, and other matters	JM 782-93	Nov. 1993
	—Determine that changes in ownership and management are reported to the SB and the KM in a timely fashion		
4.2	**Redefinition and reorganization of Superintendency of Banks**		
	—Ensure operational independence of Superintendency of Banks		
	—Develop and implement a modernization plan for the Superintendency of Banks	JM 843-93	Dec. 1993
4.3	**Implementation of a new set of financial supervision regulations**		
	—Study and, if necessary, reformulate the prudential standards adopted by the JM in 1992 as part of the financial modernization program,		
5.	**REGULATION OF SECURITIES AND CAPITAL MARKETS**		
5.1	**Draft the respective bill**		

CHAPTER FIVE

PERU: CONSOLIDATING FINANCIAL REFORM

Julio Velarde
Martha Rodríguez

This chapter has two main objectives. The first is to analyze how the stabilization and structural reform program implemented in August 1990 affected Peru's financial sector, and the second is to analyze the problems that the small business sector has encountered in obtaining credit.

The chapter is divided into seven sections. In the first, the current macroeconomic environment is analyzed, as are the most important measures included in the recent economic program. The second section describes the Peruvian financial system and its institutional framework. In the third section the historic evolution of the financial system is examined, while in the fourth the more recent performance of commercial banks is studied. The outlook for the financial sector and the growth of the financial markets are examined in the fifth section. The sixth section discusses the credit availability problems experienced by small businesses, and the last presents the conclusions and recommendations of this study.

The Macroeconomic Environment

Economic Growth Before 1990

Until the late fifties, the Peruvian economy, unlike that of other South American countries, experienced fairly steady growth in an open market context with minimal government involvement. Between 1950 and 1960, economic activity grew at an average rate of 5.7 percent annually, with average inflation of 6.3 percent (Table 5.1).

Although legislation to promote industry was enacted in 1959, an import substitution strategy was not adopted until a new government took office in 1963. This process, which was initiated with considerable caution, became extremely intense during the period of military rule between 1968 and 1980. During this period the National Register of Manufactures was established, whereby any imports that competed with national industry were prohibited, and government intervention was extended to nearly all economic activities. At the same time, not only was agrarian reform undertaken, but a broad range of sectors and businesses was nationalized, comprehensive price controls were imposed, and rules were introduced that led to near total labor stability.

Inflation, which had hovered at single-digit levels in prior years, began to climb as a result of expansive policies in a context of increasing macroeconomic distortions. By the time the military government left office, inflation was high, and the country had entered a phase of severe economic stagnation.

Between 1980 and 1985, several efforts were made to reverse this trend, most of which were neutralized by the external debt crisis. At the end of the period, inflation was still on the rise. In July 1985, the presidency was assumed by Alan García, a left-of-center leader who instituted a populist economic policy. During his presidency, between 1985 and 1990, the country experienced not only the longest and most intense inflationary process in its history, but also its worst recession (Table 5.1).

The hyperinflation in Peru during this period was caused by the pursuit of expansive policies in a context of controlled prices. Public service rates were frozen and a multiple exchange system was introduced. Moreover, the real interest rate was extremely negative, so that some prime rates were on the order of –95 percent per annum. Inflation reached 114 percent in September 1988. After that, inflation remained steady at a monthly average of about 30 percent.

Two stages in economic policy are discernible in the first quarter of 1990. Because of the nearness of the elections, an expansive policy was applied at first. Then, once the elections were over and it was no longer possible to sustain the disequilibria generated, the authorities adopted a tight money policy to prevent an inflationary explosion before the change of government. Thus, a policy of crowding out the private sector, postponing public price adjustments, and deferring government payments was pursued.

Until July 1990, owing to a marginal cash reserve of 80 percent and postponement of the reserve replenishment payment, real effective interest rates were extremely high. This situation eroded the financial position of businesses and of the banking system in general.

Moreover, the pronounced lags in the official exchange rate and in public prices became intolerable and necessitated a change in economic policy that would bring about high, corrective inflation.[1]

---

[1] See Velarde and Rodríguez (1992) and World Bank (1989).

Table 5.1. Trend of Several Macroeconomic Variables, 1950–93

(Percentage rates of growth, in five-year and annual averages)

	1950–55	1956–60	1961–65	1966–70	1971–75	1976–80	1981–85	1986–90	1991	1992	1993[a]
GDP	6.19	5.18	6.18	4.40	4.99	2.56	–0.40	–1.92	2.45	–2.91	7.0
Inflation	6.49	6.22	5.64	9.43	13.55	54.91	105.58	972.48	139.20	56.70	39.6
Exports	6.68	1027	6.35	4.18	–1.43	7.73	1.02	–4.84	–1.72	–1.33	2.9

[a]Preliminary.

Source: National Institute of Statistics and Computerized Information (INEI), *Compendio Estadístico del Perú*, 1992–93.

The Economic Program of August 1990

The new government that took office at the end of July 1990 instituted a stabilization plan on August 8 and began a series of ambitious structural reforms.

The key component of the adjustment program was closing the fiscal gap by indexing public prices and establishing a number of emergency taxes. The magnitude of the adjustment is well illustrated by the fact that fuel prices increased 34 times.[2]

In addition, the exchange rate was unified by establishing a managed float system. Monetary policy attempted to remonetize the economy through foreign exchange purchases in the interbank market.

The basic objective of the structural reforms was to deregulate markets. Quasitariff restrictions were eliminated and tariffs were lowered and reduced in number, so that by March 1991 there were only two rates of 15 and 25 percent. Most tariff and tax exemptions were also eliminated.

The labor market was made more flexible by eliminating some of the impediments to unrestricted hiring and dismissal practices. Several of the restrictions affecting the agricultural real estate market were lifted, the transportation and port administration department was deregulated, and an ambitious process of privatizing public enterprises was initiated.

Reform of the Financial System

In the financial sector, interest rates were decontrolled, ceilings were kept well above those in the market, and in March 1991 the interest rates for foreign currency transactions were deregulated. In addition, the capital account of the balance of payments was completely liberalized, the requirement of selling foreign exchange from exports to the Central Bank was eliminated, and the freedom to hold and dispose of foreign exchange was guaranteed.

In July 1991 a new Banking Law entered into force, establishing full-service banking and strengthening the supervisory role of the Superintendency of Banks and Insurance Companies (SBS).

As far as monetary policy is concerned, a substantial change occurred when the Central Bank, for the first time in many years, established an active policy and cut off credit to the government, exercising the autonomy granted it by law. As a result, the development bank, which had subsisted for years on Central Bank funds, entered a period of drastic decline that ended with its eventual closing.

It should be pointed out that in Peru, financial deregulation, both in the domestic market and in the foreign capital account, was carried out almost simulta-

---

[2] See Velarde and Rodríguez (1992a).

neously with the stabilization plan, through trade liberalization and the partial deregulation of factor markets.[3]

The Financial Sector and Its Institutional Framework

Historic Evolution

Since the creation of reserve banks in 1850–1860, the Peruvian financial system has undergone some significant changes.

Several banks were severely affected by the crisis in the 1930s, and some even failed. It was at this juncture that the government requested the sending of the Kemmerer Mission, which prepared a monetary and banking reform project. This project called for the creation of a Central Reserve Bank, based on the former Reserve Bank, in April 1931. The first Banking Law was also promulgated and the Superintendency of Banks was created, both in May 1931.[4]

The plan developed for Peru did not differ significantly from the ones proposed in other countries assisted by the Kemmerer Mission.[5] The Banking Law was liberal in inspiration, limiting banking to a strictly commercial role, i.e., operations were restricted to periods of less than one year.

The same law, although slight amended over the years, remained in force until the late 1970s. At that point, most of the regional banks that had opened with small capital requirements entered into crisis, which led many of them to close or merge.

In response to this crisis, and with a view to modernizing the banking sector, in 1968, at the end of the first Belaúnde administration, a rule was established prohibiting the creation of new commercial banks pending the enactment of a new Banking Law. This provision was ratified early in the military regime, which was in power from 1968 to 1980. During this period, the prohibition was broadened to include the opening of branches and agencies, although the founding of construction banks (commercial banks of a sectoral nature) and financial enterprises was permitted.

The Banking Law was not promulgated during the military regime's tenure of government. Moreover, the policy concerning the financial sector was decidedly interventionist. The role of state financial institutions was strengthened, certain banks that were experiencing difficulties were absorbed into the state system, and some foreign-owned banks were nationalized. Commercial banks were

---

[3] See Velarde and Rodríguez (1992b).

[4] See Bardella (1990).

[5] See Tamagna (1963).

subject to regulations that became increasingly complicated with respect to the allocation of their resources. The military regime not only made it mandatory to convert foreign currency deposits to local currency, it also compelled the opening of the safety deposit boxes of the banks' customers.

Restrictions were also placed on loans to foreign companies, and all public enterprises (including those recently nationalized) were required to keep their deposits in Banco de la Nación, the financial agent of the state. At the same time, commercial banks were required to deposit additions to their reserve funds in Banco de la Nación.

Increasingly, banks were able to make fewer choices about how to lend their funds: commercial banks headquartered in Lima had to loan at least 60 percent of any increase in their loan portfolio to sectors specified by the government.[6]

All of these interventionist measures occurred against the backdrop of interest rate controls, and even caps on officers' salaries, imposed by the government. Amid these circumstances, no new banks opened, not only because of the express prohibition against it, but also because the prevailing conditions were not conducive to the growth of the sector.

This situation began to change in the late seventies. In 1979, financial leasing operations were authorized. In 1981, finance companies were authorized to conduct certain short-term operations, and the opening of new banks was again permitted. At the same time, exercising a series of powers conferred by Congress, the government that year promulgated the new Organic Law of the Superintendency of Banks and the new charters of Banco de la Nación (founded in 1966), Banco Agrario (agricultural bank founded in 1931), Banco Industrial (industrial bank founded in 1936), Banco Minero (mining bank founded in 1942), Banco de la Vivienda (housing bank founded in 1962), and Banco Hipotecario (mortgage bank founded in 1929).

Moreover, interest rates were gradually raised to mirror inflation, and the reserve requirements were lowered for deposits in local currency and in foreign currency (which had been authorized in 1978). As a result of this deregulation of interest rates, some banks that had excessively concentrated their credits on companies with ties to the banks' owners began to experience difficulties. In 1981 Banco de la Industria de la Construcción and Financiera Andina were placed under government control, as were Banco Comercial and Financiera Comercial in 1982.

These institutions were then liquidated, with the government assuming responsibility for the payment of all deposits. Later, because of similar problems, Banco del Sur Medio y Callao was placed under administration and subsequently taken over by Banco de la Nación. The remaining banks also experienced difficulties due to the erosion of their respective loan portfolios in the wake of the

---

[6] See De la Melena (1973).

steep decline in GDP in 1983 (–13 percent), the contraction of external credit, and the sharp real devaluation that began to occur.

These initial liberalization efforts were interrupted at the start of the APRISTA administration in July 1985. Once again, interest rates began to be controlled, remittances of profits and the payment of credits abroad were prohibited, the mandatory conversion of dollar deposits to local currency was instituted, sectoral loan portfolio quotas were imposed, different reserve ratios were established depending on where deposits were received, and the funds collected in these areas could not be invested in the capital. Development banks were reactivated through the diversion of enormous amounts of Central Bank resources, and a number of development loans were granted at a zero nominal interest rate in a context of mounting inflation.

The high point of state intervention during this period occurred in July 1987 when the Law on Nationalization of the Financial System was promulgated. Although this law was never fully enforced owing to its repeal in November 1990, it promoted the growth of informal banking, which, given the existence of controlled interest rates, came to represent a large percentage of the financial intermediation.

Added to these factors were the extremely high reserve requirements, ever increasing loan portfolio quotas and the obligation to purchase growing volumes of Treasury bonds.

However, the factor that most affected the financial system during this period was the hyperinflationary process that lasted from August 1988 to July 1990, which was the longest such period in the world since the episode in Russia in the 1920s.

Fortunately, unlike other hyperinflationary processes, the physical structure of the Peruvian banking system did not expand rapidly. As hyperinflationary experiences in other parts of the world demonstrate, the number of bank offices increases disproportionately with a view to taking advantage of the enormous financial margins, so that after stabilization, operating costs are greater than potential margins, forcing many institutions into bankruptcy.[7] In Peru, due to the Bank Nationalization Law and the fact that banks pay interest on checking account deposits, this type of growth did not occur.

Even so, hyperinflation had a number of negative effects on the Peruvian financial sector. As might be expected, real liquidity in local currency decreased substantially. This also meant that the fall of quasimoney was greater than that of money, and in the case of the latter, demand deposits contracted more than the money supply. This process of disintermediation led to a greater turnover of deposits, which increased the banks' operating costs. In addition, banknotes quickly lost their real value, raising the banks' transaction costs.

---

[7] See, for example, Dornbusch (1987) and Keynes (1924).

Condition of the Financial System in August 1990

Prior to the current government's economic program, Peru had three state financial institutions: the Central Bank, Banco de la Nación, and COFIDE. There were four development banks (Industrial, Mining, Agricultural, and Housing), one state mortgage bank, seven public commercial banks (associated banking), 13 private commercial banks, and eight financial enterprises. There were also 16 mutual savings and loan banks, the Savings Bank of Lima (Caja de Ahorros de Lima) and other institutions such as municipal banks and savings and credit cooperatives. Two stock exchanges operated: one in Lima, established in 1860, and the other in Arequipa. In addition, there was an active trading board where bonds, bills of exchange, repurchases, swaps, and the like were traded.

The banking system as a whole comprised a network of 2,100 offices and around 50,000 employees. Despite the relatively high number of institutions, there was little competition. Within the banking system, Banco de la Nación held a third of the deposits, while in commercial banking, the largest bank (Banco de Crédito) had a third of the loans.

Similarly, the concentration of credit was fairly pronounced: in 1990 it was estimated that 2 percent of the borrowers accounted for 54 percent of the credit,[8] which was in turn contracting in real terms because of the acute process of financial disintermediation occurring at that time (Table 5.2). In terms of both deposits and loans, the state's participation was predominant: Banco de la Nación and the development bank handled 40.9 percent of the credit granted to the private sector.

The condition of the financial system in July 1990 was fairly critical. The development banks were running cumulative losses greater than their assets and had become almost entirely dependent on the funds provided by the Central Bank. Macroeconomic instability, interest rate controls, and high reserve requirements had adversely affected private banking.

Government intervention in the allocation of credit was excessive. Not only were vast sums being channeled to the development bank, but sectoral and regional loan portfolio quotas were being set for private commercial banks. The government also owned various commercial banks and finance companies.

In addition, the institutional and regulatory framework within which the financial sector operated was inadequate, and banking supervision was deficient.

Until the 1980s, the Superintendency had functioned more or less satisfactorily, although in later years the institution became politicized, resulting in the retirement of a large number of career officers.

---

[8] See IMF (1991).

Table 5.2. Intermediation Coefficients and Financial Saving, 1966–93
(As a percentage of GDP)

	1966	1970	1975	1980	1985	1990	1991	1992	1993[a]
1. Total financial saving[1]	10.3	9.8	10.3	9.6	12.6	3.6	5.8	7.9	9.8
L/C financial saving	8.3	8.9	10.1	5.5	4.1	1.4	1.6	2.0	1.6
F/C financial saving	2.0	0.9	0.2	4.1	8.5	2.2	4.2	5.9	8.2
2. Money[2]	8.9	9.8	10.7	6.8	4.2	1.9	1.6	2.1	2.0
3. Total liquidity (1+2)3	19.2	19.6	21	16.4	16.8	5.5	7.4	10.0	11.9
L/C liquidity	17.1	18.9	20.9	12.2	8.1	3.0	3.2	4.0	3.7
F/C liquidity	2.1	0.7	0.1	4.2	8.7	2.5	4.2	6.0	8.2

[a]Preliminary.
[1]Total deposits in the financial system, except demand deposits.
[2]Money supply plus demand deposits.
[3]Money supply plus total deposits in the financial system.
Source: Central Reserve Bank of Peru (BCRP), INEI.

In addition, the successive amendments to the Banking Law produced a proliferation of regulations that hindered the functioning of the banking sector. The greatest deficiency was the lack of technical personnel to provide preventive supervision, as well as the absence of clear-cut procedures to halt potential banking crises.

Moreover, the taxes on debits and interest receivable contributed to growing financial disintermediation and the slight growth of financial markets.[9] Thus, for example, the liquidity of the financial system (currency plus public deposits in the system), which had reached 21 percent of GDP in 1975, fell to 5.5 percent in 1990 (Table 5.2). Additionally, hyperinflation had led to the excessive growth of financial institutions, accentuating financial disintermediation and eliminating medium- and long-term credits.

Regarding monetary policy, the Central Bank had no instruments that would have allowed it to pursue a more active policy.

These problems were the consequence both of the macroeconomic policies and those that directly affected the sector, which, over the years, created growing distortions that hindered the proper functioning and development of the financial system.

Changes in the Financial System's Legal and Regulatory Framework after 1990

The most important changes in the legal and regulatory framework of the financial system are contained in the new Law on Banking, Financial, and Insurance Institutions, which was passed in April 1991 and entered into force in July of that year. However, in October 1993, a new law was enacted that retained the essence of the former but amended several of its provisions.

These laws represented a substantial change from the pre-1991 regulatory system, broadening the scope of action of the Superintendency of Banks and strengthening its regulatory and supervisory control over the financial entities.

One of the most significant measures adopted was equal treatment for all financial institutions, since the law states that "no distinction in the treatment of banks shall be made on the basis of ownership (private or public) or source of capital (domestic or foreign)." The law also states that no provisions of a general nature issued by the SBS or the Central Reserve Bank (CRB) shall include exceptions that discriminate between companies of the same type (banks, for example) or between companies of different types engaged in the same type of business (banks or finance companies, for example).

---

[9] In 1989, a 1 percent tax was imposed on all transactions involving checks and a 20 percent excise tax was levied on the interest earned on financial system credit operations.

These new rules represented a substantial change from the preferential treatment that had long existed for state-owned banks and the restrictions imposed on the participation of foreign capital in national banking.

More specific measures were also adopted regarding the spreading of risks, with a financial intermediary being prohibited, for example, from concentrating its loans in any one economic sector.

Furthermore, all banks were authorized to operate nationally, eliminating the former provisions that governed banking institutions on the basis of the geographic scope of their operations.

Perhaps one of the most important aspects of these laws was the introduction of the concept of full-service banking—insofar as the types and terms of financial operations are concerned—thus eliminating the segmentation that formerly existed. Banks were authorized to conduct operations such as factoring and financial leasing, which were previously restricted to the finance companies. Additionally, banks were allowed to act as investment banks and to operate through subsidiaries as managers of mutual funds, securities brokers, and public bonded warehouses.

As for monetary policy instruments, it was decided that interest rates would be determined by the market, and a single minimum legal reserve of 9 percent was set for all types of deposits.

Moreover, a minimum capital requirement was established for banking institutions and finance companies, which would be adjusted to account for inflation. A minimum capital requirement of approximately US$5.2 million was set for banking institutions, while the minimum for finance companies and consumer credit companies (engaged in extending credit to individuals) was approximately US$2.3 million.

Unlike the former law, which prescribed a maximum ratio of 20:1 between deposits and equity, the current legislation sets limits based on real net worth. Assets are weighted according to risk, with a weighting of zero to two. The rule is that the leverage or ratio between this group of assets, weighted on the basis of risk, and real net worth shall be no greater than a factor of 12.5.

Regarding the limits on lending, stricter limits than those established by the previous legislation were introduced, and it was prohibited to grant unsecured credits or contingency financing to economic groups in excess of 10 percent of the bank's real net worth. The limit is raised to 15 percent of the real net worth if authorized guarantees are provided.

Similarly, a Central Credit Information Office was created, and a deposit insurance fund was established to protect individual deposits of up to approximately US$4,300, an amount which is adjusted according to the consumer price index.

As far as supervision is concerned, a new Law on the Superintendency of Banks was promulgated, which, in addition to increasing the autonomy of the Superintendency, broadens its authority to supervise and audit financial entities.

It also authorizes the Superintendency of Banks to interpret the scope of the legal rules governing credit institutions.

The SBS was also authorized to intervene and close institutions engaged in informal financial activities. The new law also allows the SBS to replace directors or managers of financial institutions if they are negligent in the performance of their duties.

In addition to the Law on the Superintendency of Banks, the rules established by the SBS were amended: guidelines were issued for the uniform determination of real net worth, for valuing various types of guarantees, and for standardizing the information required by the Central Credit Information Office; also, stiffer penalties were established for delays in the submission of periodic information.

It was also stipulated that the reserve for doubtful credits (the third of the five categories for rating credits according to risk) must necessarily be formed as soon as the credit receives that rating. Previously, this reserve of approximately 25 percent was required only when that rating was assigned for two consecutive years.

A register of audit firms was also established within the SBS, providing a clearer delineation of obligations, categories, and penalties, with a view to reinforcing the work of external auditors in order that they might complement the general aspects of the SBS' mission.

An effort was also made to define more strictly those credits which are known as refinanced (i.e., involving the constant renewal of credits when due to conceal the inability of certain debtors to pay) through more specific rules concerning the suspension of interest.

For the purpose of determining the limits applicable to bank operations, a more technical definition was given of the concept of economic groups or conglomerates. In addition, the SBS implemented a reorganization plan that will reduce its staff by 60 percent. However, the SBS still does not have sufficiently qualified personnel to perform its supervisory tasks.

In November 1991 a new Securities Market Law was promulgated, and a set of rules was established, introducing a number of new institutions and instruments designed to generate more information and contribute to growth and greater competition in the financial market, including privatization of the two stock exchanges and the creation of mutual funds, credit rating and risk assessment companies, and securities clearing and settlement institutions.

It should also be pointed out that private pension funds have been in operation since 1993. These funds, which already have 800,000 contributors, will help vitalize the financial market.

Growth of the Financial Sector

Financial sector growth has been influenced by the changes that have occurred over the years in economic policy and in the regulatory framework. The most important changes that affected the sector in the last decade were the populist economic policy pursued between 1985 and 1990, which unleashed a hyperinflationary process, and then, in August 1990, the application of a drastic stabilization plan and a series of structural reforms that emphasized economic stabilization and the deregulation of markets.[10]

As for the total liquidity of the financial system (currency in circulation plus deposits in financial institutions) expressed as a percentage of GDP, from the mid-seventies until 1990, the trend was clearly downward. The rate of financial deepening, which had been 21 percent in 1975, was only 16.8 percent in 1985 and 5.5 percent in 1990. This trend responded to the control of interest rates and the prohibition against holding deposits in foreign currency, in a context of mounting inflation, which turned into hyperinflation in 1988.

With the implementation of the stabilization program of August 1990, after the initial flight of deposits and currency, the latter experienced a fairly substantial recovery. The rate of financial deepening climbed to 10 percent in 1992 and to 11.9 percent in 1993. The growth of liquidity, more than the expansion of monetary creation or liquidity in local currency, reflected the increase in the flow of capital in foreign currency (Table 5.2).

The rapid recovery of liquidity is attributable to the increase in financial savings, which grew from 3.6 percent of GDP in 1990 to 9.8 percent in 1993, while the money supply (M1) only grew from 1.9 percent to 2.0 percent. Financial savings in 1993 were even close to the 1970 level, when annual inflation was single-digit, whereas the money supply reached a level in 1993 that was only 21 percent of what it had been in 1970.

The elimination of interest rate controls and the authorization of deposits in foreign currency, together with the increased confidence of economic agents, were the factors responsible for the rapid recovery of financial savings. Moreover, as far as M1 is concerned, during the period of hyperinflation, the high cost of holding money was such that individuals and companies substantially reduced their cash holdings. This behavior did not change rapidly after the dip in inflation, there being observed, as in other countries, a lagging phenomenon.

As for total liquidity in nominal dollars, it can be seen that while the latter reached almost US$4.2 billion in 1980, it fell to just over US$1 billion in 1988 when the hyperinflationary process began. The situation improved to a certain extent until 1990 and then began to recover rapidly over the next three years. Thus, while in 1990 liquidity reached US$2.1 billion, in 1992 it was nearly US$4.7 billion, and in 1993 it reached almost US$6 billion. Although this amount is larger than the 1980 figure, the composition of liquidity changed substantially due to a marked process of dollarization (Table 5.3).

---

[10] See Cáceres and Nagamine (1991) and Macroconsult (1993).

Table 5.3. Financial System Liquidity,[1] 1980–93

Year	Amount (Billions of $)	L/C Percentage	F/C Percentage
1980	4.183	73	27
1985	2.628	65	35
1986	3.672	84	16
1987	1.911	76	24
1988	1.061	39	61
1989	2.292	60	40
1990	2.137	52	48
1991	4.359	42	58
1992	4.678	37	63
1993	5.970	31	69

[1]End of period.
L/C Local currency.
F/C Foreign currency.
Source: BCRP, *Nota Semanal*, various issues.

While obligations in local currency represented 73 percent of the total liquidity of the financial system in 1980, as compared to 27 percent in foreign currency, the situation was reversed in 1993. In that year, obligations in local currency represented only 31 percent of the total, while those in foreign currency accounted for 63 percent (Table 5.3).

The behavior of banking sector liquidity (currency in circulation plus bank deposits) largely reflects the above-described growth of the financial system. In most years, bank liquidity accounted for more than 90 percent of the liquidity of the financial system. In 1980 it was over US$3.5 billion, falling to US$996 million in 1988, and then recovering in 1990 and climbing to over US$5.6 billion by late 1993.

Similarly, deposits in foreign currency—which represented 31 percent of bank liquidity in 1980 and, following the government-ordered conversion to local currency, only 17 percent in 1986—began expanding in 1990 until reaching 70 percent in 1993.

The growing dollarization of deposits is more clearly illustrated in Table 5.4. In 1993, deposits in dollars represented 80 percent of total banking sector deposits. Mortgage bonds, which accounted for 11 percent in 1980, represented only 1 percent in 1991, the last year that Banco Hipotecario, which issued the bonds, was in business.

Deposits in local currency, on the other hand, which had represented 6 percent of all deposits in 1980 and 15 percent in 1986, fell to 3 percent in 1992 and 1993. Savings deposits, which amounted to 22 percent in 1986, reached only 8 percent in 1993, while demand deposits, which had represented 28 percent of the total deposits in 1980 and 34 percent in 1986, accounted for only 8 percent in 1993.

The growing importance of dollar deposits is a reflection of the reaction of local currency depositors to the losses they sustained during the period of

Table 5.4. Breakdown of Banking System Deposits, 1980–93
(Percentages)

	1980	1985	1986	1987	1988	1989	1990	1991	1992	1993
Demand deposits	28	23	34	31	13	16	7	9	9	8
Savings deposits	14	16	22	17	7	19	13	13	11	8
Time deposits	6	11	15	12	3	9	5	4	3	3
Mortgage bonds	11	3	4	3	1	2	1	1	0	0
Other securities	1	1	2	1	0	1	0	0	0	0
Deposits in F/C	40	46	23	36	76	53	64	72	77	80
Total	100	100	100	100	100	100	100	100	100	100

Source: INEI.

hyperinflation, due to the fact that the controls on interest rates generated significantly negative rates in real terms.

Moreover, the drop observed in demand deposits in local currency reflects the reaction of economic agents to the debit tax levied between 1989 and 1992, as well as the capital flight that occurred as a result of hyperinflation.

The banking system played a predominant role in the supply of financial system credit to the private sector, which increased as a result of the minor importance of finance companies and mutual savings and loan institutions. While in December 1990 the banking system had granted 83.4 percent of financial system credit to the private sector, in 1993 it loaned 89.3 percent.

The share of commercial banking in total credit to the private sector varied significantly between 1980 and 1993. Between 1980 and 1986, it hovered slightly above 50 percent, falling to 24.1 percent in 1987. This decrease reflected the enormous expansion of development bank credit utilizing Central Bank resources. In the latter year, development banks granted 72.3 percent of the credit to the private sector. Later, the decreased value of development bank debt due to hyperinflation and the decreased availability of funds for channeling through such banks increased the share of commercial banking in credit, which rose to 86.2 percent in 1993. In that, year development banks accounted for only 10.3 percent of loans, most of them within the failing development banking sector.

Recent Performance of Commercial Banking

Given the rising importance of commercial banking as the development banks were in the process of liquidation, the indicators of commercial banking were analyzed, highlighting its most recent growth.

Table 5.5 shows the principal accounts of commercial banks, both in absolute amounts and in terms of the share of the various categories of banks, which include private banks, state-owned commercial banks, and multinational banks. Among the latter, both the branches of foreign banks and Andean multinational banks are considered. The latter include three banks organized in accordance with certain provisions of the Andean Pact concerning the structure of ownership, by virtue of which at least two-thirds of the shareholders must be from member countries of the Andean Group. In all other respects they are subject to the same conditions that apply to Peruvian commercial banks in general.

Deposits

Expressed in nominal dollars, a sharp drop in deposits is observed between 1980 and 1988, from nearly US$2.2 billion to only US$349 million. Taking into account the fact that in 1988 there were 21 banks, the average deposits per bank

Table 5.5. Principal Accounts of Commercial Banking, 1980–93
(In millions of dollars)

	1980	1985	1986	1987	1988	1989	1990	1991	1992	1993
Deposits	2,183	1,489	2,009	836	349	1,222	1,277	3,245	3,649	5,267
Private banking	1,124	717	969	384	184	756	793	2,246	2,571	3,721
Public banking	982	668	941	424	158	437	443	846	881	1,223
Multinational banking	77	104	99	27	6	29	42	152	197	322
Assets	4,449	2,318	3,191	1,477	859	2,450	2,574	4,738	5,162	7,054
Private banking	2,115	1,014	1,460	638	416	1,373	1,391	3,055	3,483	4,833
Public banking	2,169	1,113	1,558	782	414	991	1,043	1,409	1,267	1,649
Multinational banking	165	190	174	56	29	85	141	274	412	571
Loans	1,151	879	1,215	558	263	766	779	1,970	2,074	3,046
Private banking	534	337	494	216	113	390	381	1,204	1,380	2,120
Public banking	581	460	652	319	140	333	362	658	562	734
Multinational banking	36	82	69	23	10	43	36	108	132	191
Equity	198	163	308	116	101	229	357	449	330	648
Private banking	109	103	139	58	62	145	238	292	206	436
Public banking	78	42	148	51	34	72	101	125	76	146
Multinational banking	11	19	21	7	6	13	18	31	49	66

Source: Superintendency of Banks and Insurance Companies (SBS), various publications.

were an incredible US$16.2 million. Deposits recovered in the ensuing years, totaling almost US$1.3 billion in 1990. In the last three years, the stabilization process has accelerated this recovery, more than quadrupling the deposits, which amounted to roughly US$5.3 billion in 1993 (Table 5.5).

This rapid recovery of deposits, as mentioned above, was largely a response to the increased net inflow of foreign capital, which was channeled into the banking system. This occurred as a result of the authorization to hold deposits in foreign currency in Peru, the unrestricted flow of capital, and the deregulation of interest rates.

In examining the growth of commercial banking, it can be noted that prior to 1988, state-owned commercial banks held deposits in excess of 45 percent of the total, although that performance was reversed in subsequent years. The share of public banking decreased to 34.7 percent in 1990 and to 23.2 percent in 1993, the year in which private banking increased its shared to 70.7 percent and multinational banking to 6.1 percent.

Lending

As far as lending is concerned (total loans, excluding interbank loans), a similar trend is observed. Lending decreased to US$263 million in 1988 (or US$12.5 million per bank). It subsequently recovered, particularly from 1990 onward. In the last three years, it has increased 290 percent, going from US$779 million in 1990 to over US$3 billion in 1993 (Table 5.5). Also observed in this category is the loss of state banking's share: in the last three years, while the share of private banking grew 456 percent and that of multinational banking climbed 430 percent, state bank lending only increased 102 percent, reducing its share from 46.5 percent in 1990 to only 24.1 percent in 1993.

Assets

A similar situation can be observed over the years in the case of commercial banking assets, which rose from nearly US$2.6 billion in 1990 to more than US$7 billion in 1993. As might be expected, the share of public banking contracted, decreasing from 40.5 percent in 1990 to 23.4 percent in 1993.

Despite the closing of several banks, bank equity also recovered in recent years, rising from US$357 million in 1990 to US$648 million in 1993. State banking saw its share of total equity shrink from 28.4 percent to 22.5 percent. This decrease was absorbed by multinational banking, which increased its share from 5 percent to 10.2 percent.

It is important to stress that this increase in the amount of commercial banking operations occurred simultaneously with a cost reduction process, in which both the number of bank offices and the number of personnel decreased.

Productivity

The number of commercial bank offices, which was 1,383 in 1990, decreased to 1,297 in 1991, to 856 in 1992, and to 815 in 1993. The number of employees decreased from 27,345 in 1990 to 17,692 in 1993. Although all of the banks were involved in this adjustment, the largest reduction occurred in state banks, due to the liquidation of two of them (Table 5.6).

State banking, which in 1990 had 49.3 percent of bank offices and 49.8 percent of the employees, in 1993 had only 36 percent of the offices and 33.7 percent of the employees.

This staff reduction process, together with the growth of deposits, generated a substantial improvement in some commercial banking productivity indicators such as deposits per office and per employee. Deposits per office went from US$924,000 in 1990 to US$6.46 million in 1993, while deposits per employee increased from US$47,000 to US$298,000. In that year, private banking had US$334,000 in deposits per employee, public banking US$205,000, and multinational banking US$544,000 (Table 5.7).

This cost reduction process is also reflected in the ratio of personnel expenses to deposits. This indicator, which was on the rise until 1991, shows a decrease starting that year: between 1991 and 1993, in the case of commercial banking, the ratio of personnel expenses to deposits decreased from 8.16 percent to 5.05 percent, and in private banking from 6.61 percent to 4.55 percent. However, this average conceals a fairly significant disparity between banks. For example, in 1993, the personnel expenses of Banco de Comercio were the equivalent of 15 percent of its deposits, while Banco del Nuevo Mundo showed a ratio of only 1.7 percent.

Although this decrease in the ratio of personnel expenses to total deposits largely reflects the rapid increase in deposits, the reduction in staff and the waning power of the bank employees' labor union were also important factors.

Allocation of Credit

The changes in commercial banking coincided with changes in the sectoral allocation of credit. Agriculture and livestock, which received 6.7 percent of the commercial banking credit in 1990, received 4 percent in 1993. Mining, which obtained 9.1 percent of the credits, received only 3.5 percent in 1993, while the share of credits to transportation rose from 1 percent to 5.6 percent, to real estate activities from 0 to 2.5 percent, and to construction from 1 to 2.8 percent. The most important sectors, such as industry and trade, which together accounted for 58.9 percent of the credit in 1990, received 54 percent in 1993.

What has persisted over time is a strong concentration of credit in the capital as compared with the rest of the country. In 1993, metropolitan Lima accounted for 83.57 percent of the loans and had 83.92 percent of the depos-

Table 5.6. Commercial Banking Offices and Employees, 1980–93

	1980	1985	1986	1987	1988	1989	1990	1991	1992	1993
Offices	842	1,073	1,141	1,177	1,210	1,385	1,383	1,297	856	815
Private banking	378	44	486	510	533	689	692	693	527	512
Public banking	453	60	634	648	671	690	682	595	319	292
Multinational banking	11	2	21	19	6	6	9	9	10	11
Employees	16,865	22,956	24,017	24,520	25,186	26,291	27,345	24,269	17,815	17,692
Private banking	6,972	10,774	11,131	11,305	11,537	11,963	13,419	12,831	11,108	11,129
Public banking	9,484	11,527	12,289	12,880	13,371	14,040	13,616	11,047	6,272	5,971
Multinational banking	409	665	597	335	278	288	310	391	435	592

Source: SBS, various publications.

Table 5.7. Commercial Banking Productivity Indicators, 1980–93
(Thousands of dollars)

	1980	1985	1986	1987	1988	1989	1990	1991	1992	1993
Deposits per office	2,593	1,388	1,761	710	288	882	924	2,502	4,263	6,462
Private banking	2,973	1,615	1,994	753	346	1,097	1,145	3,242	4,879	7,268
Public banking	2,168	1,099	1,484	655	236	633	650	1,422	2,762	4,189
Multinational banking	7,027	4,932	4,714	1,443	957	4,885	4,619	16,885	19,657	29,260
Deposits per employee	129	65	84	34	14	46	47	134	205	298
Private banking	161	67	87	34	16	63	59	175	231	334
Public banking	104	58	77	33	12	31	33	77	140	205
Multinational banking	189	158	166	82	21	102	134	389	452	544

Source: SBS, various publications.

its, illustrating the negligible development of banking services in the country's interior.

Concentration

Following is an analysis of the evolution of the concentration of commercial banking deposits, loans, assets, and equity.

In the years between 1980 and 1993, a high concentration of deposits is observed at the start of the period, which declines until 1990 and then rises until 1993. Thus, for example, the index of concentration in the case of the three largest banks, which was 64.61 percent in 1980, fell to 43.48 percent in 1990, and then rose to 65.51 percent in 1993. It should be noted, however, that changes occurred in the composition of the group of three largest banks. Two of them, Crédito and Continental, remained in the group, while Banco Wiese, which was in fifth place until 1988, became the second largest bank in 1993 (Table 5.8).

Similar behavior is observed in the concentration index for the five and seven largest banks, respectively. The concentration index for the five largest banks went from 71.37 percent in 1980 to 59.51 percent in 1990, and to 78.19 percent in 1993. The concentration index of the seven largest banks dropped from 81.05 percent in 1980 to 70.56 percent in 1990, and then rose again to 84.69 percent in 1993.

The Herfindahl index corroborates the growth described as it shows a decrease between 1980 and 1990, from 0.14 to 0.10, followed by an increase in the nineties, reaching 0.16 in 1993.

The loan situation is somewhat different. The index shows a downward trend during the period, falling from 0.38 in 1980 to 0.20 in 1993. This can be attributed largely to the behavior of the largest bank, Banco de Crédito, which opted for a conservative loan policy: although in 1992 and 1993 it had an average of 30 percent of the deposits in the system, its loans represented only 21 percent. Behavior similar to that of loans is observed with regard to assets and equity.

Offices and Staff

As far as the number of offices is concerned, a distinction can be made between banks operating at the national level—such as Banco de Crédito, Banco Internacional, and Banco Continental, with more than 100 offices each—and metropolitan and regional banks. Moreover, there are banks that serve specialized market segments, which have only one or two offices.

An effort to reduce the number of offices can be observed in the private banking sector. The largest bank cut the number of its offices by more than 20 percent in the last two years. It should be pointed out that the number of offices is currently only 60 percent of the 1990 figure, and there are now even fewer offices than there were in 1980.

Table 5.8. Commercial Bank Deposits, 1980–93
(Percentage shares and concentration indexes)

	1980	1985	1986	1987	1988	1989	1990	1991	1992	1993
Total commercial banking	100	100	100	100	100	100	100	100	100	100
Private banking	53	49	50	46	53	61	62	67	70	72
Banco de Crédito	28	28	26	22	26	25	22	29	31	29
Banco Wiese	9	7	6	6	6	7	9	13	17	21
Banco Comercial	6	—	—	—	—	—	—	—	—	—
Banco de Lima	4	4	5	4	4	7	6	5	5	4
Bandesco	1	1	1	1	1	1	1	1	1	1
Banco Latino	—	3	4	4	5	5	8	7	6	5
Banco Mercantil	—	2	2	1	2	2	2	2	2	2
Banco Regional del Norte	2	2	2	2	3	3	3	2	2	2
Banco del Sur del Perú	2	2	2	3	3	4	3	2	2	2
Banco Financiero	—	—	—	1	1	3	2	1	1	2
Banco de Comercio	1	—	2	2	2	2	3	2	2	1
Probank	—	—	—	—	—	—	1	1	1	1
Banco Sudamericano	—	—	—	—	—	—	—	—	—	1
Banex	—	—	—	—	—	—	—	—	—	1
Banco CCC	—	—	—	—	—	2	2	2	—	—
Associated banking	45	45	48	52	46	36	34	26	24	23
Banco Popular	12	9	9	8	6	6	5	3	—	—
Banco Internacional	8	9	11	12	9	7	8	7	9	7
Banco Continental	14	19	17	19	22	14	12	11	15	16
Banco Nor-Perú	2	2	3	3	2	3	3	1	—	—
Surmebanc	3	2	2	3	3	2	2	1	—	—
Banco de los Andes	2	1	2	2	1	1	2	1	—	—
Banco Amazónico	2	1	2	2	1	1	1	1	—	—
Caja de Ahorros	2	2	2	3	2	2	1	1	—	—

	1980	1985	1986	1987	1988	1989	1990	1991	1992	1993
Multinational banking	4	6	4	3	2	2	3	5	6	6
Citibank	1	1	0	0	1	0	0	0	1	1
Extebandes	—	1	1	1	1	2	3	2	2	2
Banco Interandino	—	—	—	—	—	—	0	2	2	1
Banco Interamericano	—	—	—	—	—	—	—	1	1	1
Banco del Nuevo Mundo	—	—	—	—	—	—	—	—	—	1
Banco de Londres	0	1	1	0	—	—	—	—	—	—
Banco de Tokyo	1	1	1	1	—	—	—	—	—	—
Bank of America	1	2	1	0	0	0	—	—	—	—
Central de Madrid	—	0	0	0	—	—	—	—	—	—
Chase Manhattan	—	0	0	—	—	—	—	—	—	—

	1980	1985	1986	1987	1988	1989	1990	1991	1992	1993
Concentration indices										
Herfindahl index										
Value	0.14	0.14	0.12	0.12	0.14	0.11	0.10	0.13	0.17	0.16
Possible minimum	0.05	0.04	0.04	0.04	0.05	0.05	0.04	0.04	0.06	0.05
Rates of concentration (%)										
RC(3)	54.61	56.34	53.06	53.10	56.58	46.91	43.48	53.18	63.83	65.51
RC(5)	71.37	71.50	67.62	67.03	68.27	61.42	59.51	67.90	78.88	78.19
RC(7)	81.05	78.13	76.07	75.11	76.77	72.02	70.56	75.63	85.80	84.69

Source: SBS, various publications.

Analyzing the increase in the number of bank employees in the last 13 years shows that almost all the banks substantially reduced their staffs in the last three years, from 27,345 employees in 1990 to 17,692 in 1993. This process is more pronounced in private banks than in state-owned banks.

As mentioned above, deposits per employee, after falling during the years of hyperinflation, began to recover in 1990 and were six times higher in 1993. The differences in the level of deposits per employee in the commercial banks are fairly wide, however, ranging from banks such as Banco de Comercio with US$91,000 or Bandesco with US$129,000, to others such as Nuevo Mundo, Wiese, and Citibank with much higher figures: US$702,000, US$663,000, and US$612,000, respectively (Table 5.9).

Uncommitted Funds

The uncommitted funds of commercial banks represent a high percentage of deposits. In December 1993, they averaged 45.8 percent in the commercial banking sector, a figure which can be attributed essentially to the Central Bank's reserve policy concerning deposits in foreign currency.

The reserve requirement for bank deposits in local currency is not high, being the same as the Banking Law's requirement for all types of deposits (9 percent). Given the continuing high turnover of deposits resulting from the hyperinflationary episode, this percentage also reflects the banks' operating requirements.

As for deposits in foreign currency, however, in August 1991 the Central Bank established a marginal reserve requirement of 50 percent, which was lowered to 45 percent in November 1993. Considering the rapid growth of deposits in foreign currency, the banks' high level of liquidity should come as no surprise.

In addition, the significant rise in deposits could not be placed in its entirety owing to natural banking prudence, so that surplus resources were generated which were not applied to loans.

Temporal Structure of Deposits and Loans

Deposits as of December 31, 1993, were 85 percent short-term and 15 percent long-term. Most of these long-term deposits consisted of years of service payments.[11] These deposits must be held until the worker retires from the company.

The potential instability of the deposits in the banking system became apparent in April 1992 after Congress adjourned: deposits in foreign currency contracted nearly 10 percent that month, although they recovered in subsequent months.

---

[11] Companies are required to deposit one month's salary per year of service for workers.

The significance of long-term loans (more than one year), which practically disappeared during the period of hyperinflation, is slight. This situation still has not changed. As of March 31, 1993, long-term loans represented only 10.53 percent of the total loans. Most of these loans originated in financial leasing or compulsory refinancing operations, or were linked to facilities of development institutions.

Interest Rates and Margins

As mentioned above, the performance of the financial sector was affected by macroeconomic policy. During the final months of the previous government, a financial bottleneck developed. The reason for this is that while money was still being created to finance the government, an attempt was made to check secondary growth by imposing marginal reserve requirements of 84 percent. This translated into extremely high real interest rates, which led to erosion of the banks' loan portfolios, a situation that was partially alleviated with the implementation of the August 1990 stabilization program. During that month, inflation reached 396 percent, greatly diminishing the value of existing debts.

Nevertheless, real interest rates remained at high levels, both in local currency and in foreign currency. As the stabilization program progressed, interest rates fell, although they remain considerably higher than the international rates. Because it was affected by exogenous and economic policy factors, this downward trajectory was not uniform over time. After the political events of April 5, 1992, for example, deposit withdrawals drove interest rates upward (Table 5.10).

The trend of interest rates affected the banks' financial margins, as can be seen in Table 5.11. While gross margins in local currency decreased, the spread between lending and deposit rates for foreign currency widened in 1991, following the deregulation of interest rates on foreign currency. In the following years this spread narrowed.

The average gross margin between lending and deposit rates on foreign currency, which was 10.36 percent in 1993, can be explained largely by the high reserve requirement applicable to deposits in foreign currency. Thus, if the cost of the reserve requirement is deducted, the before-tax margin is 4.61 percent. If, in addition, the impact of the tax on assets[12] and the contribution of banks to the SBS are deducted, the net margin drops to 3.41 percent.

---

[12] In 1992, the government established a minimum income tax, which in the case of financial enterprises is 1 percent of their assets.

Table 5.9. Deposits per Employee in Commercial Banks, 1980–93
(In thousands of dollars)

	1980	1985	1986	1987	1988	1989	1990	1991	1992	1993
Total commercial banking	129	65	84	34	14	46	47	134	205	298
Private banking	161	67	87	34	16	63	59	175	231	334
Banco de Crédito	177	74	91	34	17	55	50	190	226	314
Banco Wiese	162	56	68	28	12	58	80	243	424	663
Banco Comercial	129	—	—	—	—	—	—	—	—	—
Banco de Lima	109	68	113	42	16	107	86	178	218	297
Bandesco	213	56	57	23	10	43	45	96	82	129
Banco Latino	—	81	118	39	15	49	80	186	185	253
Banco Mercantil	—	101	109	39	25	64	73	193	200	248
Banco Regional del Norte	185	76	84	40	21	91	81	155	171	242
Banco del Sur del Perú	117	55	68	28	15	75	56	123	163	240
Banco Financiero	—	—	—	68	28	140	87	132	127	309
Banco de Comercio	—	—	63	26	9	29	50	130	129	91
Probank	—	—	—	—	—	—	149	285	310	341
Banco Sudamericano	—	—	—	—	—	—	—	—	—	231
Banex	—	—	—	—	—	—	—	—	—	271
Banco CCC	—	—	—	—	—	—	22	62	—	—
Associated banking	104	58	77	33	12	31	33	77	140	205
Banco Popular	83	39	51	21	6	19	18	38	—	—
Banco Internacional	90	50	72	30	9	26	30	78	123	150
Banco Continental	145	90	107	49	23	50	45	120	153	247
Banco Nor-Perú	139	70	112	43	13	38	60	85	—	—
Surmebanc	139	32	55	29	11	29	26	48	—	—
Banco de los Andes	70	61	84	42	10	32	68	101	—	—
Banco Amazónico	74	19	97	36	9	33	38	51	—	—

	1980	1985	1986	1987	1988	1989	1990	1991	1992	1993
Caja de Ahorros	104	216	68	25	9	23	21	56	—	—
Multinational banking	189	158	166	82	21	102	134	389	452	544
Citibank	157	119	62	32	37	36	59	104	485	612
Extebandes	—	167	263	65	17	133	164	244	360	498
Banco Interandino	—	—	—	—	—	—	75	824	676	522
Banco Interamericano	—	—	—	—	—	—	—	468	298	434
Banco del Nuevo Mundo	—	—	—	—	—	—	—	—	—	702
Banco de Londres	76	123	150	—	—	—	—	—	—	—
Banco de Tokyo	347	170	199	—	—	—	—	—	—	—
Bank of America	234	282	250	50	19	20	—	—	—	—
Central de Madrid	—	133	47	—	—	—	—	—	—	—
Chase Manhattan	—	130	181	—	—	—	—	—	—	—

Source: SBS, various publications.

Table 5.10. Nominal Interest Rates,[1] 1985–93

Year and month		Local currency[2]					Foreign currency[3]			
		Lending[4]	TAMN[5]	Savings[6]	TIPMN[5]	Rediscount Oper	Lending[7]	TAMEX[5]	Savings[6]	TIPMEX[5]
1985	December	45.00	n.a.	19.00	n.a.	n.a.	n.a.	n.a.	n.a.	n.a.
1986	December	40.00	n.a.	19.00	n.a.	n.a.	n.a.	n.a.	n.a.	n.a.
1987	December	32.00	n.a.	22.00	n.a.	n.a.	n.a.	n.a.	n.a.	n.a.
1988	December	20.00	n.a.	17.30	n.a.	n.a.	n.a.	n.a.	n.a.	n.a.
1989	December	21.50	n.a.	19.30	n.a.	n.a.	n.a.	n.a.	n.a.	n.a.
1990	August	51.00	n.a.	35.60	n.a.	n.a.	n.a.	n.a.	n.a.	n.a.
	September	40.00	n.a.	20.00	n.a.	n.a.	n.a.	n.a.	n.a.	n.a.
	October	14.08	n.a.	7.15	n.a.	n.a.	15.91	n.a.	7.21	n.a.
	November	12.51	n.a.	6.12	n.a.	n.a.	16.24	n.a.	7.46	n.a.
	December	12.45	n.a.	5.10	n.a.	n.a.	16.32	n.a.	7.84	n.a.
1991	January	17.41	n.a.	6.02	n.a.	n.a.	15.16	n.a.	7.18	n.a.
	February	22.17	n.a.	8.49	n.a.	n.a.	16.59	n.a.	6.43	n.a.
	March	23.75	n.a.	9.42	n.a.	n.a.	17.34	n.a.	6.74	n.a.
	April	18.73	19.07	7.49	n.a.	n.a.	20.80	19.41	8.40	n.a.
	May	14.94	15.40	6.67	n.a.	n.a.	20.47	19.37	9.18	n.a.
	June	17.10	17.47	7.28	n.a.	n.a.	20.21	19.18	9.51	n.a.
	July	18.20	18.32	9.28	4.91	n.a.	21.00	19.43	11.23	8.64
	August	17.29	17.76	9.62	4.44	6.86	21.55	19.56	11.31	8.89
	September	12.10	12.69	5.56	3.23	3.04	22.53	19.80	9.41	7.76
	October	9.83	10.62	4.42	2.71	2.57	22.92	19.96	8.40	7.73
	November	9.67	10.54	4.42	2.70	2.50	23.07	20.30	8.53	7.64
	December	9.86	10.48	4.44	2.73	4.40	23.18	20.33	8.54	7.76
1992	January	9.61	10.26	4.40	2.61	2.56	23.43	20.09	8.54	7.80
	February	8.56	9.15	3.93	2.29	2.00	23.26	20.64	8.43	5.92
	March	8.00	8.05	3.40	2.00	2.02	22.15	19.16	7.78	6.93
	April	7.11	7.29	2.96	1.86	2.00	19.54	17.21	6.59	6.50
	May	7.29	7.67	3.07	1.71	2.94	19.89	18.43	6.65	6.18
	June	7.81	7.84	3.17	1.67	2.50	20.37	19.03	6.59	6.28
	July	7.94	7.84	3.21	1.74	2.81	20.61	19.21	6.64	6.32
	August	7.95	7.86	3.20	1.66	2.42	20.58	19.18	6.61	6.22
	September	7.17	7.38	3.10	1.51	1.78	18.68	16.91	6.42	5.97
	October	6.85	7.24	3.03	1.48	1.75	18.17	16.79	6.29	5.88
	November	7.00	7.14	3.03	1.39	1.97	18.23	16.75	6.32	5.79

Year and month		Local currency[2]					Foreign currency[3]			
		Lending[4]	TAMN[5]	Savings[6]	TIPMN[5]	Rediscount Oper	Lending[7]	TAMEX[5]	Savings[6]	TIPMEX[5]
	December	7.05	7.39	3.02	1.42	3.35	18.30	16.92	6.28	5.80
1993	January	6.93	7.22	3.00	1.41	4.00	18.21	16.71	6.26	5.72
	February	6.90	6.98	2.98	1.40	2.50	18.39	16.50	6.16	5.77
	March	6.49	6.49	2.77	1.40	2.50	18.40	16.35	5.83	5.72
	April	6.25	5.86	2.70	1.39	2.50	18.39	16.19	5.76	5.72
	May[8]	5.91	5.57	2.67	1.36	2.43	18.37	15.96	5.89	5.69
	June	5.70	5.47	2.57	1.32	2.25	18.34	15.77	5.85	5.63
	July	5.67	5.38	2.53	1.31	3.38	18.25	15.61	5.91	5.52
	August	5.42	5.25	2.48	1.21	3.96	18.17	15.44	5.79	5.41
	September	5.30	5.19	2.35	1.24	1.54	18.07	15.34	5.63	5.30
	October	5.18	4.99	2.22	1.21	2.00	18.12	15.22	5.49	5.16
	November	5.04	4.82	2.00	1.12	1.53	18.09	15.04	5.27	5.01
	December	4.88	4.64	1.92	1.10	2.12	18.15	15.17	5.16	5.01
1994	January	4.79	4.59	1.90	1.08	1.50	18.15	15.41	5.09	4.97
	February[9]	4.68	4.61	1.82	1.06	1.50	18.18	15.36	4.98	4.87

[1] Simple average effective rates for the period. Before 1990, the source is INEI. Also during this period deposits in foreign currency were not permitted, so that there is no applicable interest rate.
[2] In monthly terms.
[3] In annual terms.
[4] In loans of up to 360 days.
[5] Average rates weighted for balances of each type:
TAMN: average lending rates in local currency.
TIPMN: average deposit rates in local currency.
TAMEX: average lending rates in foreign currency.
TIPMEX: average deposit rates in foreign currency.
[6] Beginning in March 1993, the minimum rate is considered for banking institutions reporting a range.
[7] Rate of overdrafts.
[8] Beginning in May 1993, weighted average rates reported by banking institutions are considered.
[9] With the exception of the weighted average rates, the information is the mean until February 18.
Source: BCRP, INEI.

Table 5.11. Commercial Banking Margins, 1990–93
(Distribution of the net margin: December 1993)

	December 1993		December 1992		December 1991		December 1990	
	L/C[1]	F/C[2]	L/C[1]	F/C[2]	L/C[1]	F/C[2]	L/C[1]	F/C[2]
Average lending rate	4.53	15.37	7.39	16.92	10.48	20.33	13.68	16.32
Average deposit rate	1.09	5.01	1.42	5.80	2.73	7.76	5.48	7.75
Gross margin	3.44	10.36	5.97	11.12	7.75	12.57	8.20	8.58
Reserve requirement cost	0.41	5.75	1.07	7.10	1.41	8.89	2.33	4.53
Before-tax margin	3.03	4.61	4.90	4.02	6.34	3.68	5.87	4.04
Tax cost	0.10	1.20	0.10	1.20	0.10	1.20	0.10	1.20
Assets tax	0.08	1.00	0.08	1.00	0.08	1.00	0.08	1.00
SBS Contributions	0.02	0.20	0.02	0.20	0.02	0.20	0.02	0.20
Net margin	2.93	3.41	4.80	2.82	6.24	2.48	5.77	2.84

[1] In monthly terms.
[2] In annual terms.
Source: SBS, BCRP.

Table 5.12. Structure of the Past-due Loans of Commercial Banking, 1980–93
(Percentages, end-period data)

	1980	1985	1986	1987	1988	1989	1990	1991	1992	1993
Credits overdue	37.5	9.9	12.7	14.4	24.1	42.7	42.6	47.5	42.5	27.7
Credits in court collection process	62.5	90.1	87.3	85.6	75.9	57.3	57.4	52.5	57.5	72.3
TOTAL	100.0	100.0	100.0	100.0	100.0	100.0	100.0	100.0	100.0	100.0
Past-due loans/ total gross loans	2.0	17.7	11.8	9.6	9.5	6.1	10.5	10.7	13.0	9.3

Source: SBS, Monthly Financial Report.

The trend of the margins affected net financial income (financial income less financial expenditures). Thus, despite the decrease in local currency margins, the increase in the volume of transactions allowed a sharp increase in net financial income. For foreign currency, the increase in both margins and transaction volumes explained the significant increase in net financial income.

Profitability

Due to portfolio deterioration, especially after 1992, and the consequent need for larger reserves, the rise in net financial income did not increase the profitability of private commercial banking. For example, profits relative to equity were 14.91 percent in 1992, but only amounted to 9.61 percent in 1993. Relative to assets, profits decreased from 0.95 percent to 0.88 percent.

Quality of the Portfolio

The quality of loans also declined. Before the August 1990 adjustment, most loans were in local currency, so they decreased in value due to high inflation. Later, the banks exercised greater caution in granting new loans, given the uncertainty regarding results of the stabilization program and structural reforms.

This situation remained essentially unchanged until 1992, when the recession eroded the financial position of businesses, leading to further declines in the quality of the banks' loan portfolios. In late 1992, the delinquent portfolio represented 13 percent of gross banking sector loans (Table 5.12).

Nevertheless, a banking crisis was averted. Because of the flight of foreign-currency deposits following disruption of the institutional order on April 5, 1992, the banks, already in a precarious financial situation, ended by closing their doors. During this period, not only did the development banks go out of business, but Banco Popular (state-owned), Banco Hipotecario, the CCC, the mutual savings banks, and the cooperatives also went into liquidation. The Caja de Ahorros de Lima was already in this process. Moreover, Surmeban (state-owned bank) was taken over by Banco de la Nación, and three regional banks merged with Banco Continental (state-owned bank).

Following economic recovery in 1993, a higher volume of bank transactions slightly improved the quality of bank portfolios, lowering the delinquent portfolio index from 13 percent to 9.3 percent. Nevertheless, this average conceals the disparate situations of various banks.

In late 1993, two banks had overdue portfolios exceeding 20 percent, while five others had between 12 and 20 percent of their loans overdue or in court-ordered collection. In that same year, reserves for bad debts represented 73.62 percent of the problem loans. However, several banks had a reserve percentage of less than 30 percent of their delinquent loans.

Solvency

Table 5.13 shows assets and credits weighted by risk in relation to real net worth (leverage ratio) for each bank. As the table shows, this ratio, which averaged 10.1 in 1992, remained at that level in 1993. Thus, all of the banks complied with the requirement of the 1991 Banking Law, which established a maximum leverage index of 15.

The new banking law of November 1993, however, established a minimum of 8 percent of capital relative to assets weighted by risk (i.e., a leverage ratio of 12.5). In December 1993, three banks exceeded this index and were compelled to increase their capital.

Table 5.13. Assets and Credits Weighted by Risk vs. Real Net Worth, 1992–93
(Leverage ratio, end-period data)

	1992	1993
NATIONAL COMMERCIAL BANKING		
Continental	11.2	7.8
Interbanc	7.1	12.8
Crédito	9.1	10.1
Wiese	13.5	14.0
Lima	14.1	13.8
Bandesco	6.0	6.9
Latino	8.3	11.6
Mercantil	7.6	14.1
Regional del Norte	10.9	11.8
Sur del Perú	7.9	10.3
Financiero	8.8	10.3
De Comercio	8.5	7.2
Probank	12.8	12.4
Sudamericano	4.5	8.4
Banex	6.8	11.5
FOREIGN BANKS		
Citibank	3.1	5.0
MULTINATIONAL BANKING		
Extebandes	6.1	6.1
Interandino	11.7	11.2
Interamericano	5.7	7.1
Nuevo Mundo	—	11.1
COMMERCIAL BANKING TOTAL	10.1	6.8

Source: SBS, Monthly Financial Report.

Financial Sector Perspectives

In recent years some analysts predicted a banking crisis, which, in fact, did not materialize. Although several banks went into liquidation, they had been having problems for years. Similarly, the development banks had to be closed when they no longer had access to Central Bank resources.

Several factors enabled banks to withstand the drastic stabilization and reform plan. First, they benefited from the experiences of other countries and were prudent in placing their credits. Second, the larger volume of transactions after the stabilization and higher interest rates enabled them to increase reserves to cover bad debts. Lastly, the economy's robust recovery in 1993, following the recession of 1992, helped the banks stay afloat.

Particularly since 1990, greater competition has been observed in the banking system. Although credit cards were first introduced in Peru in 1981, only during the last two years were massive campaigns mounted to promote their use. Similarly, automatic teller machines, which were introduced in 1978, have experienced significant growth in the past two years after several banks joined forces to create shared networks.

The use of checking accounts, which had diminished significantly with the onset of hyperinflation and the tax on debits, has also expanded in recent years. Although demand deposits constituted 45 percent of the money in circulation in 1990, they now represent 56 percent.

Banks have branched out into new operations authorized by the new Banking Law. For example, several banks became more aggressive in factoring operations. Two banks created their own stock brokerage firms in 1992, and five others followed suit in 1993.

Several banks also established mutual funds in 1993, and this number is expected to grow. Long-term credits have slowly started to appear. These operations were initially financed with years-of-service deposits (CTS, *compensación de tiempo de servicios*) and financial leasing bonds. In December 1993, the latter were issued at the level authorized by the National Enterprises and Securities Supervisory Commission (CONASEV), which exceeded US$155 million. Recently the use of bank-issued mortgage notes was authorized, and they are expected to play an important role in long-term financing.

Reinforcement of structural reform and the stabilization process, as well as capital inflow into Latin America, have helped vitalize the financial market in recent years. The amount traded on the Lima and Arequipa stock exchanges, which was US$417 million in 1989, climbed more than to US$2 billion in 1993 (Table 5.14). In the secondary stock market, this growth was even more pronounced, rising from US$55 million in 1989 to nearly US$2 billion in 1993.

In bills of exchange and other commercial instruments, trading has decreased: although the amount traded in 1992 was US$612 million, the figure was only US$90 million in 1993. Bills of exchange backed by banks, once an important trading instrument on the board, have virtually disappeared.

The growth of the stock exchange in recent years was reflected in a significant rise in the stock exchange capitalization index (ICB, *índice de capitalización bursátil*): 318 companies listed shares on the exchange in 1992. Although the ICB on the Lima stock exchange was then US$2.6 billion, it grew by more than 93 percent in 1993, reaching almost US$5.1 billion by year's end.

Moreover, in the over-the-counter market where banks and brokerage firms trade, CONASEV estimates the volume of transactions at US$60 million in 1993, 50 percent of this in notes and bills.

With June 1993 as the start-up date, the Pension Fund Administrators (AFP, *Administradores de Fondos de Pensiones*) by May 1994 had a cumulative fund of US$96 million, a figure expected to climb to US$200 million by the end of 1995.

Table 5.14. Lima and Arequipa Stock Exchanges: Volumes Traded, 1970–93
(Millions of dollars)

Years	Exchange segments		Total
	Session	Board	
1970	27.3	—	27.3
1971	30.3	—	30.3
1972	32.7	—	32.7
1973	31.7	—	31.7
1974	31.9	—	31.9
1975	22.3	—	22.3
1976	25.6	—	25.6
1977	40.3	—	40.3
1978	50.9	—	50.9
1979	94.9	—	94.9
1980	144.7	—	144.7
1981	98.2	—	98.2
1982	52.7	—	52.7
1983	33.9	5.8	39.7
1984	31.4	19.4	50.8
1985	37.3	19.7	57.0
1986	246.6	10.1	256.7
1987	148.2	3.6	151.8
1988	25.1	1.6	26.7
1989	55.3	361.9	417.2
1990	92.2	612.0	704.2
1991	209.8	413.9	623.6
1992	558.7	186.9	745.6
1993	1,993.4	90.3	2,083.7

Source: CONASEV.

One factor contributing to the buoyancy of the financial market is the privatization of public enterprises, since the privatized companies are expected to list their shares on the securities exchange.

Financing for Small Businesses

Obstacles to Credit Availability

Peru's financial system contained a number of deficiencies that hampered long-term financing and limited credit to certain sectors. The small business sector's lack of access to credit worsened after the development banks disappeared.

The tightness of long-term credit is not surprising, given the macroeconomic instability and the fact that property rights were in jeopardy in Peru for many years. As the process of macroeconomic stabilization gathers momentum, it is hoped that the growth of the financial market will give impetus to long-term credits.

The lack of credit availability of some sectors is often due to inadequate information or the high cost of obtaining it. As banking is an information-intensive activity, this constraint causes banks to refrain from participating in the financing of certain sectors. This is especially true for small businesses and small agricultural units.[13]

Another factor blocking small businesses' access to credit is the high cost of processing and tracking small loans. Although these costs could be recovered in higher interest rates, the high financial cost would make lending more risky.

Moreover, financial institutions do not participate in financing an activity with which they have no experience. This has happened when credit for a specific type of enterprise was monopolized by development banking for a prolonged period.

Costs imposed by the institutional framework must also be considered. Lack of adequate records on collateral guarantees and tedious or confusing legal procedures may deter the granting of loans.[14] In addition, because of the rules established by the Superintendency of Banks, companies without current financial statements have difficulty obtaining credit. Another problem hindering the access of small businesses to credit is the informal character of the operations of most small productive units.

Regarding the collateral guarantees required by credit institutions, some progress has occurred in recent years. For example, in 1988 the property register was expanded to include marginal real estate developments when the People's Mortgage System was created, which is still operating precariously.

Later, under the current government, Legislative Decree 653 was promulgated, which, in addition to repealing rules on agrarian reform, permitted the furnishing of mortgages on rural properties, but only if these properties were larger than five hectares.

Moreover, Legislative Decree 637 provided a series of guarantees for banks and financial institutions covering properties offered as collateral, thereby more effectively ensuring recovery of the credits. This rule provides that unless there is an agreement to the contrary, any property pledged or mortgaged in the bank's favor, backs all the debtor's debts or transactions with that institution.

As far as procedural matters are concerned, a special mortgage and pledge foreclosure procedure was established: in case of default, the financial institution can petition the competent judge to auction the mortgaged or pledged property. The debtor can only oppose the court-ordered auction by discharging his obligation or proving that it was previously discharged. This has significantly stream-

---

[13] See Calomiris (1993) and Stiglitz (1993).

[14] See World Bank (1989a) and (1990).

lined the foreclosure procedure. The time and cost savings of these procedures have helped revitalize this type of collateral.

The area where no progress has occurred is in the credit histories of small business owners. Although a central credit information office was established for larger borrowers, it does not cover small businesses. The lack of information about the credit rating of borrowers is largely responsible for their limited access to financing.

Regarding consumer credit and personal credit, the fundamental information needed to assess credit risk has been identified, which substantially reduces the cost of processing loans. However, no major advances have been made in this type of credit that affect small businesses.

The Superintendency of Banks now requires a formal presentation on the credit recipient, including information about the recipient's financial circumstances and cash flow position. In the case of investment credits, a financial evaluation of the project is needed. These requirements reduce the banks' degree of flexibility in extending credit.

The Small Business Sector

Over the years, employment in small businesses and micro-businesses (mostly in the informal sector) has been gaining in importance, largely in response to macroeconomic instability and the sharp increase in the economically active population.[15] In 1987, only 28.8 percent of manufacturing jobs were in medium-sized and heavy industries, while 71.2 percent of such jobs were concentrated in establishments with fewer than 20 workers.

A recent study by the Central Reserve Bank and the U.S. Agency for International Development (USAID) estimated that in 1989, in metropolitan Lima, there were 775,102 establishments with fewer than 50 workers, which together employed 1.3 million people. The commercial sector accounted for 66.7 percent of the units, while the industrial sector accounted for 9.5 percent. Similarly, micro-businesses (1–4 workers) represented 96 percent of the units and 80.9 percent of the individuals employed. Small businesses (5–50 workers) had only 19.2 percent of the employed workers (Table 5.15).

Neither the financial entities nor NGOs that finance the small business sector have been important sources of financing.[16] Various studies show instead that the most common financing arrangements are, in order of importance, loans from relatives, supplier's credit, credit from informal lenders, pawnshops, and collective funds *(panderos and tanamoches)*. However, many of these financing arrangements are used in combination with facilities granted by the NGOs.

---

[15] See Villarán (1992).

[16] See Velarde (1987).

Table 5.15. Distribution of Enterprises by Size, 1989

	Micro (1–4 employees)	Small (5–50 employees)
Commerce		
Enterprises	506,915	10,064
Employment	716,019	72,022
Industry		
Enterprises	66,379	7,074
Employment	112,467	60,600
Services		
Enterprises	80,896	8,081
Employment	136,750	61,370
Other sectors		
Enterprises	89,284	6,409
Employment	110,553	61,121
Total		
Enterprises	743,474	31,628
Percentage	95.9	4.1
Employment	1,075,789	255,113
Percentage	80.9	19.2

Source: BCRP, United States Agency for International Development. Preliminary findings.

Peru's Experience in Financing Microenterprises and Small Businesses

The initial experiments in small business financing took place under the military government. In the 1980s, financing programs began to be extended to this sector through the NGOs. Various NGO officials were interviewed for this study. Following is a discussion of the three most important experiments: Community Action, CARE, and IDESI.[17]

Community Action began operating in 1982, under the auspices of International Action (AITEC) and USAID. Unlike the subsequent experience with other NGOs, it was basically oriented toward the poorest micro-businesses. It generally granted very short-term credits (60 days), with weekly payments and interest rates slightly above market rates.

In the 1982–92 period, 85 percent of the credits went to commerce and averaged US$180, while 15 percent were oriented toward industrial micro-businesses and averaged US$96. In 1991, 93.9 percent of the loans were directed to commerce and only 6.1 percent to production, with the loans averaging US$1,815. During that same year there were 1,986 borrowers and the total amount loaned was US$3.6 million.

Community Action requires joint and several guarantees for group loans and personal collateral for individual credits. It also conducts training and technical assistance programs in conjunction with the financing. In general, its bad debts

[17] These experiments are described in Chávez and Chacaltana (1994).

have not exceeded 3 percent, although its delinquency ratio has climbed higher in some years.

CARE began by granting technical assistance and financial guarantees to owners of small businesses and micro-businesses. Later, under an agreement concluded with a cooperative bank, the CCC, it expanded its functions, acting as a qualifier and supervisor of loans granted by that financial institution. In general, these credits were for 12 to 14 months, with current bank interest rates.

The program ran successfully for five years, with a delinquency rate of less than 10 percent. This experiment was later copied by other Latin American countries. When the CCC ran into trouble, CARE began using its own funds, serving more than 5,000 users in ten Peruvian cities. In 1993 CARE loaned approximately US$5 million, with average loans of US$1,200 for terms of eight months at market interest rates.

IDESI began its activities in 1986 with a small guaranty fund of US$10,000 granted by the International Labor Organization (ILO), which was used to channel CCC credits five times larger than the fund.

Later, in 1987, the Central Bank granted it a facility of US$10 million, creating the Informal Sector Credit Fund (FONCRESI). IDESI's roles is that of qualifier and supervisor of the credits, while the banks act as administrators. At first, the guaranty requirements were minimal in order to quickly expand the coverage of the loans.

In 1987, IDESI granted US$12 million to nearly 50,000 users. In 1993 it loaned a total of US$3 million to 5,000 borrowers. During that same year, the delinquent portfolio was less than 5 percent, while loans considered uncollectible accounted for less than 1 percent of all the funds.

In general, a learning process is observed over the years among the NGOs involved in financing small businesses. At first, they tried to reach a larger number of users in the poorest segments of the population, regardless of their payment capacity. Later, they ascribed greater importance to the quality of the loans, targeted businesses with greater growth potential and modified their operating procedures.

Thus, in the early experiments, priority was given to the use of revolving funds, with joint and several guarantees. The credits were graduated and small in scale, with weekly or monthly payments, and were used primarily for working capital. The terms of these loans were generally 2–6 months. Delinquency, due in large part to pressure from the members of the groups, rarely exceeded 10 percent and the credits considered unrecoverable were generally less than 3 percent.

Later, especially in 1987 and after, the guaranty funds were promoted as a means of qualifying small business owners for bank credit. The attitude toward assistance also changed, and greater importance was assigned to productive units with better growth perspectives. These funds later became Association Guaranty Funds, the objective being to organize small business owners into trade associations.

These mechanisms improved the efficiency of small business financing programs as well as the methods of tracking and control. Delinquency ratios were lowered and a certain degree of specialization according to the line of business and geographic area emerged. Operating costs, however, were not lowered significantly, given that in some instances the operators themselves had no precise knowledge of the magnitude of such costs.

Following implementation of the August 1990 economic program, the credit functions of the NGOs began to change. A Program to Support Industrial Micro-businesses and Productive Services (PAMIS) was formed, consisting of nine NGOs financed by the Catholic Relief Service (CRS).

This group tries to work cooperatively. Each NGO in the group specializes in a given field, and the alternative NGO is in charge of directing the credit program. For this purpose, a guaranty fund was created with grants of US$48,000 from the CRS to each NGO, which can temporarily use the funds of other NGOs in case of cash flow problems.

Perhaps the most important innovation was the creation of a central credit information office, which has begun collecting information. It is expected that this will alleviate the problem of defaulting companies applying to other NGOs.

In addition, in 1990, COPEME was created, a consortium of 15 NGOs that operates at the national level as a second-tier financial institution. This consortium expects to serve 27,000 users in 1994.

In the public sector, now that the development banks are no longer functioning, mention should be made of the Municipal Savings Banks and some funds within the Ministry of Industry.

In 1990, the Municipal Savings Banks instituted small business financing programs. Loans were granted at market interest rates with the amounts graduated over time. In 1992, the number of loans granted was 24,366 and the average amount was US$664.

One of the most important funds dedicated to supporting small businesses and micro-businesses is FONCODES (Social Compensation and Development Fund), managed by the Ministry of the Presidency. In 1994, it plans to provide direct financing for small businesses and micro-businesses totaling approximately US$21 million.

Also worthy of mention is FONDEMI (Micro-Industry Development Fund), which is administered by the Ministry of Industry and which, according to ministry sources, has channeled loans totaling US$3 million in the last three months. This fund, which has resources of US$10 million granted by the European Economic Community, loans funds on the basis of the credit rating provided by COPEME and the banking services offices of the Wiese, Continental, and del Sur banks. Loans are granted in dollars at an interest rate of 14 percent—7 percent of which goes to the fund itself, 6 percent to the COPEME NGO, and 1 percent to the intermediate bank.

FOGAPI (Small Industry Loan Guaranty Fund), despite its small size, has been relatively dynamic. In 1993, FOGAPI guaranteed loans totaling US$2,747,449 with a fund of only US$550,000. Of the amount guaranteed, only US$49,879 had to be paid, and of this amount US$13,545 had been recovered by December 1993. It recently signed new agreements with international cooperation organizations enabling it to expand its operations. In general, FOGAPI guarantees credits with the financial system for 50 percent of the loan, which must not exceed US$10,000.

Discussions with the NGOs have generally revealed that they can handle a larger number of operations and that defaults have not been a very important factor in the experience of these institutions.

Conclusions and Recommendations

- In July 1990, the Peruvian economy in general and the financial system in particular were in a state of profound crisis. The magnitude of the stabilization adjustment and the intensity of the structural reforms raised expectations of great change and created fear about the future of the banking system.
- Fortunately, the results of the economic policy have been positive so far, and the financial sector has been able to deal with the changes, having largely overcome its problems thanks to the recovery of economic activity and the strong growth of financial savings.
- During the last three years, a far-reaching financial reform was carried out. Not only were interest rates and the capital account of the balance of payments decontrolled, but the legal and institutional framework within which the financial system operates was modernized. This reform was achieved concurrently with the stabilization plan and other structural reforms.
- New laws were promulgated, both for the Central Bank and the Superintendency of Banks, as well as for the banking system in general. In addition, a series of rules on banking prudence and transparency in the securities market was established.
- As a result of these rules, not only is full-service banking now available but the supervisory powers of the Superintendency of Banks have been greatly enhanced. The new provisions signify greater transparency and modernity both in the banking sector and in the financial market generally.
- Although some problems remain, the banking liquidity and solvency situation is relatively acceptable and is rapidly improving.

- In recent years banking costs have been reduced by closing offices and cutting staff. Moreover, particularly in 1993, commercial banking made a significant effort to increase its reserves for bad debts, which in many cases represented 10 percent of the total loan portfolio.
- Regarding the financing of small businesses, many of the obstacles are created by institutional barriers, either through excessive regulation or the lack of adequate institutions.
- Tedious and costly legal procedures remain, many urban and rural properties are not recorded, the functioning of public registers is excessively slow, and the procedures for formalizing small business units are lengthy and costly.
- A number of small business financing experiments have been tried, many by NGOs. These experiments, after a period of trial and error, were generally successful and have had low delinquency ratios. It is expected that the efforts of the NGOs will be reinforced in the future.
- Nevertheless, the amounts channeled through these efforts were relatively small. Generally, banking sector participation in this financing has been slight, although there are at least three banks that have established departments to serve small businesses.
- Very little progress has been made in establishing a central credit information office for small and medium-sized businesses to provide financial institutions with the credit history of potential clients in this sector.
- Nor has it been possible to develop a set of financial indicators and ratios to determine the solvency and the payment capacity of small and medium-sized businesses. Consequently, the cost of processing credit operations for this sector has not decreased as it has with respect to consumer credit.
- It is expected that the growth of the financial market and the larger volume of funds handled by banks will enable the latter to pay more attention to the small business sector.

Bibliography

Aghion, P. et al. 1992. "The Economics of Bankruptcy Reform." National Bureau of Economic Research. Mimeo.

Andean Report. 1985–92. "Peru Banking and Insurance Portfolio." Lima.

Bahtt, V. 1986. "Mejoramiento de la estructura financiera en países en desarrollo." *Finanzas y desarrollo.*

Barbe, M. 1991. "El papel de la banca central en el marco de la liberalización financiera: el caso de Chile." Santiago, Chile. Mimeo.

Bardella, G. 1990. *Un siglo en la vida económica del Perú 1889–1989.* Banco de Crédito, Lima.

Basombrío, I. 1983. *Bancos: elementos para un debate.* Universidad del Pacífico, Lima.

Baltensperger, E. 1980. "Alternative Approaches to the Theory of the Banking Firm." *Journal of Monetary Economics.* Vol. 6.

Benston, G., and G. Kaufman. 1986. "Risks and Failures in Banking: Overview, History and Evaluation." *Federal Reserve Bank of Chicago.*

Brock, P., ed. 1992. *If Texas were Chile: A Primer on Banking Reform.* Institute for Contemporary Studies.

Bruno, M. 1988. "Opening Up: Liberalization with Stabilization." In Dornbusch, R. and Helmers, eds. *The Open Economy.* Oxford University Press.

Bruno, M., et al. 1991. *Lessons of Economic Stabilization and its Aftermath.* M.I.T. Press.

Cáceres, A., and J. Nagamine. 1991. "Política Económica y Desarrollo del Sistema Financiero Peruano," Grade. Lima.

Calomiris, Ch., and Ch. Himmelberg. 1993. "Directed Credit Programs for Agriculture and Industry: Arguments from Theory and Fact." World Bank. Mimeo.

Caprio, G., and I. Atiyas. 1992. "Policy Issues in Reforming Finance: Lessons and Strategy." World Bank. Mimeo.

Caravedo, B., and F. Villarán. 1991. *Pequeña empresa: desarrollo moderno.* Lima.

Central Reserve Bank of Perú. 1985–93. Nota Semanal, various numbers.

_______. 1980–92. *Memoria anual.* Various numbers.

Chávez, E., and J. Chacaltana. 1994. *Como se financian las microempresas y el agro.* CEDEP, Lima.

Cho, Y. J. 1986. "Inefficiencies from Financial Liberalization in the Absence of Well Functioning Equities Markets." *Journal of Money Credit and Banking.* Vol. 18.

Cho, Y. J., and D. Khatkhate. 1989. *Lessons of Financial Liberalization in Asia: A Comparative Study.* World Bank.

Cobo del Prado, M. 1984. *Diagnóstico del mercado de capitales peruano.* Conasev. Lima.

Collier, P., and C. Mier. 1989. *Finance and Economic Development.* Special Number of the *Oxford Review of Economic Policy.* Vol. 5, No. 4.

CONASEV. 1984. *Flujo de fondos financieros en el Perú: 1979–1983.* Lima.

_______. 1989. *Flujo de fondos financieros en el Perú: 1985–1987.* Lima.

_______. 1989. *La desintermediación financiera.* Lima.

Corbet, J. 1992. "Structure and Behavior in the Japanese Financial System: Lessons from Eastern Europe." St. Anthony's College, Oxford University. Mimeo.

Corbo, V., J. De Melo, and J. Tybout. 1985. *What Went Wrong with the Recent Reforms in the Southern Cone.* World Bank.

_______. 1986. What Went Wrong with the Financial Reforms in the Southern Cone." *Economic Development and Cultural Change.*

Coricelli, F., and A. Thorne. 1992. "Dealing with Enterprises' Bad Loans." World Bank. Mimeo document.

De la Melena, G. 1973. *La reforma financiera: octubre 1968–octubre 1973.* Ministry of Economy and Finance. Lima.

Dornbusch, R. 1987. "Lessons from the German Inflation Experience of the 1920s." In Dornbusch and Fischer, eds., *Macroeconomics and Finance. Essays in Honor of Franco Modigliani.* Cambridge.

_______. 1991. "Lessons from Experiences with High Inflation." Massachusetts Institute of Technology. Mimeo.

Dornbusch, R., Sturzenegger, F. and Wolf, H. 1990. " Extreme Inflation: Dynamics and Stabilization." Massachusetts Institute of Technology. Mimeo.

Economic Commission for Latin America. 1992. "Regulación y supervisión de la banca: experiencias en América Latina y el Caribe." Colección Estudios Políticos y Sociales.

Edwards, S. 1984. "The Order of Liberalization of the External Sector in Developing Countries." *Princeton Essays in International Finance.* No. 156.

_______. 1985. "Stabilization with Liberalization: An Evaluation of Ten Years of Chile's Free Market Policies, 1973–1983." *Economic Development and Cultural Change.*

Feldstein, M. ed. 1991. *The Risk of Economic Crisis.* University of Chicago Press.

Frenkel, J. 1982. "The Order of Economic Liberalization: Discussion." In Brunner and Meltzer, *Economic Policy in a World of Change.*

Fry, M. J. 1988. *Money, Interest and Banking in Economic Development.* Baltimore, MD: The Johns Hopkins University Press.

Giorgio, L. A. 1988. "El sistema financiero argentino. Evolución y estructura actual." Centro de Estudios Monetarios Latinoamericanos—CEMLA. Mexico City.

_______. 1991. "Crisis financiera, reestructuración bancaria e hiperinflación en Argentina." Buenos Aires. Mimeo.

_______. 1992. "Opening the Capital Account: A Survey of Issues and Results." World Bank. Working Paper.

Hanson, J., and J. De Melo. 1985. "External Shocks, Financial Reforms and Stabilization Attempts in Uruguay 1974–1983." *World Development.* Vol. 13.

Held, G., and R. Szalachman, editors. 1991. *Regulación y supervisión de la banca. Experiencias en América Latina y el Caribe.* Vols. 1 and 2.

Hidalgo, R. 1988. "Eficiencia económica: el caso del sistema bancario comercial peruano." In *Ciencia Económica.* No. 20. Lima.

Hoschi, T., A. Kashyap, and D. Scharfstein. 1989. "Bank Monitoring and Investment: Evidence from the Changing Structure of Japanese Corporate Banking Relationship." NBER.

IMF (International Monetary Fund), 1991. "Perú: evolución reciente, aspectos institucionales del sistema financiero y marco actual para el control monetario." Washington, D.C. Mimeo.

_______. 1991a. "Perú: un programa de gestión monetaria basada en el mercado." Washington, D.C. Mimeo.

Keynes, J. M. 1924. *Monetary Reform.* New York.

King, R., and R. Levine. 1992. "Financial Indicators and Growth in a Cross Section of Countries." World Bank. Working Paper.

Klingenberger, J. 1987. *Supervisión bancaria en el Perú.* Lima.

Lima Stock Exchange. 1980–93. *Vademecum bursátil y Boletín diario.* Various issues.

Mayer, C. 1991. "The Role of German Banks in Controlling and Restructuring Private Enterprises." World Bank. Mimeo.

_______. 1992. "In the Image of the West: Creating Financial Systems in Eastern Europe." City University Business School, London. Mimeo.

McKinnon, R. 1982. "The Order of Economic Liberalization: Lessons from Chile and Argentina." In Brunner and Meltzer, eds., *Economic Policy in a World of Change.*

_______. 1988. *Financial Liberalization and Economic Development: A Reassessment of Interest Policies in Asia and Latin America.* International Center for Economic Growth.

_______. 1991. *The Order of Economic Liberalization: Financial Control in a Transition to a Market Economy.* Johns Hopkins University Press, Baltimore.

Moore, B. J. 1986. "Inflation and Financial Deepening." *Journal of Development Economics.*

Morris, F. 1990. "Los sistemas bancarios en América Latina en los años 80s: un estudio comparativo de doce países." World Bank. Discussion Paper.

Superintendency of Banks. 1980–94. *Memorias y Boletines Estadísticos.* Various numbers. Lima.

Perú Report. 1990. *The Peruvian Financial System.* Perú Reporting ERL. Lima.

Portocarrero, J. 1987. *Promoción de la artesanía y la pequeña empresa en el Perú.* Fundación Ebert. Lima.

Rossini, R. 1991. "Liberalización comercial y estabilización económica." In *Foro Económico.* Lima.

Stiglitz, J., and A. Weiss. 1981. "Credit Rationing in Markets with Imperfect Information." *American Economic Review.* Vol. 71.

Stiglitz, J. 1993. "The Role of the State in Financial Markets." World Bank. Mimeo.

Stone, A., B. Levy, and R. Paredes. 1991. "Public Institutions and Private Transactions: The Legal and Regulatory Environment for Business Transactions in Brazil and Chile." World Bank. Policy Research Working Paper.

Sundararajan, V., and T. Baliño. 1991. *Banking Crises: Cases and Issues.* IMF.

Tamagna, F. 1963. *La banca central en América Latina.* CEMLA. Mexico City.

Thorne, A. 1988. "El mercado financiero no organizado en el Perú: determinantes de la oferta de fondos prestables: 1966–1986." Grade. Lima.

_______. 1992. "The Role of Banks in the Transition: Lessons from Eastern European Countries' Experience." World Bank. Mimeo.

Velarde, J. 1988. "Los efectos de la hiperinflación sobre el sector bancario." Apoyo. Lima. Mimeo.

_______. 1987. "El Problema de Financiamiento del Sector Informal." Fundación Ebert. Lima.

_______. 1987. "El potencial de servicios bancarios para el sector informal." Banco de Crédito. Lima.

Velarde, J., and M. Rodríguez. 1992. "De la desinflación a la hiperestanflación. Perú: 1985–1990." CIUP, Lima. Working document.

_______. 1992a. "El programa de estabilización de agosto de 1990: evaluación del primer año." CIUP, Lima. Working document.

_______. 1992b. "Los problemas del orden y velocidad de liberalización de los mercados." CIUP, Lima. Working document.

Villarán, F. 1992. *El nuevo desarrollo: la pequeña industria en el Perú.* Lima.

World Bank. 1989. World Development Report 1989. Washington, D.C.

_______. 1989. "Peru: Policies to Stop Hyperinflation and Initiate Economic Recovery." Washington, D.C. Country Study.

_______. 1989a. "Report of the Task Force on Financial Sector Operations." Washington, D.C.

_______. 1990. "Financial Sector Adjustment Lending: A Preliminary Assessment of the Bank Experience." Washington, D.C.

Yaron, J. 1992. "Assessing Development Finance Institutions: A Public Interest Analysis." World Bank. Discussion Paper.

CHAPTER SIX

URUGUAY: CREDIT PROMOTION AND MARKET EFFICIENCY

Nelson Noya

This chapter presents an overview of the functioning of Uruguay's financial system, with special emphasis on the aspects that determine the greater or lesser credit availability of micro-, small, and medium-sized businesses.

The first section explains the evolution of the Uruguayan financial system after its liberalization in the mid-1970s. We summarize the most recent developments in the system's regulation and the behavior of economic agents, and describe the process of financial disintermediation. The second section identifies the financial intermediaries that are most important to micro-, small and medium-sized businesses, and the third discusses the most common contracts. In the fourth section, the characteristics of small businesses are analyzed, distinguishing those in the urban environment from those in rural areas. The last section contains economic policy recommendations aimed at promoting wider credit availability and increased efficiency in financial market operations.

Recent Trends in the Financial System and Its Regulatory Context

Profound changes took place in the Uruguayan financial system in the last 20 years. These developments are an essential point of reference for understanding many of its current characteristics, particularly the behavior of economic agents and their strategies.

Liberalization, Crisis, and Adjustment

Uruguay undertook financial deregulation between 1974 and 1977. The corresponding measures included the deregulation of interest rates for both lending and deposit; completely unrestricted international capital movements; and the possibility of concluding contracts in foreign currency or in any unit of account.

Restrictions on the composition of intermediary portfolios were lifted, and risk limits for economic groups or businesses were moderated. The government relaxed the limits on deposit-taking based on an institution's capital and eased the rules governing entry into the system. Deregulation was so extensive that between 1979 and 1983 there were no minimum legal reserve requirements. Except for reinstatement of reserve requirements, the deregulation was not reversed.[1]

This deregulation changed the levels of financial intermediation before inflation soared upward in the eighties. In Table 6.1 the growth of that intermediation, can be seen from the ratio of credit granted to GDP, and by increasing monetization of the economy (ratio of bank deposits to GDP). However, this increase in financial intermediation did not reflect higher rate of savings, but resulted from private agents shuffling the aggregate financial portfolio.

The most significant shift in this portfolio was from foreign financial assets or dollar-denominated assets generally (outside the formal financial system), toward the assets of the formal domestic financial system. This also helps explain why the levels of financial intermediation were restored by increased intermediation in dollars. The proportion of credits in foreign currency rose to 70 percent in the 1970s, and is currently at 90 percent.

As in other countries that undertook financial deregulation in the Southern Cone, Uruguay suffered a financial crisis in 1981 and 1982. Negative external shocks to the economy and errors and inconsistencies in macroeconomic policies caused a financial crisis that very nearly resulted in insolvency (see Banda, 1990, and Pérez-Campanero and Leone, 1991).

When the stabilization policy based on pre-announced exchange rules was abandoned in late 1982, Uruguay's currency depreciated significantly. Since most credits had been granted in dollars, real devaluation intensified the problem of delinquent portfolios caused by the recession that began in 1981. In this way, the insolvency of businesses also endangered many banks.

Thereafter the government took steps to rescue financial intermediaries and businesses, incurring considerable fiscal costs, estimated at 8 percent of GDP between 1982 and 1984. Transnational banks managed to exchange their overdue portfolios for external loans from their headquarters to the Uruguayan government, but loans were extremely rare following the Mexican external debt crisis. Meanwhile, nationally owned private intermediaries, and some regionally owned, were failing one after another. The national private banks gradually disappeared in this process. The three largest national private institutions survived, with the difficulties inherited from the crisis, until they were taken over between

[1] Between 1984 and 1985, upper limits were set for interest rates on loans in local currency. Moreover, for non-banking operations, a multiple of the average bank rate served as the upper limit.

Table 6.1. Bank Credits and Deposits Relative to GDP, 1975–92
(Percentages)

	Credits					Deposits			
Year	BCU	BROU	BHU	Private banking	Total	BROU	BHU	Private banking	Total
1975	0.5	7.6	3.3	6.3	17.7	2.2	1.1	7.5	10.8
1976	0.6	8.2	3.6	7.7	20.1	2.8	1.4	10.7	14.9
1977	0.2	8.5	3.7	9.8	22.1	3.1	1.3	13.8	18.2
1978	0.1	8.5	3.9	12.6	25.1	3.5	1.3	17.3	22.1
1979	0.1	7.5	3.4	15.0	25.9	3.8	1.2	18.4	23.4
1980	0.0	7.8	4.3	19.9	32.1	3.8	1.1	20.7	25.6
1981	0.0	8.3	6.2	24.1	38.7	5.1	1.7	26.0	32.8
1982	0.4	10.9	9.6	30.5	51.4	7.2	2.7	33.6	43.5
1983	4.1	13.5	9.6	31.9	59.1	9.2	2.9	30.9	43.1
1984	8.8	12.9	9.1	23.4	54.2	10.9	3.3	28.9	43.1
1985	7.5	13.5	10.0	19.0	49.9	13.0	3.5	24.5	41.0
1986	5.1	12.6	10.3	15.8	43.8	13.1	3.6	22.8	39.5
1987	3.6	12.0	10.1	14.3	39.9	12.8	3.4	20.9	37.2
1988	2.6	13.0	10.5	14.6	40.7	14.5	4.3	22.4	41.2
1989	1.9	13.7	10.4	13.6	39.6	16.8	4.9	26.1	47.8
1990	0.4	15.0	10.6	12.0	38.0	20.2	6.0	32.5	58.6
1991	0.7	11.4	10.5	13.8	36.4	19.6	6.2	30.3	56.1
1992	0.2	11.0	11.0	10.0	32.2	18.7	6.2	28.6	53.5

Note: Credits include credits in local and foreign currency to the resident private sector. Deposits include demand, savings and fixed-term deposits in local and foreign currency, excluding those of nonresidents. Both are annual averages of monthly balances over nominal GDP.
BCU: Central Bank of Uruguay. BROU: Banco de la República. BHI: Banco Hipotecario (Mortgage Bank).
Source: BCU, Boletín Estadístico, various numbers.

1985 and 1987. Once under government control, these institutions became known as "administered" banks.

Resolving the crisis was delayed because of the heavy indebtedness of many businesses to the country's banking system. In 1982, the Central Bank of Uruguay (BCU) acquired overdue bank credits in the above-mentioned rescue operations, although it was practically impossible to recover these credits. Similarly, between 1981 and 1992, measures were adopted calling for the mandatory refinancing of overdue bank credits, which included, in addition to portfolios held by the Central Bank, many private banks' portfolios. Beginning in 1985, these measures were adopted through laws that were approved in the Uruguayan Congress, the last of which dates from 1992. These laws significantly eroded the quality of contracts and the value of guarantees, creating a basic obstacle to the growth of the credit market.

The crisis had various effects on the functioning of the system. Between 1983 and 1987, credit to the private sector contracted by 20 percent of GDP. Deposit levels, after an initial period of low confidence, steadied and even increased in response to the bank rescue policy. Private banks lost ground to public banks, and especially to Banco de la República (BROU). That institution and Banco Hipotecario (BHU), which together make up the public banking sector, attracted deposits equivalent to 9 percent of GDP in 1982; by the late eighties, their share had increased to 26 percent of GDP (20–34 percent of the total). Private banks closed offices and reduced their staffs, concentrating credits on a few large, secure customers (see Tables 6.A.5–6.A.11 in the Appendix). To offset their fixed costs as traditional activities declined, banks offered a wider range of nonbanking services (foreign trade, credit cards, etc.) and expanded their external operations (Table 6.A.3 in the Appendix).

Consequently, toward the mid-eighties, a clear segmentation of the banking system was observed. Foreign banks adopted a wholesale strategy regarding both credit and deposits. Small customers were relegated to the BROU and to the small segment of savings and credit cooperatives (which had a market share of less than 2 percent). The national banks taken over by foreign interests in the first rescue operation of 1982 had been characterized by extensive networks and a wide range of operations of varying volumes. After the change in ownership, their physical networks were reduced. Between 1985 and 1987, the banks taken over by the government, which were the major competitors of the BROU, lost market share when they were reorganized before being reprivatized.

Due to system-wide adjustments in both establishments and staff, most banks lost the store of information and basic experience necessary for smaller credit operations.

In the nineties, some changes in business strategies occurred. Comercial, the only reprivatized bank, adopted an aggressive strategy with certain retail characteristics, and was even assisted by several foreign banks (Boston, ING). Financial cooperatives continued their previous strategy and significantly expanded their networks. Nevertheless, these changes did not result in an expansion of credit to productive enterprises, especially those owned by Uruguayans.

Changes in the credit portfolio were related primarily to an increase in personal consumer credit and credit to import companies (Table 6.A.4 in the Appendix). In the field of consumer financing, banks began to crowd out nonbanking sources (finance companies, suppliers, trade, etc.). This was due in part to the risks associated with legal changes in private contracts and the difficulties of enforcing guarantees. The mandatory refinancing imposed by law affected businesses, particularly those owned by Uruguayans, and above all those in the agricultural and industrial sectors. It is not surprising, therefore, that personal loans had a competitive edge, because they were not greatly affected by these changes.

Recent Changes in the Regulatory Framework

Once the most urgent problems caused by the crisis had been solved and the failure of banks prevented, the system was again placed under regulation. The basic objectives of this process were to strengthen the powers of the BCU and modernize its supervision, to rationalize the reserve requirements policy, and to standardize the treatment of public and private banks.

Prudential Regulations and Capital Adjustment

Until late 1989, the capital adjustment procedure was based on the establishment of a maximum ratio between liabilities and capital. Specifically, this ratio was set at 20 times the net worth requirement (RPN, *responsabilidad patrimonial neta*), plus secure assets (reserves, BCU deposits, public securities and Uruguayan external debt notes). It has been estimated that this type of adjustment entailed capital of approximately 4.8 percent of the risk assets (Amoroso and Xavier, 1988). The limits were based on each institution's RPN.[2] The minimum required by the BCU until then was adjusted on the basis of inflation, and set according to the intermediary's legal form (locally organized subsidiary or corporation, or cooperative) and number of offices.

In late 1989, a ratio was established directly involving the risk assets, net of reserves, in conformity with the international rules known as the Basel Committee regulations. Assets are weighted increasingly according to their risk characteristics (based on the schedule shown in Table 6.A.17 in the Appendix). The ratio between capital, measured by the minimum net worth requirement (RPNM, *responsabilidad patrimonial neta mínima*), and the assets so weighted steadily increased until reaching 8 percent in late 1992 (this growth is illustrated in Table 6.2).

At the same time, the reserve requirements were changed. Before 1989, borrowers were rated not according to risk, but according to whether they were current in their obligations on the last day of the month. Reserves were established as a percentage of debtors in collection (more than six months in arrears) and portfolio write-offs were required for arrears of more than 150 days. Under the new rule, financial institutions had to rate direct and contingent risks constantly, according to objective and subjective criteria. Thus, they rated debtors in the nonfinancial sector by five categories: normal risks, potential risks, real risks, high risks, and unrecoverables.[3]

---

[2] Consisting of book equity less several adjustments such as the deduction of investments in branches abroad, shares of other enterprises, movable and immovable property not in use and accounts with the head office and branches abroad.

[3] Reserves are established in the following manner: from 0 to 0.5 percent in the normal risks category, 5 percent in the potential risks category, 20 percent in the real risks category, 50 percent in the high risks category, and 100 percent in the unrecoverables category. The criteria for rating a debtor in each category are summarized in Table 6.A.16 of the annex.

Table 6.2. Capital Adjustment Rules since 1989

Capital shall simultaneously be:

1. Greater than the basic net worth requirement (absolute amount set by the BCU, adjusted on the basis of domestic wholesale prices).

2. Greater than a percentage of the risk assets, net of reserves, appropriately weighted, i.e.:

At end–1989	5 percent
1990	6 percent
1991	7 percent
1992	8 percent

3. Greater than 4 percent of assets and contingencies, net of reserves

Source: Rules for Regulating and Auditing the Financial System, Central Bank, Montevideo.

The amended rule should prevent distortions in the treatment of the portfolio in local currency, as compared to the dollar portfolio. Partial adjustment of interest on high risk and unrecoverable debtors is allowed. Conversely, if a credit in local currency is not adjusted, at least at the rate of devaluation, it deteriorates relative to a credit of similar quality in foreign currency.

However, the above prudential regulations are not particularly stringent requirements for very small credit operations. Financial institutions can rate customers with credits of less than 0.3 percent of the basic net worth requirement for banks (RPBB, *responsabilidad patrimonial básica para bancos*), which is currently US$15,000, according to whether they are current in their obligations. That eliminates the need for rating risks on the basis of a more thorough and more costly analysis. This rating is allowed if the credits are not a significant percentage of the total portfolio and statistical studies on the unrecoverable portion of the portfolio do not indicate above-average indices. Rules for financial cooperatives are stricter, however, because the above limit was set at 0.05 percent of the RPB (or approximately US$2,500).[4] These institutions tend to specialize in the smaller customers segment and, consequently, their credits are smaller. As a result, cooperatives incur a high information cost for rating small credits, although not for very small credits (under US$2,500).

As for mid-sized credit operations, according to the assessment of financial system operators, most of smaller companies are rated as real risks and high risks (categories three and four, with reserves of 20 and 50 percent). This is because criteria based on the last two fiscal years' earnings are rarely satisfactory for these companies, which sometimes undervalue earnings to avoid paying income

[4] Consultation No. 31/93, Superintendency of Banks.

tax (IRIC, *impuesto a las rentas de industria y comercio*) and may conceal assets to evade payment of net worth tax.[5]

There are also limits on the individual credit risk, which cannot exceed 25 percent of each bank's RPB. This limit may be exceeded up to 50 percent, counting guarantees in cash and others. In addition, financial intermediaries cannot hold shares or make investments in other local activities, except temporarily for capitalizing enterprises or recovering guarantees. Investment banks are the only exception, but no companies of this type are in operation. Similarly, banks may not incur credit risks in excess of their net worth: their net asset or liability position in local or foreign currency is limited by the RPB.

Information Requirements and Risk Control

Changes in these areas began with the introduction of a new, more analytical banking chart of accounts in 1989. Nevertheless, the most important changes relate to the information that intermediaries must keep on their credit customers.

For decades, the law required all credit applicants to submit certificates attesting to the fulfillment of their tax obligations (General Tax Directorate or DGI, *Dirección General de Impuestos*) and their contributions to the social security system (Social Insurance Bank or BPS, *Banco de Previsión Social).* In addition, since early 1993, extensive provisions have required the Superintendency of Banks to compile other information,[6] for assessing the quality of risks. Consequently, these regulations on information requirements are related to those summarized above on rating portfolios. In many cases, these requirements make access to credit very expensive.

The rules require keeping a folder for each customer that contains a risk analysis and information on financial standing. All the information in this folder must be updated annually, no more than 120 days after the close of the fiscal year.

The information requirements [illegible]ut are determined by certain considerations, such as the customer's in[illegible]ess to the financial system as a whole

[5] The avoidance and evasion of both taxes is [illegible]le[illegible]ged t[illegible] e extensive in Uruguay. The low level of revenue from both taxes and the high t[illegible] are proo[illegible] of this. The ratio of IRIC receipts to private, nonagricultural GDP reached a ten-yea[illegible] 1994. On average, it was 1.8 percent during this period. On the other hand, net worth tax receipts did not exceed 1.7 percent of private, nonagricultural GDP. The current IRIC rate is 40 percent (30 percent prior to 1990), while the rate of the net worth tax for businesses is 2 percent. The net worth tax is also levied on individuals above a certain nontaxable minimum. It is estimated that 80 percent of the receipts come from the tax on personal net worth, which, unlike the figure on private GDP, reinforces the idea that tax avoidance and evasion are widespread among businesses.

[6] BCU Circular 1444 of February 1, 1993, supplemented by documents 93/60 of May 28, 1993, and 93/81 of July 1, 1993.

(national and foreign), and the risk the customer represents for the particular financial institution. The term of the credit, type of customer (resident or non-resident), and type of institution (financial or nonfinancial) are required. Other factors include whether the customer pays certain taxes (on fictitious income in the agricultural sector or on small businesses in the urban sector), whether the guarantees are easily enforced (cash collateral), and whether the customer is a member of a group of companies.

Regarding the level of indebtedness to the financial system, categories are established on the basis of the minimum capital required of banks by the central bank (i.e., the RPBB). There are three categories of requirements: less than 15 percent of the RPBB, between 15 and 30 percent, and over 30 percent. In mid-1993, those categories were the following: less than US$780,000, between US$780,000 and US$1,560,000, and over US$1,560,000.

For short-term loans (less than three years for these purposes) involving the largest debtors, the requirements are: financial statements for the last three fiscal years (balance sheet, income statement, statement of changes in net worth, statement of source and allocation of funds) and the corresponding notes, prepared in accordance with standard accounting principles. A cash flow statement—annual or for the term of the credit—is also required. This statement must be prepared by a professional and must be updated every six months, including an itemized list of financial debts and commercial debtors and creditors. All the reports must be accompanied by the opinion of an independent auditor.

In the intermediate category of indebtedness (between 15 and 30 percent of the RPBB), an outside auditor's statement may be replaced by a report on a limited audit prepared by a qualified professional, not necessarily independent.

For customers with low indebtedness (less than 15 percent of the RPBB), a cash flow statement signed by a professional is not mandatory, and the financial statements need not be adjusted for inflation. Instead of the limited audit report, the information can be accompanied by a report prepared by a qualified professional.

Whenever the term of the loan is under three years, if exposure is greater than 4 percent of the RPBB (approximately US$208,000), an investment proposal with technical and economic components is mandatory, as well as a financial evaluation by a financial institution or a specialized firm. For exposure below this limit, a cash budget or "quasi-proposal" is sufficient.

If indebtedness is low (less than 15 percent of the RPBB), but the debtor is an individual who does not own a company (personal credits), the information is limited to a notarized statement of accountability and proof of income.

Some exceptions in the case of small credits make the information requirements less costly. If the exposure is less than 0.3 percent of the RPBB (US$15,600), the financial and economic data need not be monitored but merely obtained when the credit is granted or renewed. The same is true in the case of housing credits. For personal loans in this category, all that is required is proof of income.

Moreover, even a company with risks below 15 percent of the RPBB, which pays the small business tax (IPE), needs only a statement of income and expenditure from the bank and an itemization of assets and liabilities.[7]

Microbusinesses are most likely to experience difficulties in obtaining bank credit because of the above measures. Data from a sampling of small businesses in the Montevideo region suggest that many businesses with more than five employees now use accounting records.

Licenses and Deposit Insurance

Authorizations for establishing new financial institutions are governed by the September 1992 law on financial intermediation. The Executive Branch is responsible for authorizing the founding of new financial institutions, but it must first obtain the favorable opinion of the BCU. Each year the number of banks founded must not exceed 10 percent of those already in existence.

Banks must be either corporations or subsidiaries of foreign companies. In the past, bearer shares were permitted and could be transferred simply by notifying the monetary authority. But a 1989 amendment provided the central bank with better information and greater control over the holdings of financial agents, by stipulating that shares must be registered and all transfers must be authorized by the central bank.

Though the system of licenses has not changed substantively since 1982, the central bank has thoroughly evaluated the reputation and creditworthiness of all who wish to purchase existing banks or open new ones. Apparently, a criterion sine qua non is that any new bank or purchaser must be either a first-line international banking institution or a consortium of agents in which such an institution has a significant interest.[8]

This policy appears to use administrative barriers as a policy tool to safeguard the system. In particular, it can be interpreted as a means of avoiding responsibility for an implicit deposit guarantee.

Before the September 1992 law, there was no official deposit insurance system, although the rescue operations of the past three decades make it reasonable

---

[7] Companies below the limit of gross sales required for exemption from the IRIC and also from charging VAT on sales are liable for the small business tax. In compensation, the taxpayer cannot deduct the VAT charged on its purchases. This gross sales limit is adjusted annually and is about US$22,000 at annual rates ($92,000 at 1993 prices). A monthly fixed amount is paid, which is currently the equivalent of approximately US$500 at annual rates ($224 per month for 1994).

[8] An example of this rule is the refusal to sell one of the administered banks to a consortium formed by Crédit Agricole (the largest bank in the world in terms of assets, except for the Japanese banks), a Chilean bank, and one of the savings and credit cooperatives, apparently because Crédit Agricole's equity holding was insufficient.

Table 6.3. Companies that Keep Accounting Records
(Percentages)

	Number of employees		
Existence of accounting records	2–5	5–19	20 or more
Yes	71.6	93.6	90.5
No	27.4	6.0	9.5
Don't know/no response	1.0	0.4	0.0
Total	100.0	100.0	100.0

Source: Alberti and Melgar, 1992.

to assume that depositors relied on an implicit form of insurance. The 1992 law expressly states that the government is not responsible for the failure of private institutions. The central bank may offer special financial assistance in the discounting of risk-free instruments, but is limited to a maximum determined by the financial institution's capital. Thus, the central bank and the national government will cooperate to aid institutions experiencing insolvency crises.

Reserve Requirements

Once the exchange policy of pre-announced rules was abandoned, monetary policy became active, and after 1982 the reserve requirement was reinstated. The resulting high, non-interest-bearing reserve ratios affected the level of lending rates. Moreover, transactions in local and in foreign currency were treated differently, making foreign currency more advantageous.

Toward the end of the eighties, the rules were changed: The level of the non-interest-bearing reserve ratio was lowered and the treatment of local and foreign currency were treated alike. Policies for public and private banks were standardized, as were those for public agencies' deposits in public banks.

However, because inflation remains high, the sunk cost of the portion of non-interest-bearing reserves in local currency is higher than that of the foreign currency portion. Banks can offset this negative effect on operating costs in pesos because there is a demand for sight deposits, on which very low interest rates are paid.

Reorganization of Public Banks

These reforms are especially relevant with regard to small credits, owing to the specialization of the banks involved in these operations: the BROU and the "administered" banks.

The four administered banks were originally Pan de Azúcar, Comercial, Caja Obrera, and de Italia. Three of these were the largest private banks in the market, operating in market segments close to those of BROU's loan clientele. The smallest (de Italia) merged with Caja Obrera. When first taken over, these banks were placed under the BROU's control. But in 1990 they were separated and placed under the direction of a public institution originally created to manage the business rescue process, the National Development Corporation (CND).

With technical and financial assistance from the World Bank and the IDB, recapitalization policies were applied with a view to reprivatizing the banks. The privatization process succeeded only for the largest bank (Comercial), which was in private hands once more in 1990. As mentioned above, the central bank, when it tried the licensing policy, imposed fairly strict conditions on regional and national institutions wishing to buy banks. The result was that in at least three instances these negotiations were abandoned and the sales process resumed.

The BROU, having increased its share of the deposit market from 1983 until very recently, accumulated a sizable liquidity surplus, which it could not invest in its entirety. The problem has been particularly acute in the case of funds in dollars.

The policy's focal point has been to harmonize regulation of the BROU with that of other banks. Because the BROU's charter was identical to that of the central bank, the BCU could not legally supervise the BROU or apply the same rules to it as to private banks. A new financial intermediation law in late 1992 partially resolved the situation.

Nevertheless, the most important changes occurred in the policy of fixing rates. Prior to 1991, the BROU had a special reserve arrangement, the most salient feature of which was its capacity to attract public sector funds monopolistically with lower reserve requirement rates. This gave it a differential base of resources since it thus received the inflation tax on these funds. These resources allowed it to finance a fairly low rate of credits in local currency for concessional credits. Toward the beginning of 1991, this reserve arrangement was changed: new funds were given the same treatment as private sector funds, and the central bank established a 100 percent reserve requirement for central government funds.[9]

This point is important for our purposes because the BROU is a significant source of small credits. The private banks working in the adjacent segments were the "administered" banks, which were in the process of adjusting and decreasing their activities.

---

[9] Other specific considerations make it impossible to speak of the complete harmonization of reserve requirements, but these factors do not affect the marginal cost of the financial resources.

Figure 6.1 BROU and Private Banking Margin
(In local currency at 180 days)

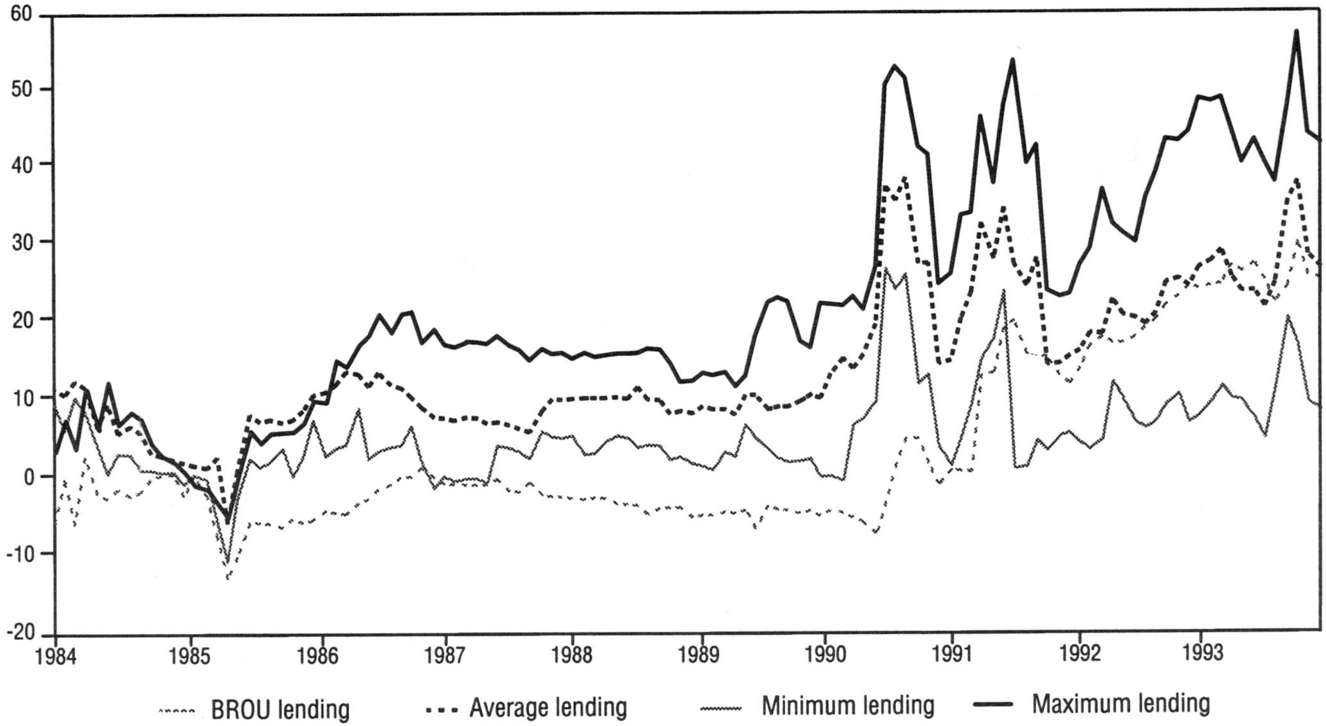

Source: BCU, *Boletín Estadístico*, various numbers, and Oikos, *Panorama financiero*, various numbers.

The change in policy regarding reserve requirements and the fixing of the BROU's rates substantially increased its gross margin. Along with these changes, the margins of private banks also increased, which suggests that the BROU's higher lending rates carried those of private banks along with them. Figures 6.1 and 6.2 show the trend of the ex ante gross margin or spread, calculated as the difference between lending and deposit rates, less the effect of the sunk cost of non-interest-bearing reserves. The margins calculated in this manner should cover operating costs, potential risks, and the payment of banking capital.

Four margins are shown in each figure: three for private banking (with maximum lending rates, for customers with higher risks or approval costs, and with average and minimum lending rates, for first-line customers) and one for the BROU (using the most representative lending rate, known as the basic rate). Each figure represents the gross margin of operations in local currency or in dollars. Table 6.4 shows the annual averages of the margins. To compare the two exercises, margins in local currency were calculated using equivalent interest rates in dollars (consequently there are more variations, since real and not anticipated devaluation is used). The ex post aggregate margin for private banks is calculated in Table 6.5.

As the sunk cost of BROU reserve requirements prior to 1991 is unavailable due to the rule's enormous complexity, this cost was calculated by assuming that the reserve arrangement was similar to those of private banking, which is definitely the case for the marginal cost of operations from 1991 onward.

These figures show that the cost of financial intermediation increased substantially for second- or third-line accounts in local currency. From the viewpoint of private banks, the strategy seems to be based on setting lending rates at the opportunity cost of their customers' credit.[10]

Given these margins, the cost of intermediation in the system, measured via the gross margins, is extremely high: more than 25 percent per annum in dollars for average rates on credits in local currency. However, the same is not true in dollars, in which case the cost of intermediation is reasonable. The private banking margins on medium-quality credits (calculated with average lending rates) are similar to those of the BROU.

These differences can be explained by the dissimilarity of risks or selection costs among applicants for different currencies, by the greater instability of infla-

[10] This interpretation accords with the observation that for first-line accounts in dollars, the gross bank intermediation margin is practically insignificant. Moreover, for this same type of customer, the intermediation margin is zero or negative in local currency, because banks make operations with these customers profitable by providing other services. The opportunity cost for sound customers is the cost of credit at the international level; such customers are generally multinational companies (see Noya and Dominioni, 1992).

Figure 6.2 BROU and Private Banking Margin
(In dollars at 180 days)

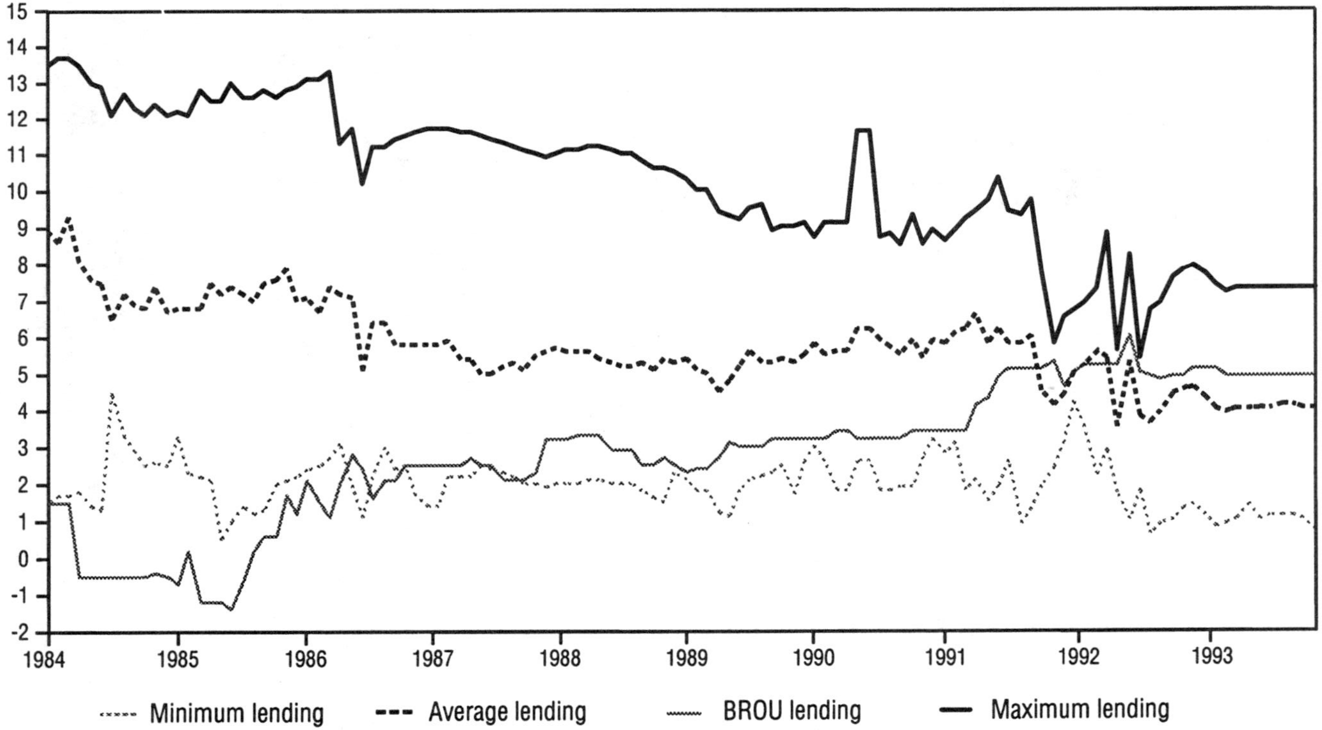

Source: BCU, *Boletín Estadístico*, various numbers, and Oikos, *Panorama financiero*, various numbers.

tion in pesos as compared to dollars, or by a situation of disequilibrium, or transaction costs. Noya and Dominioni (1992) support the hypothesis of disequilibrium caused by the upward movement of the price of the bank with the highest marginal cost (the BROU).

The ex post aggregate margin figures shown in Table 6.5 are heavily influenced by the operations in dollars, which represent more than 80 percent of the balances. Thus these figures do not reflect a high intermediation cost. (This is also due to the inferior standing of the "administered" banks, which have a fairly large weight in local-currency operations.)

The high margin on credits in local currency explains the high real interest rates on credits in that currency, unlike the rates for credits in dollars and for deposits in dollars or local currency (Table 6.6). Because the recent higher costs of intermediation in local currency reflect the BROU's own inefficiencies (lower productivity, higher operating costs, etc.), policies to eliminate such inefficiencies are critical.[11] The increase in competition, which results in lower opportunity costs for agents who work with the BROU, points in the same direction. Thus, prompt reprivatization of the "administered" banks would contribute to achieving this objective, if their new owners' business strategies correspond with the strategies previously applied to virtually all types of credits.

Reforms in Progress

A bill providing a new central bank charter, currently under discussion in the Uruguayan congress and passed by one chamber, attempts to give the central bank greater autonomy. Nevertheless, even if the bill passes, Uruguay will still be far from having an autonomous central bank like that of Chile. Constitutional restrictions still permit removal of the bank's board of directors by the Executive Branch, and the bill's provisions pertaining to autonomy are fairly weak compared to other countries. Still they do provide a greater degree of autonomy than currently exists (by setting limited objectives and placing restrictions on financing the treasury, for example).

Uruguay's present constitution treats public banks and the central bank as equal institutions. However, this new bill would give the Superintendency of Banks greater authority and independence: for example, the Superintendent's term of office would be longer than those of the board of directors.

---

[11] It is impossible to estimate with any degree of accuracy what the cost of BROU operations is compared to those of private banking; first, because BROU's income statement is not available and, second, because the quality of the institution's accounting information is admittedly poor.

Table 6.4. ***Ex ante*** **Gross Financial Intermediation Margins (Rates Effective at 180 Days), 1983–1993**
(Annual average of monthly data)

	Operations in pesos				Operations in dollars			
	Private banking				Private banking			
Year	Maximum lending	Average lending	Minimum lending	Basic BROU	Maximum lending	Average lending	Minimum lending	Basic BROU
1983	−12.0	−4.8	−9.8	0.0	13.7	8.5	3.1	0.0
1984	6.5	7.3	4.1	−1.6	12.8	7.6	2.3	0.0
1985	2.2	3.6	−0.6	−5.8	12.6	7.2	1.8	−0.1
1986	16.8	11.2	4.0	−2.1	11.8	6.4	2.2	2.1
1987	16.6	7.5	2.3	−1.4	11.3	5.4	2.1	2.5
1988	15.0	9.6	3.6	−3.7	10.9	5.4	2.0	2.8
1989	17.0	9.2	2.5	−4.8	9.3	5.2	2.0	3.0
1990	33.5	22.5	10.7	−1.6	9.3	5.8	2.3	3.3
1991	35.9	23.0	7.8	12.4	8.6	5.5	2.2	4.6
1992	38.3	22.2	7.6	20.0	7.2	4.5	1.6	5.1
1993[a]	44.4	27.4	10.6	25.5	7.3	4.0	1.0	4.9

[a] Average through October.
Note: The margins are calculated on the basis of blackboard data on lending and deposit operations. The only cost deducted is the sunk cost of non-interest-bearing reserves. For purposes of comparing operations in pesos with operations in dollars, the effects of devaluation of the peso with respect to the dollar are deducted from the margins on the former.
Source: Prepared on the basis of Central Bank, *Boletín Estadístico,* various numbers, and Oikos, *Panorama financiero*, various numbers.

The new bill would overturn the provisions approved in late 1992 concerning the rescue mechanisms implemented during banking crises. Current law prohibits the central bank and any public agency from guaranteeing the other banks' obligations and limits central bank assistance to the amount of the banks' capital. The new bill, however, would permit almost unlimited assistance to banks, a return to the system of implied or discretional deposit guarantees.

Nonbanking Financial Processes[12]

A fully developed private securities market has never existed in Uruguay. The stock exchange operates essentially as a placement mechanism and as a secondary market for government bonds. Apart from the Treasury, only Banco Hipotecario places a significant volume of resources in this way.

[12] See Talvi and Viana (1991).

Table 6.5. Private Bank Margins According to Income Statements, 1987–92
(Annualized percentage rates converted to dollars)

Item	1987	1988	1989	1990	1991	1992
1) Average return on credits	7.4	11.6	11.4	17.9	18.4	16.9
2) Average financial cost	3.8	5.9	4.7	6.7	5.2	3.5
3) Gross intermediation margin (1)–(2)	3.6	5.7	6.7	11.2	13.1	13.4
4) Ratio of credits to deposits	67.6	65.5	56.3	44.7	39.7	39.6
5) Yield of other assets	0.4	2.0	3.8	5.4	4.3	5.6
6) Average variable operating cost						
a) Low hypothesis	6.9	6.6	6.1	7.3	7.6	8.9
b) High hypothesis	4.1	4.5	4.7	5.8	6.1	5.6
c) Average hypothesis	5.5	5.6	5.4	6.6	6.8	7.2
7) Variable intermediation margin (1)–(4)/100–(2)+(5)–(6)						
a) Low hypothesis	–5.3	–2.9	–0.5	–0.6	–1..2	–0.1
b) High hypothesis	–2.4	–0.9	0.8	0.9	0.2	3.1
c) Average hypothesis	–3.8	–1.9	0.1	0.2	–0.4	1.6
8) Net earnings from deposit services	1.8	2.0	1.8	1.9	1.8	1.8
9) Variable banking margin (7)+(8)						
a) Low hypothesis	–3.4	–1.0	1.3	1.3	0.6	1.7
b) High hypothesis	–0.6	1.1	2.7	2.8	2.0	4.9
c) Average hypothesis	–2.0	0.1	1.9	2.1	1.4	3.4
10) Fixed costs per deposit						
a) Low hypothesis	1.4	1.5	1.1	1.0	0.8	0.5
b) High hypothesis	4.2	3.5	2.5	2.6	2.2	2.1
c) Average hypothesis	2.8	2.5	1.8	1.8	1.5	1.3
11) Total banking margin (9)–(10)	–4.8	–2.4	0.2	0.3	–0.2	1.2

Source: Based on unpublished BCU data and Dominioni and Vaz, 1991.

Some indicators provide clear evidence of this. In recent years, transactions in the secondary private securities market have been less than one percent of the transactions on the stock exchange. Primary offerings of private securities have been virtually nonexistent. Private securities transactions on the stock exchange have not exceeded 0.2 percent of GDP since 1960, and almost without exception the trend has been downward since the early forties. At present, private securities represent 0.05 percent of GDP. The number of companies quoted on the stock exchange has decreased since the late 1940s and since 1987 has never been more than 20, with four of these companies accounting for more than 80 percent of the transactions.

Among the factors that contribute to this situation, macroeconomic instability is usually considered the root cause. Despite this instability and low rate of investment, however, according to Talvi and Viana's estimate (based on a cross-section regression with a sample of 39 underdeveloped countries), Uruguay's private securities market should be 10 times larger. Thus, institutional and microeconomic factors account for much of this underdevelopment.

One microeconomic factor is the small scale of Uruguayan private companies: the largest corporation has sales of US$60 million. Private companies are

Table 6.6. Real Interest Rates of Private Banks, 1984–92
(Annual averages of monthly values, in annualized percentages, deflated by consumer prices)

	Lending						Deposits	
	Credits in local currency			Credits in dollars				
Year	Maximum	Average	Minimum	Maximum	Average	Minimum	In pesos	In dollars
1984	13.2	12.4	9.0	42.7	36.3	30.3	3.8	26.8
1985	6.2	6.0	1.5	7.4	1.8	–3.8	0.3	–6.4
1986	16.7	9.4	2.0	5.2	–0.6	–5.0	–3.2	–7.8
1987	28.2	15.1	8.7	20.0	12.8	8.7	3.9	5.6
1988	19.8	10.9	3.8	11.1	5.0	1.1	–2.4	–1.6
1989	22.2	9.9	2.4	14.0	9.2	5.5	–17.3	–12.1
1990	27.5	12.3	–0.9	3.0	–0.7	–4.4	–25.3	–23.4
1991	45.5	29.0	12.3	1.8	–1.3	–4.7	0.3	–7.5
1992	37.3	22.8	7.8	–0.9	–3.6	–6.6	0.1	–8.8

Source: Based on Central Bank of Uruguay, *Boletín Estadístico*, various numbers.

distributed according to line of business, and most are owned and managed by families. In more developed Latin American financial markets, the largest companies quoted on stock exchanges are engaged in financial services, mining, fuel production, or utilities. But in Uruguay, these are not fields for private business, either due to lack of natural resources or because certain sectors have been reserved for public enterprises.

The institutional factors holding back Uruguay's economic development include constraints imposed by the regulation of certain key agents, limitations imposed by laws and regulations governing the corporate system, and a certain degree of discrimination in the tax system.

Until last year, no government agency was assigned to regulate or supervise the stock exchange; this role is now filled by the central bank. The previous, self-regulating mechanism would have allowed existing issuers to raise barriers against the entry of new offerors, although conflicts of this type did not occur.

On the other hand, the laws and regulations governing companies were amended in 1989, changing legislation that dated back to the nineteenth century. The changes in this aspect were designed to give shareholders greater control. Nevertheless, government supervisory agencies focused on compliance with formalities concerning the compatibility of business contracts with legislation, and publication requirements, without concern for the quality of information provided to shareholders. A key point is that external audits conducted to certify financial statements are not obligatory. In any case, the legislation prohibits the issuance of bonds in excess of 50 percent of the paid-in capital and reserves, not counting the reserves for the revaluation of assets.

The tax system discriminates in favor of government bonds and bank deposits: both are exempt from the tax on net worth. In 1944, another tax disadvantage related to the issuance of private negotiable bonds (as opposed to bank debt) was eliminated: the balance of the bond issue was not computable among the liabilities to be deducted in the case of corporate property tax (2 percent). There is still another limitation, however: the interest on negotiable bonds is deductible from income tax (IRIC) only up to a limit determined by the application of the interest rates on BROU deposits. However, excluding a few insignificant exceptions, no bond issues have been recorded.

There are no institutional investors in Uruguay, which surely constitutes a limitation on the development of instruments that spread risk and lower the fixed operating costs of the securities market. Apart from potential cost-benefit factors, the restrictions are essentially legal and regulatory. The social security system functions primarily through government institutions. Though some quasi-official institutions exist for small groups (university professions and bank employees) and social security funds may be established to supplement public funds, in such cases institutions are not authorized to hold private securities portfolios, being restricted to public debt and real estate. Moreover, until this year, the securities market was virtually monopolized—legally—by a public institution. But both this institution and private companies have the same restriction on their portfolio management that the social security institutions have. Finally, there are no provisions in Uruguayan law concerning the organization of investment funds, nor are their activities regulated. Although a law authorizing the founding of investment banks was passed in 1990, there has been no interest in opening this type of specialized bank.[13]

In 1993, regulations governing stock exchange transactions were changed, to deregulate the entry of agents and permit institutional brokers to participate (particularly financial institutions). The stock exchange was also interconnected with others in the region and an electronic exchange was created with many banks participating. But these changes had absolutely no effect on the offering of private securities. The only noticeable change is the upsurge in foreign securities transactions, including private securities.

In 1983, the formation of savings consortiums or circles was authorized. Companies dealing in these instruments are under the control of the central bank, which assigns a minimum capital (currently US$250,000). Initially dedicated to the purchase of housing and automobiles, the savings circles later extended their activities to nonspecific credits, even for companies. Although data on these operations are incomplete, they are significant only with respect to automobile purchases.

---

[13] One of the reasons mentioned for this lack of interest is the double income and capital tax to which the loan portfolio of this type of institution would be subject.

There are no methods of "securitization," given the various obstacles to such procedures. In particular, simultaneous security transfers and the guarantees they entail are not clearly defined by law. Investment funds, as independent assets without legal status, are not permitted under Uruguayan law, which is a major barrier to private pension funds (Olivera, 1992). Finally, companies that subscribe to investment fund issues would be subject to double taxation (although individuals would not, since there are no taxes on personal income from profits or interest).

Financial Intermediaries as Suppliers of Small Credits

Uruguay's formal financial system includes one public bank with commercial and some development bank functions (BROU), and one public housing bank (Banco Hipotecario). There are 22 private commercial banks, eight savings and credit cooperatives, 12 financial houses, and six foreign financial institutions. Tables 6.7 and 6.8 show the composition of the deposits and credits market according to the various institutions, as well as the structure of liabilities and assets.

Some of these financial agents have institutional characteristics that disqualify them as suppliers of small credits, either to companies or to individuals. This is the case with the financial and banking houses, distinguished from banks in that they accept deposits only from nonresidents and, consequently, deal almost exclusively in dollars. Although authorized to serve residents, in recent years they have reduced this function and focused on offshore operations. Having very small physical networks, they do not operate in the small credits segment. Foreign financial institutions can only conduct offshore operations and, consequently, do not deal with residents.

The private commercial banking sector consists of two banks still under government control as a result of rescue operations ("administered banks") and the other banks, which are foreign-owned. As mentioned, this fairly atypical ownership structure was responsible for the disappearance of national banks. Among private banks, the two administered banks and the one already privatized have larger networks and more personnel and generally operate with a more diversified portfolio, including small loans (Tables 6.A.6–6.A.8 in the Appendix).

The BROU is heavily involved in small credits, and its participation in rural credits is extremely important. For smaller urban companies, the BROU has had a special department since the mid-1980s. But small-business credit is more frequently channeled through the bank's commercial and industrial accounts. In both urban and rural areas the BROU is practically the only institution offering long-term credit for investment purposes. Its credit operations are generally based on the existence of solid guarantees, which results in a low level of demand relative to the bank's liquidity. These strict guarantee requirements can be attrib-

Table 6.7. Share of Various Groups of Institutions by Financial Instrument, June 1992
(Percentages)

	BROU	BHU	Private banks: Administered	Private banks: Others	Private banks: Total	Financial houses	Cooperatives	Total
				Credits				
Local currency	49.2	0.0	17.1	18.7	35.8	0.1	14.8	100.0
Adjustable units	0.0	100.0	0.0	0.0	0.0	0.0	0.0	100.0
Foreign currency	37.8	0.0	13.5	32.3	45.9	11.6	4.7	100.0
Residents	47.2	0.0	n.a.	n.a.	44.0	2.9	5.9	100.0
Nonresidents	0.0	0.0	n.a.	n.a.	53.4	46.6	0.0	100.0
Total	28.4	29.2	10.1	20.9	31.0	6.5	4.8	100.0
				Deposits				
Local currency	33.9	0.0	27.3	26.5	53.6	0.0	12.2	100.0
Demand	18.6	0.0	n.a.	n.a.	81.5	0.0	n.a.	100.0
Savings	66.7	0.0	n.a.	n.a.	31.3	0.0	n.a.	100.0
Fixed term	46.4	0.0	n.a.	n.a.	53.6	0.0	n.a.	100.0
Adjustable units	0.0	100.0	0.0	0.0	0.0	0.0	0.0	100.0
Foreign currency	30.4	6.8	14.9	31.2	46.1	14.3	2.4	100.0
Residents	39.8	11.0	n.a.	n.a.	45.3	0.0	3.9	100.0
Nonresidents	15.4	0.0	n.a.	n.a.	47.5	37.1	0.0	100.0
Total	29.4	10.3	15.6	29.3	44.9	12.0	3.4	100.0

Source: Prepared on the basis of Central Bank of Uruguay, *Boletín Estadístico,* various numbers, and unpublished data.

uted to the risk-avoidance behavior of loan officers, in reaction to the institution's internal control mechanisms designed to avoid risk. The result is that the bank's portfolio of small credits is extremely sound. Conversely, the large account portfolio is frequently subject to social and political pressures and is not strictly governed by banking logic, so that its quality is very poor. BROU operations are slow and bogged down in red tape, but its competitiveness lies in the fact that in many cases it is the only institution providing the services.

The savings and credit cooperatives or the financial cooperatives can receive current account deposits, attract any type of deposit and, since late 1992, are authorized by law to use checks to do current account business.[14] Their financial operations are subject to the same restrictions as those of banks, but they are subject to different reserve requirements and a more favorable tax system.[15] They

[14] Since 1979, various instruments similar to checks had been used to attract deposits. After 1990, these instruments could be cleared in the clearinghouses of the other intermediaries.

[15] They are not subject to IRIC nor to the tax on net worth (2.8 percent in the case of banks). The interest on the personal loans they grant is not subject to VAT and, until very recently, they did not pay the tax on bank assets (1.5 percent per annum on balances). From the viewpoint of central bank regulations, the most important difference is that they are subject to a smaller minimum capital requirement and a more lenient reserve system (the obligatory, non-interest bearing reserve requirement is 10 percent for banks and 4 percent for cooperatives).

Table 6.8. Credit and Deposit Structure by Type of Institution, June 1992
(Percentages of total credits or deposits)

	BROU	BHU	Private banks: Administered	Private banks: Others	Private banks: Total	Financial houses	Cooperatives
				Credits			
Local currency	25.6	0.0	25.1	13.2	17.1	0.1	45.1
Adjustable units	0.0	100.0	0.0	0.0	0.0	0.0	0.0
Foreign currency	74.4	0.0	74.9	86.8	82.9	99.7	54.9
Residents	74.4	0.0	n.a.	n.a.	63.7	20.0	54.9
Nonresidents	0.0	0.0	n.a.	n.a.	19.2	79.6	0.0
Total	100.0	100.0	100.0	100.0	100.0	100.0	100.0
				Deposits			
Local currency	13.1	0.0	19.9	10.3	13.6	0.0	41.1
Demand	2.2	0.0	n.a.	n.a.	6.8	0.0	n.a.
Savings	2.8	0.0	n.a.	n.a.	0.8	0.0	n.a.
Fixed term	8.0	0.0	n.a.	n.a.	6.0	0.0	n.a.
Adjustable units	0.0	44.5	0.0	0.0	0.0	0.0	0.0
Foreign currency	86.9	55.5	80.1	89.7	86.4	100.0	58.9
Residents	70.1	55.5	n.a.	n.a.	52.2	0.0	58.9
Nonresidents	16.8	0.0	n.a.	n.a.	34.1	0.0	0.0
Total	100.0	100.0	100.0	100.0	100.0	100.0	100.0

Source: Prepared on the basis of Central Bank of Uruguay, *Boletín Estadístico,* various numbers, and unpublished data.

can choose to become cooperative banks, in which case they must comply with the tax and regulatory system of banks. Up to a certain limit, they can also conduct operations with non-partners. But the requested payment of partners' shares to conduct liability-creating operations is insignificant; the payment of capital is usually used as a means of limiting risk in lending operations.

These cooperatives have grown significantly in recent years, after going through a rapid merger process (in 1982 there were 40 institutions). Nevertheless, they represent only 7 percent of the national financial market and 1.5 percent in dollars. Their share of small credits is larger, however, and the minimum credits of the two largest cooperatives are around US$300 (in private banks it is difficult to find loan amounts under US$5,000).

As already explained, in the eighties, foreign-owned commercial banks adopted an adjustment strategy and restricted their credit operations to the largest companies. In the nineties, increased competition in small credit operations has been observed, but the vast majority are credits to individuals. Evidence supporting the theory that commercial banks—except the BROU, the "administered" banks, and Banco Comercial—are not interested in dealing with small and medium-sized businesses is provided by the IDB-CND (National Development Corporation) experiment with concessional credit to small and medium-sized companies. This facility, totaling US$10 million, was granted at concessional rates and was created for long-term loans. Except for Banco Comercial and the cooperatives, none of these funds were channeled through private banks.

At the periphery of the formal intermediaries sector is an informal credit system with various components. For example, some NGOs channel international concessional funds to micro- and small businesses at lower costs than the cooperatives (which are subject to central bank regulations). Furthermore, as nonprofit organizations, the NGOs are tax-exempt as well. Generally, their rates are slightly above those of the BROU's facilities.

The NGOs providing support to the small and medium-sized business sector emerged in the 1980s. Most of them sponsored programs with assistance objectives, which meant that their loan capacity was considerably reduced at the end of the decade as a result of the loss of real value of the funds. Since then, a change of focus has been observed and many of them are turning to a mix of technical assistance and credit, especially for the establishment of new businesses. In any case, their significance is slight compared to the other sources of small credits. (For a complete summary of the programs associated with this group, see Alberti, 1992).

Suppliers also provide financing, a practice which is widespread. Finally, there are informal lenders that make loans at high interest rates to businesses hobbled by a lack of funds.

The intermediaries in the formal system work under varying conditions of cost and regulations. Mention has already been made of the differences in the reserve requirements, the integration of net worth, and the tax system of banks and cooperatives. The cost considerations of state banking are unknown since its income statements are not published. Table 6.9 presents a statement of the income of private sector agents. The large physical network of cooperatives and the specialization of their smaller credit operations result in higher operating costs.

Common Small Credit Instruments

The banking system channels resources to small and medium-sized businesses almost exclusively in the form of loans and by discounting negotiable instruments. Loans are channeled in the form of fixed-term or amortizable loans. The principal amount of the former is repaid at the end of the period, whereas a fixed amount of the latter is paid each month. Amortizable loans are more common in personal credit. The average term of commercial operations is rarely more than 180 days, even in operations in dollars, except for the borrowing facilities of the BROU, wherein credit is granted for up to 10 years. In the last two years, borrowing facilities of more than a year have appeared in the private banking sector.

An extended credit arrangement, especially for medium-sized enterprises, is the discounting of deferred checks. As its name implies, the deferred check

Table 6.9. *Ex post* Banking Margin of Banks and Cooperatives, 1991 and 1992
(Annualized rates of return in dollars, percentages)

	Private banks		Financial cooperatives	
Item	1991	1992	1991	1992
1) Average return on credits	14.0	13.1	45.7	40.7
In local currency	28.2	31.0	66.8	65.3
In foreign currency	10.8	9.0	16.0	15.1
2) Average financial cost of deposits	3.5	2.9	11.2	9.9
In local currency	–6.6	–2.3	16.9	16.4
In foreign currency	5.1	3.6	4.8	4.2
3) Gross intermediation margin (1)–(2)	10.5	10.3	34.5	30.8
In local currency	34.8	33.4	49.9	49.0
In foreign currency	5.8	5.4	11.2	11.0
4) Ratio of credits to deposits	45.6	49.2	77.2	89.9
In local currency	64.7	72.0	85.6	97.8
In foreign currency	42.8	45.9	67.9	82.9
5) Reserves net of recovery	9.0	2.4	4.3	5.1
In local currency	11.9	11.6	7.4	9.9
In foreign currency	8.3	0.3	0.0	0.0
6) Intermediation margin net of reserves (3)–(5)	1.5	7.8	30.2	25.8
In local currency	22.9	21.8	42.5	39.0
In foreign currency	–2.5	5.0	11.2	11.0
7) Intermediation return to assets	–1.0	–1.8	17.8	18.8
8) Financial return of other assets	5.9	5.2	6.2	2.0
In local currency	–5.4	3.4	6.9	–0.6
In foreign currency	6.8	5.3	5.8	4.0
9) Financial cost of other liabilities	3.9	2.8	–0.8	7.3
In local currency	–6.3	–5.0	–5.0	–0.5
In foreign currency	4.6	3.2	6.1	27.4
10) Financial return to assets	2.0	4.3	19.5	18.9
11) Net earnings for services to assets	1.4	1.3	0.9	0.4
12) Operating costs to assets	6.6	6.7	21.1	19.3
Personnel costs to assets	3.8	3.8	13.7	11.1
Other net income	1.8	1.6	1.1	2.6
Return to assets	–1.4	0.6	0.3	2.6
Return to capital	–30.1	11.8	3.0	26.9

Source: Based on unpublished BCU data.

is a check with a date subsequent to the operation. These are different from ordinary checks, which are drawn on current accounts. Banks issue booklets of deferred checks to customers who maintain a certain minimum balance in a current account and, in turn, open a discount line for checks that the latter receive from third parties. The principal advantage of these operations is their flexibility. The security of the system is further ensured by the existence of stiff criminal penalties for violations. Approximately 4 percent of all credit is extended in this form.

Financial leasing operations are relatively rare: they represent only 0.25 percent of the entire system's credit to the private sector. They are hampered by obstacles of two types: taxes and legal uncertainty. The tax obstacles stem from the fact that the amount of the leasing operation is subject to VAT, which is not the case with interest when the borrower is liable for income tax and its debts were contracted with the financial system. The obstacles involving legal uncertainty derive from judicial practice, which makes it easier to recover goods with a chattel mortgage than it is to recover leased goods.

Factoring operations have existed for a short time. Although the invoice represents an enforceable document, it does not offer any security as regards collection. The only accounts receivable that enjoy confidence are those issued in connection with projects carried out with government agencies.

The operators of the system recognize that in addition to the above-cited problems concerning the uncertainty of contract performance due to mandatory refinancing or stays of enforcement, there are other problems associated with the system of guarantees. For example, pledges of agricultural property are rarely executed. The laws on pledges and mortgages date from the early decades of this century. The high cost of recording mortgages—approximately 3.5 percent of the amount of the contract—make them unattractive as a means of securing short- and even medium-term credits. The cost of chattel mortgages is lower, but still considerable, and there is a tendency to avoid these costs by recording the existence of a pledge only when recovery is extremely doubtful or signs of default appear.

Small and Medium-Sized Businesses as Credit Recipients

In this section the main characteristics of micro, small, and medium-sized Uruguayan businesses and their financial practices are discussed. The different nature of rural and urban activities requires that they be considered separately.

The Urban Sector

The only reliable estimate of the significance of this sector in the Uruguayan economy is the one provided by the preliminary survey of the 1988 Economic Census, conducted in 1987. Since the survey criteria of this census, which are very specific, are different from the criteria used earlier, comparisons with prior data are irrelevant.[16] Tables 6.10 and 6.11 contain a summary of this information.

---

[16] Several documents on the subject fall into the error of comparing these data with those of the 1978 Economic Census, inferring significant growth among micro, small and medium-sized enterprises. This result is obtained because the earlier study practically ignored establishments with less than 20 employees. This is the case with Kritz, Marín, and Viera (1989) and IDB (1990).

Table 6.10. Personnel Employed by Businesses, by Number of Employees and Line of Business, 1988

	Number of employees							
Line of business	Total	1	2–4	5–9	10–19	20–49	50–99	100 or more
Total	894,426	82,361	129,270	80,614	68,325	71,270	45,768	416,792
Working of mines and quarries	1,828	57	235	295	134	639	312	156
Manufacturing industries	217,153	9,641	19,226	20,582	21,554	25,995	20,475	99,680
Electricity, gas, and water	18,976	4	10	14	31	0	0	18,917
Construction	27,085	1,970	2,017	1,868	2,634	4,130	4,153	10,313
Commerce, restaurants, and hotels	170,266	22,781	63,017	30,966	18,354	15,212	7,135	12,801
Transportation, warehousing, and communications	53,592	3,829	8,337	3,709	3,113	3,934	1,412	29,258
Financial establishments and business services	65,986	16,040	11,637	5,402	3,726	3,669	2,280	23,232
Community, social, and personal services	339,337	27,974	24,721	17,736	18,779	17,691	10,001	222,435
Miscellaneous activities	203	65	70	42	26	0	0	0

Source: National Institute of Statistics, III National Economic Census.

Table 6.11. Number of Businesses, by Number of Employees in Each Company, According to Line of Business, 1988

Line of business	Number of employees							
	Total	1	2–4	5–9	10–19	20–49	50–99	100 or more
Total	157,433	84,119	51,824	12,526	5,233	2,410	676	645
Working of mines and quarries	229	60	86	45	11	21	5	1
Manufacturing industries	23,338	9,813	7,268	3,150	1,635	857	303	312
Electricity, gas, and water	15	4	4	2	2	0	0	3
Construction	3,514	2,016	784	289	194	132	58	41
Commerce, restaurants and hotels	55,762	23,244	25,529	4,900	1,407	526	106	50
Transportation, warehousing, and communications	8,475	4,093	3,385	589	230	131	21	26
Financial establishments and business services	22,123	16,115	4,671	854	283	123	35	42
Community, social, and personal services	43,663	28,497	10,069	2,690	1,469	620	148	170
Miscellaneous activities	314	277	28	7	2	0	0	0

Source: National Institute of Statistics, III National Economic Census.

The 158,000 urban enterprises with less than 10 employees represented 94 percent of the country's urban enterprises and provided 32 percent of all urban jobs. The micro-, small, and medium-sized Uruguayan businesses are concentrated in the commercial and services sectors, which represent 69 percent of all enterprises (and 78 percent of those with less than 10 employees) and account for 75 percent of the employment in all medium-sized and small businesses.

Unlike the situation in other Latin American countries, micro-, small and medium-sized businesses in Uruguay are not predominantly the refuge of the low- income or poverty-level segments of the population. This can be attributed to the minor importance of internal migratory movements and, above all, to the small size of the rural population.[17] Thus, the educational level of the owners of micro-, small, and medium-sized businesses is higher than the average for the population as a whole, which has led many authors to assume that their incomes are also above average (Table 6.12).

Another element pointing in the same direction is that the number of street vendors counted in the 1988 economic census was not above 3,000, despite the fact that their ranks have obviously swelled. All these data suggest that most micro-businesses were not started because of self-employment or survival strategies.

The census records indicate that the failure rate of business is fairly high; the average life is estimated at five years. A relatively broad sampling of small and medium-sized businesses in the Montevideo metropolitan area (Melgar and Alberti, 1992) revealed several characteristics of this sector, in particular as a user of credit.[18]

The businesses' initial investment almost always involves their own capital (84 percent) and some family loans (10 percent). Bank loans do not exceed 5 percent.

The external resources are almost always short-term, with supplier credits being the type most commonly used: they are extended to 71 percent of businesses. The credit is used primarily to purchase inputs. The use of bank and other types of loans is very uncommon: only 26 percent of the businesses contracted such loans in the last two years (21 percent in the case of bank loans). In this context, the existence of bank credits with more than a year's term is significant: 6 percent of the cases. Although it is impossible to tell from the survey what institution the credit came from, it is very likely that it was concessional credit from the BROU. Four percent were loans from non-banking institutions.

---

[17] The rural population was 19 percent in 1963, and in 1991 was estimated at 11 percent of the total.

[18] The survey covered establishments employing between 2 and 50 people. The sample was taken from 459 cases in Montevideo and the neighboring departments of Canelones and San José. It was conducted in 1991, using the universe of the above-cited preliminary survey of the 1987 Economic Census, so that it includes only units in business three years or more.

Table 6.12. Educational Level of Business Owners and the Population

	Educational level						
	Elementary						
	Complete	Incomplete	Secondary[1]	Vocational	University	Others[2]	Total
Economically active population							
Country as a whole	12.8	25.0	33.5	13.8	10.1	4.7	100.0
Montevideo	9.7	22.4	35.5	12.9	15.6	4.0	100.0
Canelones	13.3	32.4	30.3	16.2	3.5	4.4	100.0
Sample of small business owners							
Total	14.2	1.6	48.3	14.4	19.5	1.9	100.0
Manufacturing industry	14.3	1.3	51.2	15.7	15.8	1.8	100.0
Freight transport	18.7	4.2	43.8	12.5	18.7	2.1	100.0
Data processing	5.6	0.0	38.9	5.6	44.4	5.5	100.0
Advertising and market research	3.4	0.0	23.4	3.4	66.6	3.3	100.0

[1] Includes secondary complete and incomplete.
[2] Groups the teaching profession, those without education, and others, for the data from the 1991 On-Going Household Survey, and including those who do not know or did not answer for the sample of small and medium-sized businesses.
Source: Prepared on the basis of National Institute of Statistics figures, On-Going Household Survey, 1991, and Alberti and Melgar, 1992.

The bank loans are highly correlated with the educational level of the business owner and the size of the business (measured by the number of employees). Long-term credits bear a certain correlation with the age of the business and revealed a negative correlation with the owner's age.

The cost of supplier credits was about the same as that of the borrowing facilities offered by the formal banking system. In the case of regular customers, the nominal cost of supplier credits rose in 1991 to figures close to 6–8 percent per month (100 to 152 percent annualized). Since the monthly rate of inflation was 5 percent, this meant annualized real rates of about 20 to 72 percent annually.

Other non-bank credit arrangements such as the discounting of commercial paper—relatively important because they are traditionally used by larger companies—are insignificant as far as small and medium-sized businesses are concerned.

The small share of bank credits is related to the strict guarantee requirements imposed by banks. Since the system for enforcing guarantees in Uruguay is fairly insubstantial and slow, banks require a high percentage of real guarantees to extend credit. Consequently, over time, a financing system focused on supplier transactions has evolved. Comparing the costs of this financing with bank financing does not reveal any major differences. In addition to the similar rates, the sample mentioned above shows that the weight of financial expenses does not vary among those who have a different distribution of liabilities between suppliers and banks.

There does not appear to be an unsatisfied demand for credit, or one that is relatively more unsatisfied in the case of small and medium-sized businesses in comparison with other segments of businesses. Various facts support this interpretation. One of the most important is that few businesses claim to be limited by capacity (13 percent) or working capital financing (19 percent); on the contrary, most indicate that the problem is lack of demand (56 percent).

One possible interpretation of this situation is that investment demand among businesses is small because of macroeconomic factors linked to the uncertainty caused by economic instability, changes in policy, and the viability of the liberalization process.

Similarly, the low opportunity cost of equity capital—a consequence of the reduction in real interest rates in the nineties—has the same effect of minimizing the role of financial constraints.

Several indicators from a recent survey of investment projects in manufacturing companies with more than 50 employees highlight this situation (Torello and Noya, 1992). In the owners' opinions, financial constraints do not seem to be the principal limitation on investment (only in less than 10 percent of the cases), and this opinion is not correlative to the size of the businesses. This limitation is even cited by a sizable percentage of large companies. Moreover, investment projects planned with a three-year horizon are financed almost exclusively with equity and not bank capital. Bank financing represents 12 percent of the investment in medium-sized enterprises (50 to 99 employees) and 40 percent in those with more than 100 employees.

Small Rural Enterprises

The significance of small rural establishments can be seen in the preliminary figures from the last General Agricultural Census, which was conducted in 1990. The census figures provide information on all farms with more than one hectare in productive use.[19] A summary of this information is presented in Table 6.13.

Farms smaller than 200 hectares—the traditional limit for identifying small-scale production in Uruguay—represent 73.2 percent of the total, employ 56 percent of the labor in the sector and occupy 13.7 percent of the country's agricultural land area. Since there is wide diversity in production functions, soil capabilities, and the location and capitalization level of farms, land area alone does not determine the small rural producers. Table 6.14 presents a measurement of small agricultural production by type of activity.

---

[19] It is estimated that there are 12,000 units under one hectare, which are essentially residential in nature. This represents approximately 25 percent of all rural households.

Table 6.13. Number of Agricultural Establishments, Area Worked and Full-Time Workers According to the Size of the Establishment, 1990

Size of the farm in hectares	Number of establishments	Area in hectares	Full-time workers		
			Paid	Not paid	Total
1–4	5,085	14,757	718	7,088	7,806
5–9	7,398	49,728	1,612	11,439	13,051
10–19	7,240	98,413	2,042	12,116	14,158
20–49	9,121	285,504	2,703	15,849	18,552
50–99	7,049	491,644	3,066	11,586	14,652
100–199	6,119	843,730	3,230	9,879	13,109
200–499	7,004	2,172,495	8,496	9,326	17,822
500–999	4,230	2,905,255	9,913	4,169	14,082
1,000–2,499	3,056	4,600,398	15,302	2,517	17,819
2,500–4,999	851	3,699,027	9,201	663	9,864
5,000–9,999	189	1,266,709	3,064	117	3,181
10,000 or more	12	200,176	874	1	875
Total	57,354	15,627,836	60,221	84,750	144,971

Source: Directorate of Agricultural Economic Research, 1991.

According to these criteria, small producers represent almost 60 percent of the country's total rural establishments. More than half of this total consists of livestock farms, 5 percent of which are dairy farms; vegetable and fruit growers represent approximately 30 percent. However, this large number of small farms occupies a very small area: less than 10 percent of the total area of the country.

In a survey conducted recently to assess the extent and characteristics of rural poverty, data were obtained concerning access to credit by rural establishments (Equipos Consultores Asociados, 1992).[20] The results are shown in Table 6.15, dividing the population between households with incomes below the poverty line and households with incomes above the poverty line.[21]

Generally speaking, Chile's small producers have access to credit of fairly significant proportions, compared to other developing countries. According to this survey, approximately one-third of small producers obtained credit from vari-

[20] Although the sample covered the universe of rural properties under 200 hectares, its objective was consumption units, so that the units surveyed are the families of the producers and those of the rural wage-earners of these establishments. The sample comprised 399 rural producers and 250 rural wage-earners on properties under 200 hectares. For comparative purposes, 61 rural properties over 200 hectares were added.

[21] The concept of income used corresponds to that of purchasing power available for consumption, measured as the gross income from any source, including income generated away from the rural property, less operating and investment costs, plus credits. The poverty line, based on a basket of basic goods and services defined according to ECLAC methodology, was US$3,200 per household per year in March 1992.

Table 6.14. Small Rural Producers According to Productive Specialization, 1986

Activity	Establishments: Number	Establishments: Percentage[1]	Area: Hectares	Area: Percentage[2]	Maximum area (in hectares)
Livestock	17,820	60.1	1,068,188	6.8	200/100[a]
Dairy	1,650	42.3	51,742	11.2	50
Crop farming	2,240	52.1	62,311	7.9	50
Vegetables	4,950	49.8	27,735	15.2	10
Fruit-wine	5,050	71.2	19,098	14.8	10
Crops-livestock	844	72.5	34,572	14.3	200/100[a]
Vegetable-fruits-wine	47	33.8	404	12.1	10
Others	448	39.8	7,622	11.3	20
Total	33,049	60.1	1,271,672	8.1	

[1] Percentage of total establishments in each activity.
[2] Percentage of total land area of establishments specializing in the activity.
[a] Percentage under 200 hectares in the center, north and east of the country and less than 100 hectares in the rest of the country.
Source: Directorate of Agricultural Economic Research, 1986, and International Fund for Agricultural Development, 1991.

ous sources, although there were obvious differences among the various activities. Thus, access to credit is considerable in the case of dairy and crop farming, where a little less than half the small producers had access to financing. In the case of vegetable farming, however, barely 12 percent of producers received credit. Still there are no major differences between the two income segments as far as the degree of access to credit is concerned.

The BROU is the most important financing source utilized. In the case of dairy farming, and especially for producers below the poverty line, the conduit for a large percentage of the credits is the National Diary Producers Cooperative (CONAPROLE).[22]

With regard to livestock production, the financial cooperatives also play a fairly significant role in the financing of small producers below the poverty line, which is true for both livestock activities and crop farming. Finally, as noted above, private banks play virtually no part in the financing of this segment of producers. The only exception is the share of bank credits in non-vegetable (crops) production, where the level of credits is significant, although only in the case of producers above the poverty line.

The most problematic cases in terms of access to credit are observed in vegetable farming, followed by livestock raising, regardless of income level.

[22] CONAPROLE is responsible for more than 80 percent of the supply of fluid milk. The financing channeled through this enterprise constitutes one of the few examples of unconventional financing with full participation by low-income producers.

Table 6.15. Credits to Small Rural Producers, June 1991 – June 1992
(Average amounts in dollars for all establishments in each category)

Institutional credit source	Below the poverty line					Above the poverty line				
	Dairy	Livestock	Vegetables	Others	Total	Dairy	Livestock	Vegetables	Others	Total
BROU	3,467	2,773	4,823	3,875	3,486	5,304	5,788	2,757	14,670	6,360
Financial cooperatives	0	3,170	0	2,372	2,372	2,076	2,290	0	7,640	2,543
CONAPROLE	1,937	0	0	136	136	1,532	0	0	0	107
Private banks	0	0	0	0	0	2,397	0	0	30,000	5,268
Others	239	0	398	684	684	0	199	0	12,000	2,116
Average total credit	873	463	500	595	595	1,791	695	321	6,889	1,714
Average total credit from those that obtained (it).	2,532	2,297	3,938			4,447	4,012	2,757	14,586	
Proportion of establishments that obtained credit (%)	42	28	13			40	18	12	46	
Establishments included (universe estimate)	1,260	8,736	3,657	3,450	17,103	5,740	6,864	3,243	8,050	23,897

Note: The poverty line is US$3,200 per year per family.
Source: Equipos Consultores Asociados, 1992.

In contrast to the situation of small urban establishments, most of the resources come from the formal financial system. This may be due to differences in the contracts and amounts of transactions with suppliers. Nevertheless, the differences relative to the urban sector are remarkable only in the case of dairy operations and grain crops.

It is therefore likely that increased access to bank credit is determined by the greater certainty of credit recovery in the marketing stage of production. In both dairy and vegetable farming, the initial stage of processing primary production is relatively concentrated, and this lowers the costs of tracking the credit. In many cases, the companies that own the processing plants act as guarantors of the credits. In contrast, there are few suppliers for vegetable farming and livestock raising, and there is no strong tradition of permanent ties with the commercial or industrial users of the products. Moreover, livestock farms, regardless of income, have little access to credit, even where abundant use is made of land. Land seems to be of minimal value as a means of securing credits, and the same can be said of livestock.

Policy Recommendations and Suggestions

This section contains a number of policy suggestions, which are discussed in three stages, according to the nature of the problems involved. The first part addresses the more general problems associated with the regulation and control of economic activities within their institutional framework, including problems of a macroeconomic nature. The second section deals with aspects related to the supply of bank credits, i.e., the banking policy aspects. The considerable importance of public banking justifies separate treatment in the next section. Finally, a number of aspects related to the demand for credit are considered, essentially the tax implications of certain financial instruments that could play an important role in deconcentrating credit and expanding access to financial services.

Macroeconomic Background of Economic Activity

A series of problems affects the development of financial markets—both banking and nonbanking—with repercussions on economic agents in particular, regardless of the size of their operations. In Uruguay, these problems are related to economic instability, the legal uncertainty of contracts, and the transparency and credibility of the financial information provided by businesses.

Economic instability affects the length of the terms of lending operations and limits the possibility of using long-term credits to finance investment, as well as the development of financial markets. High inflation destroys the informational value of the system of prices and thus impacts negatively on resource allocation. These effects are well-known, and Uruguay's experience of more than three decades offers a clear example of their consequences. But Uruguay's experience also shows that the use of financial assets shielded against inflation, which is the reason for the extensive use of foreign currency in contracts, does not represent a solution to these problems.

Although the legal uncertainty of contracts in Uruguay—especially those related to the credit market—is of long standing, the situation was considerably worsened by the financial crisis of the eighties and the subsequent government policies aimed at assisting and rescuing banks and businesses. The growth of the credit market was impeded as operations became less and less secure and as guarantees lost their value. The ensuing compulsory refinancing of bank debts, even as late as a decade after the crisis erupted, was a clear indicator of the problem. Since most of the recent refinancing operations were mandated by the legislature, except for the imposition of constitutional restrictions limiting the action of the branches of government in this sphere, there was no other route than political compromise.

There are other sources of uncertainty stemming from the legal structure of certain contracts. It is generally acknowledged that the system of collateral and mortgage securities, which dates from the early decades of this century, is costly and entails a high degree of legal uncertainty. No specific recommendations concerning this point can be made, given the lack of diagnostic information. However, it seems that certain registration and certification costs should be decontrolled. Similarly, the review of the system should be oriented toward permitting the "securitization" of operations. Another topic is the relative slowness of collection proceedings, although the recent changes in the judicial procedures constitute a step in the right direction.

Regarding the transparency and the quality of economic data, despite the lack of specific diagnoses, it is safe to say that some of the factors involved are the deficiencies of the tax audit agencies, the slight economic advantages for companies that issue securities, and the competitive drawbacks of being the only provider of information. In the latter case, there is a coordination problem, which leaves room for public intervention. The imposition of modern prudential standards by BCU supervisors was an important step in this direction, although it was only partially effective. Given the recent implementation of these standards, their effects are only beginning to be seen. A thorough reform of the tax inspection and audit systems and reinforcement of the tax administration would be effective in this regard, irrespective of the direct impact on revenue.

General Regulations for Banking Operations

The first recommendation concerns easing the requirements for entry into the system, which would require a decision by the executive branch, with input from the BCU. As a result of the crisis in the early eighties, private intermediaries disappeared in Uruguay. Foreign-owned banks, with certain exceptions, have shown little interest in small-scale credit operations, except when extended to individuals. The merger and growth of financial cooperatives can thus be viewed as the market's response to this new situation.

In evaluating the greater or lesser relaxation of the entry requirements, the degree of competition in the system must be taken into account. Since financial markets—especially credit markets—exhibit different degrees of segmentation due to various types of informational imbalances, competition in all market segments must be evaluated. When financial systems are in severe crisis, with high fiscal adjustment costs, public policies give priority to the objectives of rehabilitation and solvency. But once the adjustments are made and the institutions rehabilitated, active competition must be given greater weight among the objectives of the regulatory agencies.

If the conservative approach taken by the BCU to date is due to problems with the system's security, then another policy instrument should be selected. For example, the BCU discarded the objective of competition in favor of controlling entry into the system, as a means of addressing its largest problem, i.e., security. If determining the rules of entry begins to give greater importance to competition, however, then problems of security must be solved with another instrument. For example, some type of deposit insurance could be established. A large percentage of the financial intermediaries enjoy a solid international reputation or, because they are public, have the government as guarantor of their obligations.[23] In these cases, the payment of deposit insurance premiums should be optional, but would be compulsory for entities without international or government backing.

Inasmuch as there are still publicly-owned banks which are going to be privatized, a first step in easing the entry requirements would be to apply this greater flexibility in qualifying the prospective buyers of these institutions.

A second aspect is related to the increased transparency and publication of information about the system. If no changes are made in the system's regulations concerning the security of deposits (as regulations assume that the depositors' evaluation disciplines banks), a clear policy should be adopted to provide information about evaluating the management of these institutions. At present, information about their earnings is scarce or nonexistent. The legal basis for this secrecy is usually claimed to be a banking secrecy rule and a very broad interpretation of its purpose. Banking secrecy should be restricted to borrowing operations, whereas the concept of professional secrecy should not affect public evalu-

---

[23] The obligations of the BROU and the BCU are expressly guaranteed by the government, pursuant to their charters.

ation. The introduction of some type of explicit deposit insurance should not stand in the way of changes of this type.

The crisis in the eighties brought down a number of intermediaries that had a banking strategy more focused on small credits, thus destroying part of the store of information needed for certain banking practices. The experience of recent years shows that the market reacts slowly as a result of this void. Specific programs aimed at small and medium-sized businesses, apart from trying to satisfy their demand for credit, should serve as a learning experience about small credits.

Public Banks

Given its relative importance in the system (particularly with regard to granting small credits), efficient management of the BROU is a crucial topic. In addition to its participation in the market, the BROU's role assumes even greater importance if it is remembered that it is practically the only permanent source of long-term credit in the entire system. Although the institution is in the process of restructuring its management with technical assistance from international organizations, its progress has been slow. Following are some general guidelines for this restructuring process.

First, the degree of decentralization of credit decisions should be increased. This means, essentially, raising the credit authorization ceilings for each rung on the management ladder (which currently range from US$30,000 to US$60,000) and lowering the weight of the board of directors' decision. In addition, the staff incentive policy needs to be revised. At present, there are no performance awards for loan officers. Incentives are provided only at the branch level and, consequently, cover more than just the loans. In this same vein, the policy for recruiting management personnel should also be revised and based on fairly standard, routine, internal merit evaluations.

Second, more efficient management requires an infrastructure for the compiling and processing of information, which currently does not exist. The bank has no way of obtaining a complete, up-to-date picture of its position with each customer, the degree of execution of each borrowing facility, etc.

Third, the Bank should radically alter its policy concerning the publication of its earnings. The BROU has not published an income statement for decades, which, given its size and public character, sends its managers the wrong message concerning public opinion.

Fourth, the fairly successful experience with credits channeled to small rural producers through associations or cooperatives—particularly in the dairy sector and, to a lesser extent, in the wool sector—could be experimented with on a limited basis in other sectors. The promotion of these associations, especially in the vegetable and livestock sectors, is an alternative that should be explored.

This subrogation of evaluation seems more difficult to achieve in the urban sector, although it should depend on the characteristics of the markets penetrated.

Finally, an aspect that goes beyond management and involves legal reform of the way the bank is governed should aim at minimizing the role of political representatives in its governance. Currently, the bank's board of directors consists of five members appointed at the start of each administration by the executive branch, with Senate approval. Although this aspect affects the management of the bank with regard to large-volume credits, because the larger lenders are more capable of exerting political pressure, the poor quality of the large portfolios reduces the bank's capacity to operate in the other credit segments. In fact, the return on smaller credits has traditionally been higher.

Tax Aspects

The tax treatment of certain contracts that are especially important in managing small credits should be separated from changes in the tax status of specific financial agents.

In the first category is the change in the VAT treatment of leasing arrangements, whereby the tax on payments to lease durable consumer goods (12 percent) is eliminated, so that lease payments receive the same treatment as the interest on a credit. In the same way, the treatment of these lease payments in the rules governing the payment of corporate income tax (IRIC) should also be changed. Insofar as the allowable expenses include the interest on bank debts but not payments to lease durable consumer goods with an option to buy, the latter are discriminated against.

The double taxation of profits that affects the operations of investment banks and financial intermediaries in general is a stumbling block to the creation of coparticipation funds, especially to reduce follow-up costs and to spread risk in the start-up phase of businesses, or in long-term funds, in the case of both small and large companies.

Bibliography

Alberti, J.P. 1991. *Programas de apoyo a la micro y pequeña empresa en el Uruguay.* Montevideo, Uruguay. Mimeo. Servicio de Aprendizaje para el Desarrollo.

Alberti, J.P. and Melgar, A. 1992. *Caracterización, inserción y promoción de pequeñas unidades productivas.* Serie Investigaciones No. 67, Montevideo, Uruguay: Centro Latinoamericano de Economía Humana.

Amoroso, M.J. and Xavier, J. 1988. *Adecuación de capital en empresas de intermediación financiera.* Document presented at the Third Economic Seminar, Central Bank, Montevideo, Uruguay.

Asociación de Bancos del Uruguay. *Memoria anual,* various numbers. Montevideo, Uruguay.

Banco de la República Oriental del Uruguay. *Memoria anual.* Various numbers. Montevideo, Uruguay.

Banda, A. 1990. "Regulación bancaria, crisis financiera y políticas consecuentes: el caso uruguayo." In G. Held and R. Szallachman, editors, *Ahorro y asignación de recursos financieros,* Buenos Aires, Argentina: Grupo Editor Latinoamericano.

Central Bank of Uruguay. *Boletín Estadístico.* Various numbers. Montevideo, Uruguay.

_______. *Normas de Regulación y Contralor del Sistema Financiero,* various numbers. Montevideo, Uruguay: Central Bank of Uruguay.

Dirección de Investigaciones Económicas Agropecuarias. 1991. *Censo Agropecuario 1990. Datos Anticipados.* Montevideo, Uruguay: Ministerio de Ganadería, Agricultura y Pesca.

Dominioni, D. and Vaz, D. 1991. *Riesgo crediticio y concentración de cartera. Un enfoque de optimización.* Paper presented at the Sixth Economic Seminar. Central Bank, Montevideo, Uruguay.

Equipos Consultores Asociados. 1992. *Perfil y caracterización de la probreza rural. Encuesta socioeconómica a productores y asalariados agropecuarios.*

Montevideo, Uruguay: International Agricultural Development Fund—Ministerio de Ganadería, Agricultura y Pesca. Mimeo.

Instituto Nacional de Estadística. 1992. *III Censo económico nacional.* Montevideo, Uruguay.

_______. 1991. *Encuesta continua de hogares.* Montevideo, Uruguay.

Inter-American Development Bank. 1990. Uruguay. *Programa global de préstamo para la pequeña y micro empresa (UR-0033).* Washington, D.C.: Inter-American Development Bank. Mimeo.

Kritz, E.; C. Marín, and C. Viera. 1989. *Bases para la implementación de un programa nacional de apoyo a la micro, pequeña y mediana empresa.* Consultative report for the Inter-American Development Bank, Montevideo, Uruguay. Mimeo.

Lepp, A., G. Schor and E. Terberger. 1991. *Analisís de sector financiero del Uruguay, con especial consideración de la situación de financiamiento de micro y pequeñas empresas.* Interdisziplinäre Projekt Consult GmbH. Frankfurt, Germany.

Noya, N., and D. Dominioni. 1993. *El fortalecimiento del sistema financiero en el proceso de ajuste. Liberalización y regulación. El caso uruguayo.* Working document 144 DES-Network of Centers, Washington, D.C., United States: Inter-American Development Bank.

Oikos. *Panorama Financiero,* various numbers. Montevideo, Uruguay: Consultora Oikos.

Olivera, R. 1992. *Aspectos jurídicos del financiamiento a la vivienda.* Montevideo, Uruguay. Mimeo.

Pérez-Campanero, J., and A. Leone. 1991. "Liberalization and financial crisis in Uruguay, 1974–1987." In V. Sundararajan and J.T. Baliño, editors, *Banking crisis: causes and issues,* Washington, D.C., United States: International Monetary Fund.

Talvi, E., and L. Viana. (1991) *Inversión y mercado de capitales.* Montevideo, Uruguay: Centro de Estudios de la Realidad Económica y Social.

Torello, M. 1993. *Incertidumbre macroeconómica e inversión en el Uruguay.* Working document, Economic Commission for Latin America. Montevideo, Uruguay.

Torello, M., and N. Noya. 1992. *Las políticas de incentivos a la inversión privada,* Serie Informes de Investigación No. 23. Montevideo, Uruguay: Centro de Investigaciones Económicas.

APPENDIX

Table 6.A.1. Principal Macroeconomic Indicators, 1970–92

Year	GDP[1]	Domestic gross investment[2]	Domestic gross saving[2]	Tax receipts[2]	Inflation[1]	Terms of trade 1985 = 100	Current account balance[2]
1970	4.7	11.1	9.7	–1.8	16.4	137.5	–1.8
1971	0.1	12.6	10.8	–5.8	24.0	147.4	–1.8
1972	–1.6	11.8	11.8	–2.6	76.5	192.3	–0.1
1973	0.4	12.6	13.6	–1.4	97.0	252.7	1.0
1974	3.1	11.5	8.4	–4.4	77.2	133.4	–3.2
1975	5.9	13.5	8.2	–4.5	81.4	107.3	–5.3
1976	4.0	14.8	12.4	–2.6	50.6	117.2	–2.4
1977	1.2	15.2	10.8	–1.2	58.2	113.1	–4.4
1978	5.3	16.0	12.2	–1.3	44.5	118.2	–3.8
1979	6.2	17.3	12.1	0.2	66.8	116.9	–5.2
1980	6.0	17.3	10.8	0.1	63.5	111.6	–6.5
1981	1.9	15.4	10.8	–0.1	34.0	109.1	–4.5
1982	–9.4	14.4	7.8	–14.7[a]	19.0	105.0	–5.1
1983	–5.9	14.2	10.9	–12.2	49.2	102.6	–3.5
1984	–1.1	12.1	10.0	–8.9	55.3	103.0	–2.6
1985	1.5	11.4	9.8	–6.8	72.2	100.0	–2.5
1986	8.9	11.2	12.6	–5.2	76.4	113.5	0.9
1987	7.9	14.3	12.7	–4.1	63.6	116.7	–1.8
1988	0.0	13.2	14.0	–4.5	62.2	124.5	0.4
1989	0.5	11.3	13.3	–6.2	80.4	126.1	1.6
1990	0.9	11.5	13.3	–3.0[b]	112.5	125.5	2.0
1991	1.9	13.0	13.7	–1.8	102.0	n.a.	0.4
1992	7.4	12.0	11.6	0.3	68.5	n.a.	–1.8

[1] *Annual variation.*
[2] As a percentage of GDP.
[a] As of 1982, includes the quasifiscal deficit.
[b] As of 1990, includes the operating losses of administered banks.
Source: Central Bank, *Boletín Estadístico*, various numbers.

Table 6.A.2. Matured Credits as Percentage of Total Credits, Private Banks, 1980–92

Year	"Administered" banks	Other private banks	Total private banks
1980	9	9	9
1981	1	14	15
1982	31	29	30
1983	33	17	25
1984	31	14	2
1985	58	14	2
1986	68	34	45
1987	51	22	31
1988	36	15	21
1989	35	18	18
1990	35	8	18
1991	9	3	12
1992	10	2	3

Source: Unpublished data of the Central Bank of Uruguay.

Table 6.A.3. Offshore Operations of Private Banking, 1978–92
(Percentages of GDP)

Year	Balances of credits to nonresidents
1978	0.2
1979	0.7
1980	0.8
1981	0.9
1982	1.5
1983	2.1
1984	2.2
1985	3.6
1986	3.7
1987	2.6
1988	3.4
1989	4.8
1990	5.0
1991	4.5
1992	4.3

Source: Central Bank of Uruguay, *Boletín Estadístico,* various numbers.

Table 6.A.4. Credits by Private Banking Sector, 1982–93
(Balances at end of December, percentages)

Year	Agriculture	Industry and construction	Trade	Services	Consumption
1982	19.5	39.0	22.0	10.2	9.4
1983	20.2	43.6	20.9	8.9	6.3
1984	18.1	45.4	20.6	10.4	5.5
1985	15.3	49.7	20.7	9.2	5.0
1986	17.6	47.5	21.6	8.2	5.1
1987	17.4	46.8	21.9	7.8	6.1
1988	15.0	45.8	24.2	8.8	6.1
1989	12.4	47.6	23.2	7.3	9.5
1990	13.0	46.9	22.8	8.3	8.9
1991	11.2	44.6	26.0	9.0	9.1
1992	12.9	37.9	28.8	10.4	10.1
1993[a]	11.2	35.0	29.5	10.7	13.6

[a] Calculated using end-October balances.
Source: Central Bank of Uruguay. *Boletín Estadístico,* various numbers.

Table 6.A.5. Number of Banks to Which Businesses are Indebted, December 1990

Number of banks	Percentage of businesses	Percentage of credit
1	37.7	27.3
2	21.0	14.1
3	13.9	10.7
4	8.9	9.3
5	6.8	9.1
6	4.3	7.4
7	2.4	4.7
8	1.9	4.6
9	1.2	4.2
More than 9	3.1	8.4

Source: Dominioni and Vaz, 1991.

Table 6.A.6. Share of the Largest Debtors in Each Bank, 1982 and 1990
(Percentages)

	Debtors					
	5 largest		10 largest		20 largest	
Banks	1982	1990	1982	1990	1982	1990
Citibank	31.1	78.1	43.0	88.5	55.1	93.6
Trade Development/Am. Express	20.5	45.5	28.1	64.5	40.7	80.0
Londres/Lloyds	9.8	36.6	15.1	56.3	23.2	80.3
Nación Argentina	21.5	35.8	32.2	53.3	46.7	66.2
Do Brasil	39.7	35.3	44.2	45.2	50.8	52.2
Discount	19.5	31.4	27.7	47.0	39.4	66.7
Boston	28.1	28.6	39.4	38.4	52.4	52.0
UBUR/Banesto	20.2	24.2	27.9	33.0	36.8	44.6
BAFISUD/NMB	21.7	20.2	30.7	31.7	43.9	45.5
BANFED/Exterior	19.5	20.0	26.1	31.5	35.8	44.1
Holandés	19.1	18.1	29.6	33.0	42.1	51.1
Panamericano/Centrobanco	27.4	17.7	43.1	30.9	63.3	46.6
Sudameris	21.7	17.1	32.8	26.0	46.7	40.0
De Crédito	10.8	15.7	17.6	26.6	28.0	40.7
Montevideo	10.9	14.1	18.8	23.4	29.3	37.6
Caja Obrera	63.7	13.0	10.5	20.2	16.2	32.0
Real	4.9	12.2	8.3	21.1	13.6	33.8
Comercial	7.5	11.8	13.1	16.7	20.5	22.2
Pan de Azúcar	8.3	11.5	13.2	17.8	21.0	26.2
del Litoral/Santander	7.1	11.0	11.8	19.7	18.6	32.9

Source: Dominioni and Vaz, 1991.

Table 6.A.7. Herfindahl Equivalent Number of the Portfolio of Private Banks: 1980, 1985, and 1990

Bank	1980	1985	1990
Real	9.72	8.72	10.97
Montevideo	8.82	9.69	9.72
UBUR/Banesto	9.45	9.76	9.26
Holandés	10.09	7.61	8.80
Boston	10.94	5.73	8.47
Pan de Azúcar	7.20	8.93	8.23
Panamericano/Centrobanco	7.32	5.81	7.97
Sudameris	10.26	8.19	7.87
BAFISUD/NMB	11.58	7.24	7.60
Londres/Lloyds	10.84	8.85	7.55
Nación Argentina	8.67	6.29	7.52
del Litoral/Santander	7.98	10.70	7.50
Crédito	5.70	7.37	6.94
Caja Obrera	6.41	8.43	6.78
BANFED/Exterior	5.41	1.79	6.20
Comercial	4.95	5.42	5.86
Discount	8.31	6.91	4.98
Do Brasil	11.56	10.02	4.81
National Republic of New York	—	—	4.01
Trade Development/American Express	—	5.96	3.90
Citibank	6.79	6.22	2.94
Del Plata	9.51	—	10.62
Bank of America	5.27	4.22	—
Average	8.42	7.33	7.20

Note: The Herfindahl equivalent number is the number of businesses which, with an identical share, would equal the value of the Herfindahl concentration index.
Source: Dominioni and Vaz (1991).

Table 6.A.8. Herfindahl Equivalent Number of the Portfolio of Private Banks, by Sector of Activity, 1980, 1985, and 1990

	1980	1985	1990
Agriculture	11.3	10.1	7.7
Livestock	7.5	7.1	6.7
Industry	18.8	17.8	15.4
Food	15.2	12.2	10.9
Meats	12.0	6.0	6.5
Dairy	14.9	4.0	1.6
Fish	7.2	8.0	5.8
Oils	7.5	1.8	2.0
Canning and preserving fruits and vegetables	8.4	3.5	3.2
Meals	6.7	4.0	7.0
Sugar	6.2	4.7	2.9
Other foods	13.4	11.4	11.7
Beverages	7.6	8.0	8.7
Liquors	5.9	3.5	3.3
Wines	3.7	4.8	5.0
Beer and malt	7.1	4.8	6.0
Nonalcoholic beverages	7.8	3.7	5.5
Tobacco	9.6	4.4	1.5
Textiles	16.2	15.1	12.2
Clothing and leather	16.3	13.9	13.4
Leather and leather products	12.1	13.6	11.6
Footwear	10.9	8.6	5.9
Clothing	14.2	8.8	12.4
Wood and cork	12.1	5.6	3.8
Paper and printed materials	15.8	10.7	12.3
Paper and by-products	12.6	9.4	7.7
Printed materials	15.1	5.8	9.9
Rubber	11.0	8.0	10.9
Chemical products	15.9	15.2	12.0
Plastics	16.1	10.0	6.0
Other chemical products	12.6	12.4	10.8
Metals	14.9	10.9	9.9
Basic metals	13.3	8.2	6.4
Metals except machinery and equipment	13.0	9.2	9.8
Electrical equipment	10.6	11.1	8.7
Transportation machinery and equipment	10.0	6.5	10.6
Construction and repair of machinery	9.9	5.8	6.0
Transportation, construction and materials	11.7	4.7	7.8
Others	15.6	8.1	13.2
Nonmetallic minerals	11.0	3.8	6.7
Other manufactures	14.4	7.1	12.6
Construction	15.0	12.1	9.0
Wholesale trade	16.4	12.9	13.3
Retail trade	10.6	12.4	12.4

Note: The Herfindahl equivalent number is the number of businesses which, with an identical share, would equal the value of the Herfindahl concentration index.
Source: Dominioni and Vaz (1991).

Table 6.A.9. Distribution of Credit to the Private Sector, by Sector and Bank, 1980 and 1990
(Percentages)

	Sectors									
	Agriculture		Industry		Trade		Services		Families	
Banks	1980	1990	1980	1990	1980	1990	1980	1990	1980	1990
Do Brasil	20.0	44.2	44.8	32.8	13.8	18.3	6.2	3.9	15.3	0.9
BANFED/Exterior	41.4	33.1	21.3	31.8	21.1	18.3	6.2	13.2	10.3	3.5
Caja Obrera	37.0	32.5	27.3	34.2	20.3	17.0	7.9	12.1	7.5	4.2
Comercial	43.0	28.8	31.0	19.8	21.3	30.9	2.1	3.6	3.0	16.9
Crédito	41.0	27.1	22.0	31.7	19.8	25.9	4.7	10.4	12.4	4.8
del Litoral/Santander	27.6	24.6	31.0	31.5	27.6	28.9	7.0	9.2	6.9	5.7
UBUR/Banesto	20.4	13.6	35.0	53.3	22.4	17.8	11.8	10.3	10.5	5.0
Pan de Azúcar	32.4	8.4	39.4	40.0	16.3	22.3	6.1	7.3	5.7	22.0
Real	14.2	4.9	45.2	56.5	17.3	17.8	21.4	17.5	1.8	3.3
BAFISUD/NMB	7.0	4.9	55.1	51.0	18.2	28.3	14.2	12.3	5.6	3.6
Nación Argentina	7.3	4.8	53.4	61.9	34.7	25.6	4.6	5.7	0.0	2.0
Panamericano/Centrobanco	0.5	3.0	86.6	65.5	8.5	20.1	1.6	2.2	2.8	9.2
Londres/lloyds	11.8	2.9	52.2	64.4	25.9	28.6	5.0	3.2	5.0	0.9
Montevideo	1.4	2.5	65.8	61.4	22.6	24.4	0.9	6.3	9.4	5.4
Sudameris	6.6	2.5	50.0	46.4	24.2	29.3	8.6	5.3	10.6	16.6
Boston	5.1	1.3	58.5	52.6	13.5	23.3	18.6	3.6	4.3	19.2
Discount	0.0	0.9	63.3	54.2	19.4	35.6	13.5	4.5	3.8	4.9
Holandés	3.6	0.6	62.7	66.0	18.5	22.9	2.8	4.9	12.5	5.7
Citibank	33.0	0.4	49.3	73.4	11.4	3.4	5.4	19.0	1.0	3.9
Trade Dev./Am. Express	—	0.2	—	38.4	—	19.8	—	2.3	—	39.2
National Republic of NY	—	0.0	—	33.2	—	4.7	—	39.7	—	22.5
Bank of America	41.2	—	32.6	—	9.6	—	11.5	—	5.1	—

Source: Unpublished BCU data, according to Dominioni and Vaz, 1991.

Table 6.A.10. Number of Branches of Private Banks, by Bank Owner's Nationality, 1974–91

Years	Total	Europeans except Spanish	Spanish	Latin American	North American	Other
1974	238	30	63	3	8	134
1975	239	31	63	3	8	134
1976	238	31	63	3	9	132
1977	245	32	63	9	8	133
1978	257	35	65	14	10	133
1979	265	36	66	14	11	138
1980	280	41	68	19	13	139
1981	291	44	69	20	13	145
1982	290	44	69	20	13	144
1983	304	45	73	19	20	147
1984	303	43	76	19	24	141
1985	309	43	85	19	26	136
1986	304	38	80	17	26	143
1987	277	36	69	18	19	135
1988	268	36	58	18	21	135
1989	264	37	56	18	22	131
1990	253	37	52	16	21	127
1991	237	36	37	13	25	126

Source: Asociación de Bancos del Uruguay, *Memoria anual,* various numbers.

Table 6.A.11. Bank Employees, by Bank Owner's Nationality, 1975–91
(In December of each year)

Years	Total	Total private banks	Europeans except Spanish	Spanish	Latin American	North American	Other	BROU
1975	9,598	5,342	1,041	1,138	162	281	2,720	4,256
1976	9,736	5,667	1,103	1,194	236	312	2,822	4,069
1977	9,995	5,944	1,150	1,303	289	347	2,885	4,051
1978	10,490	6,169	1,199	1,352	345	365	2,908	4,321
1979	10,788	6,609	1,285	1,454	417	425	3,028	4,179
1980	11,378	7,090	1,353	1,552	486	513	3,186	4,288
1981	11,816	7,523	1,383	1,626	493	598	3,423	4,293
1982	11,784	7,360	1,354	1,548	482	615	3,361	4,424
1983	11,692	7,106	1,309	1,483	470	613	3,231	4,586
1984	11,906	7,003	1,283	1,429	447	636	3,208	4,903
1985	12,459	6,857	1,270	1,432	430	661	3,064	5,602
1986	12,463	6,617	1,196	1,288	415	663	3,055	5,846
1987	12,089	6,140	1,144	1,124	412	532	2,928	5,949
1988	11,952	6,142	1,163	1,071	423	562	2,923	5,810
1989	11,967	6,010	1,206	993	399	597	2,815	5,957
1990	11,477	5,591	1,242	843	388	645	2,473	5,886
1991	11,112	5,372	1,242	708	353	667	2,402	5,740

Source: Asociación de Bancos del Uruguay, *Memoria anual,* various numbers, and BROU, *Memoria Anual,* various numbers.

Table 6.A.12. BROU Market Share, 1982–93
(Balances in December)

	Deposits in local currency			Deposits in foreign currency		Credit to residents	
Years	Demand	Savings	Time	Residents	Nonresidents	Local currency	Foreign currency
1982	22.0	30.0	15.0	n.a.	n.a.	30.7	25.5
1983	20.3	31.7	21.4	24.4	16.3	40.9	30.9
1984	21.1	31.4	26.9	31.7	17.1	36.6	37.6
1985	17.4	38.3	28.5	40.4	23.4	49.2	40.8
1986	19.7	45.4	33.8	37.1	21.8	50.6	38.9
1987	20.6	54.9	41.1	41.2	22.1	53.2	41.1
1988	29.7	59.7	42.5	43.9	19.1	59.4	41.3
1989	25.6	65.1	44.9	45.4	17.3	65.3	47.1
1990	28.8	69.7	50.0	47.0	16.3	66.9	51.6
1991	25.7	69.1	49.3	48.3	15.9	58.9	51.7
1992	18.4	67.2	47.7	47.6	14.4	52.6	46.2
1993[a]	24.8	68.9	40.6	46.8	13.3	52.0	48.2

[a] Balances in October.
Source: Central Bank of Uruguay, *Boletín Estadístico,* various numbers.

Table 6.A.13. Physical Indicators of the Private Banking System, 1984, 1989, and 1991
(In December of each year)

	1984[a]	1989[a]	1991[b]
Depositors	543,193	430,887	450,380
In local currency		276,485	267,832
In foreign currency, residents		113,643	134,725
In foreign currency, nonresidents	83,186	40,759	47,823
Investors		80,288	172,590
In local currency		67,552	154,223
In foreign currency, residents		11,731	16,435
In foreign currency, nonresidents	7,365	1,005	1,932
Number of employees	335	6,429	6,522
Number of branches	74	290	328
Deposits per employee	11	67	69
Investments per employee	85	12	26
Total per employee		80	96
Activity per branch	1,870	1,764	1,899

[a] Private banks only.
[b] Includes savings and credit cooperatives.
Source: Unpublished BCU data.

Table 6.A.14. Structure of Credit and Deposit Terms in the Private Financial System, June 1993
(Percentages)

	Currency	
	Local	Foreign
Deposits	100.0	100.0
Sight	64.5	39.2
Under 30 days	2.3	1.5
30–360 days	32.6	54.6
One year or more	0.5	4.7
Credits	100.0	100.0
Sight	1.4	0.1
Under 30 days	3.9	19.9
30–360 days	73.2	64.3
One year or more	21.4	15.7

Source: Unpublished data of the Central Bank of Uruguay.

Table 6.A.15. Obligatory Reserve Rates, 1974–93
(Percentages at December 31 of each year)

Years	1974	1975	1976	1977	1978	1979	1980	1981	1982	1983
In local currency										
S.D. and under 30 days	30	40	40	50	50	—	—	—	—	14
S.D. 30–180 days	10	20	20	35	50	—	—	—	—	14
S.D. over 180 days	10	20	20	35	50	—	—	—	—	14
S.D. 360 days or more	—	—	5	12	6	—	—	—	—	14
Additional excl. deposit	—	20	—	—	20	—	—	—	—	—
In foreign currency										
S.D. under 180 days	20	20	20	32	20	0	0	0	0	0
S.D. over 180 days	20	20	20	32	20	0	0	0	0	0
Additional excl. deposit	0	0	0	0	20	0	0	0	0	0
Corr. credit pend. conf.	0	0	0	0	0	0	0	0	0	0

Years	1984	1985	1986	1987	1988	1989	1990	1991	1992	1993
In local currency										
S.D. and under 30 days	15	24	24	24	25	25	25	23	10	10
S.D. 30–180 days	5	11	11	11	12	12	12	10	4	4
S.D. over 180 days	0	5	5	5	6	6	6	6	2	2
S.D. 360 days or more	0	5	5	5	6	6	6	6	2	2
Additional excluding deposit	0	0	0	0	0	0	0	–	0	0
In foreign currency										
S.D. under 180 days	3	10	10	10	10	10	10	10	10	10
S.D. over 180 days	0	4	4	4	4	4	4	4	4	4
Additional excluding deposit	0	0	0	0	0	0	0	0	0	0
Corr. credit pend. conf.	3	10	10	10	10	10	10	0	0	0

S.D. Sight deposits.
Source: Central Bank of Uruguay, Rules for Regulating and Auditing the Financial System.

Table 6.A.16. Risk Assessment Criteria

1. Normal risks
   - — operations current or no more than 30 days overdue;
   - — no doubt about recoverability on a timely, normal basis,
   - — full knowledge of solvency, amount, and source of regular income;
   - — good record;
   - — adequate earning capacity;
   - — indebtedness proportional to asset and income structure;
2. Potential risks
   - — operations current or no more than 90 days overdue;
   - — occasional late payments;
   - — deficiencies stemming from situations that could affect payment capacity on the agreed terms (for example, negative trends in the economic situation that could affect the normal flow of income used as the source of payments, such as increased indebtedness without real investments, or a decline in sales and net profits; changes in the management, board of directors, or ownership that affect its efficiency);
   - — market conditions that could affect the sector of economic activity;
   - — negative net earnings resulting from the initiation of a capital project;
3. Real risk:
   - — low rating for debtors with operations more than 90 days overdue;
   - — delay of up to 60 days in providing information;
   - — insufficient information or contradictions that cast doubt on the financial statements—negative accrued earnings that do not significantly affect net worth—low rating for debtors with conditions, terms, and interest rates different from those prevailing in the market;
4. High risks:
   - — low rating for debtors with operations to be recorded as debtors in process of collection;
   - — delay of more than 60 days in providing information;
   - — attachments that impede the normal conduct of business;
   - — symptoms of eroding solvency (such as negative accrued earnings for the current and previous fiscal years that significantly affect net worth);
5. Unrecoverables:
   - — low rating for debtors with operations recorded as delinquent credits;
   - — debtors in process of collection with a delay of more than 180 days in providing information;
   - — debtors who are absent, declared in bankruptcy, or in meeting of creditors;
   - — debtors against whom legal action has been instituted but with little chance of collection;
   - — obvious erosion of solvency;
   - — incapacity to generate funds to pay debts.

Source: Central Bank of Uruguay, Rules for Regulating and Auditing the Financial System.

Table 6.A.17. Weighting of Assets for Capital Adjustment
(Summary based on major assets)

Percentage	Asset
0	Cash Precious metals National government securities (except Banco Hipotecario adjustable mortgage obligations) Assets in the Central Bank of Uruguay Uruguayan external debt securities
5	Current credits with terms of less than 30 days with domestic financial institutions Other assets and contingencies with domestic financial institutions Checks and other clearable instruments
10	Current credits with terms of less than 30 days with foreign banks Current credits with terms of 30–360 days and contingencies with domestic private companies Current credits and contingencies with the public sector
20	Current credits and contingencies with the nonfinancial sector for the part covered by easily enforced chattel mortgages Current credits with terms of 30–360 days and contingencies with foreign banks Foreign government securities Contingencies corresponding to credit card loans
50	Current credits with domestic private companies with terms of more than one year Current credits with foreign banks with terms of more than one year Contingencies corresponding to documentary credits

Source: Central Bank, Rules for Regulating and Auditing the Financial System.

Index